BEN SHAHN

HOWARD GREENFELD

RANDOM HOUSE   NEW YORK

BEN SHAHN

AN ARTIST'S LIFE

Grateful acknowledgment is made to the following for
permission to reprint previously published material:

George Braziller, Inc., Publishers: Excerpts from *Ben Shahn:
Paintings* by James Thrall Soby. Copyright © 1963 by
James Thrall Soby. Reprinted by permission of
George Braziller, Inc., Publishers.

Harvard University Press: Excerpts from *The Shape of Content*
by Ben Shahn (Cambridge, Mass.: Harvard University Press,
1975). Copyright © 1975 by the President and
Fellows of Harvard College. Copyright renewed 1985
by B. B. Shahn. Reprinted by permission.

Alfred A. Knopf, Inc.: Excerpt from *Washington Goes to War*
by David Brinkley. Copyright © 1988 by David Brinkley.
Reprinted by permission of Alfred A. Knopf, Inc.

Library of Congress Cataloging-in-Publication Data

Greenfeld, Howard.
Ben Shahn: an artist's life / Howard Greenfeld.
p.   cm.
Includes bibliographical references and index.
ISBN 0-679-41932-2 (hardcover)
1. Shahn, Ben, 1898–1969.   2. Artists—United States—Biography.
I. Shahn, Ben, 1898–1969.   II. Title.
N6537.S5G74   1998
760'.092—dc21   97-46748
[B]

Random House website address: www.randomhouse.com

Book design by Carole Lowenstein

For Bob Rosenstiel,
a good man

PREFACE

I knew Ben Shahn during the 1960s, the last decade of his life. I spent time with him in Paris, in New York, and at his home in Roosevelt, New Jersey. A man of great charm and wit, of warmth and dignity, he was enormously intelligent, possessed of great intellectual curiosity. I thoroughly enjoyed his company.

Several years after Shahn's death, I had a chance meeting with his widow, Bernarda Bryson Shahn. In the days following this meeting, I began to wonder why there had been no biography of Ben Shahn since an early one, published during his lifetime. I knew that this once immensely popular artist's fame had diminished since his death in 1969, but I firmly believed that he remained one of the most significant figures in the history of twentieth-century American art. Knowing Ben and greatly admiring his work, I felt qualified to write this biography.

I would not have undertaken this project without the initial encouragement and cooperation of Shahn's widow, which she graciously offered to me. It is impossible for me to express adequately my gratitude to her. Mrs. Shahn was unfailingly generous with her suggestions, submitted to lengthy and frequent interviews, and introduced me to men and women who had been important to her husband both personally and professionally.

She never interfered with nor did she in any way attempt to control the direction of my work. Needless to say, in spite of her selfless cooperation (which was given without restrictions), this remarkably intelligent and vital woman is in no way responsible for any errors of fact or interpretation in this biography; the responsibility is mine alone.

Special thanks are also due to Judith Shahn Dugan, the artist's daughter by his first wife, without whom it would have been extremely difficult to present a rounded portrait of the artist's early years. I am grateful to her for her help and for her willingness to share her memories, and to do so with intelligence and sensitivity.

I would also like to express my gratitude to the following people for their help: Mirella Bentivoglio, Martin Bressler, Donna Briggs, Rabbi Herbert Brockman, Humphrey Burton, Jason H. Cohen, Mildred Constantine, Robert Conway, Jack Delano, Morris Dorsky, Susan H. Edwards, Malcolm Evans, Julie Fawcus, W. H. Ferry, Doris Fortes, Lawrence Fleischman, Martha Fleischman, Peggy Frank, Fred W. Friendly, Geoff Gehman, Irving Geis, Raymond Gordon, Ed Grazda, Johanna Hecht, John Hill, Richard Hudson, Dr. Alexander Kirschenbaum, Mary Laing, Peggy Lewis, Diana Linden, Leo Lionni, Estelle Thompson Margolis, Mira Nakashima, Barbara Novak, Francis V. O'Connor, Ted Ormai, Susan Osborn, Bernard Perlin, Philip Pochoda, Belinda Rathbone, Alan Reitman, Hilda Robbins, Warren Robbins, Louise Rosskam, Irma Rudin, Charlotte Safir, Leah Schwartz, Tony Schwartz, Pearl Seligman, Abby Shahn, Ezra Shahn, Jeb Shahn, Jonathan Shahn, Yashiaki Shimizu, Amanda Slamm, Bud Stillman, Kitsi Watterson, Gertrude Weber, Jake Wien, Anna Williams, Martin Wolf, and Deborah Yaffe.

I am also grateful to Judy Throm and Elizabeth Joffrion of the Archives of American Art; Ron Becker of the Special Collections, Rutgers University; Amy S. Doherty of the E. S. Bird Library, Syracuse University; Barbara Dunlap of the City College of New York; Janis Ekdahl of the Museum of Modern Art; Richard Fyffe of the University of Connecticut; Eulalie Drury of the Marine Biological Laboratory, Woods Hole; Nathan Gluck of the American Institute of Graphic Arts; Cathy Henderson of the Harry Ransom Research Center, University of Texas; Marguerite Lavin of the Museum of the

City of New York; Tom Owen and Bill Carner of the University of Louisville; Robert Panzer of VAGA; Rona Roob of the Museum of Modern Art; Jeffrey Ryan of the Museum of Modern Art; Alice Rwabazaire of the Oral History Collection, Columbia University; Richard Strassberg of the Labor-Management Documentation Center, Martin P. Catherwood Library, Cornell University; Deborah Whythe of the Brooklyn Museum of Art; and Barbé Hammer of Random House.

I could never have completed this book without the patient support of my extraordinary editor, Bob Loomis. His insights and suggestions were invaluable. My son Daniel was encouraging in every way, and I am also deeply indebted to my wife, Paola, for her unfailing understanding and compassion as well as for her skills as a researcher.

Shortly after embarking on this project, I learned of the existence of the Ben Shahn Archive, in Berkeley, California. Dr. Stephen Lee Taller, its founder and director, proved to be of immense help. A successful physician, Taller had spent many years amassing an astoundingly complete collection of writings by and about Shahn, which he generously shared with scholars from all parts of the world. He made himself available day and night to offer help and advice to me and to others who studied the life and work of Ben Shahn.

Stephen Taller died in October 1997, before he could see this book, but not before he had a chance to read the manuscript. We had become friends, and I shall always remember his friendship as well as the essential role he played in enabling me to write this biography.

While I knew him, but even more in the course of writing this book, I became aware of Ben Shahn's personal failings: his frequently selfish and arrogant behavior, his sometimes uncontrollable temper. These flaws, impossible to ignore, were, I felt, outweighed by his generosity, his integrity, and, above all, his extraordinary gifts as an artist. I hope I have made this clear in the pages that follow.

CONTENTS

BEN SHAHN

CHAPTER ONE

The
Early Years:
Kovno and Vilkomir

IN 1906, SHORTLY AFTER BEN SHAHN ARRIVED IN THE UNITED States from Lithuania, he became aware of what he later called "the whole business of the Mayflower and ancestry." He was eight years old and had been taught that Abraham, Isaac, and Jacob, the great biblical figures, were his ancestors, and they seemed unquestionably more directly related to him than did Columbus and the Pilgrims. It was puzzling. He recognized that he had parents and two sets of grandparents and many aunts and uncles, but he knew nothing of the kind of ancestry that appeared valued in his new country. In an attempt to establish this lineage, he nagged his father incessantly. He knew that his father was a woodcarver, as were his father's father and his father's grandfather, but he wanted to know more. Finally, exasperated, the young boy's father answered by drawing a picture of a man on a gibbet. When Ben wanted to know who that was, his father angrily answered that the man was an ancestor, a horse thief, adding, "If I ever catch you asking about ancestors . . . ! Only what *you* do counts, not what your ancestors did."

In spite of these words, there is no doubt that many of Ben's characteristics can be traced to his ancestors. His father, Hessel, born in 1871, was a skilled craftsman who loved to work with his hands, as would his son. He taught himself to draw at an early age, as would Ben, and he was a born storyteller, just as his son would become, in his art as well as in his conversation. Finally, Hessel was an idealist, whose liberal political convictions must surely have influenced Ben.

Ben's mother, Gittel Lieberman, born in Lithuania in 1872, was descended from a family of peasants, but her father educated himself and became an innkeeper, and later even worked as a schoolteacher. She, too, was a natural storyteller, whose fanciful tales delighted her son. One of many children, she was apprenticed as a kind of indentured servant to a wealthy family of wholesale grocers. Because she was a girl, she wasn't taught to read or write Lithuanian—she was taught these skills by her husband, after their marriage—though she learned to work as a bookkeeper, making out invoices in a language she couldn't understand. Gittel was strong-willed and keenly intelligent, as was her son. She was often described as quarrelsome and angry, as Ben would become.

"Most facts are lies; all stories are true," Ben told his friend Edwin Rosskam. And Ben told many stories. If a large number of these were invented, they are still worth recounting; they reveal as much about the artist as would the truth. He was the sum of his stories.

Certainly his memories of his earliest years in Kovno, where he was born on September 12, 1898, were, inevitably, confused—and, as he admitted, most likely inaccurate, since he spent only four years of his life there. These early memories include brutal incidents of religious discrimination and political terror. At the time of Ben's birth, Kovno, where more than 25,000 Jews lived (they made up approximately 30 percent of the town's population) was a center of Jewish cultural activity. These Jews lived in their own section, separated from the Gentiles. Crossing the non-Jewish sector was so dangerous that they walked through it hurriedly, never strolling in a leisurely fashion. They were even harassed at home and at work. Many Russian soldiers were stationed in Kovno, and when these recruits, most of them far from home, drank too much, they would smash the windows of the Jewish-owned homes and shops. Ben remembered a rock coming through the window of the Shahn home at least once. His family knew, however, that it would be futile to protest since any complaint to the authorities would be considered anti-czarist and result in harsh punishment.

Not all of Ben's memories were unhappy ones, however. On occasion he enjoyed playing with friendly soldiers on the parade ground where military drills and maneuvers were held. In Kovno, he ate ice cream for the first and only time before moving to America. An Armenian or a Turk carried on his head a huge wooden bucket filled with a container of the sweet frozen dessert, packed in ice. There was an uncle who played him to sleep with his trumpet each night when he stayed with Ben's family while on furlough from the army. And Ben remembered with great affection his father, whose stories entertained him, and who carried him on his shoulders to large gatherings, most likely socialist meetings.

Ben was too young to remember the birth of his brother Philip in 1900, but he did recall the birth of his sister Hattie in June 1902, when he was not yet four years old. She was born in a small room, separated from a larger one by a curtain with a peacock design; an old man—a cousin or a neighbor—sat on a nearby stool, cutting his toenails so close to the flesh that each toe bled.

That year of 1902 was a traumatic one for the young child. Not long after the birth of his sister, his father, politically active as an enemy of the czarist government, was arrested by the authorities. According to Gittel, her husband had been framed—revolutionary leaflets, she maintained, had been planted on him. However, in spite of her pleas, Hessel was exiled to Siberia, leaving his wife alone to bring up their three small children, and his eldest son heartbroken at the loss of a father.

Shortly after Hessel's departure, Gittel decided to move back to Vilkomir, forty miles away, where she and her husband had been born. A river divided the town, and the two parts were connected by a bridge. Most of Vilkomir's more than 7,000 Jews (half the population of the town) lived "across the river." Gittel's friends, as well as her parents and Hessel's, still lived in Vilkomir, and she felt certain that life would be far easier for a single mother there than in Kovno.

In Vilkomir, Ben formed one of the deepest attachments of his

*Ben's father, Hessel, came to America
shortly before Ben, who arrived with
younger brother Phil, his sister Hattie,
and their mother in 1906.*

life, with his paternal grandfather. He also first learned to express himself through drawing, and began to question the fundamental doctrines of his religion.

Ben's paternal grandfather, Wolf-Leyb ("Wolf-Lion"), was a huge man, known throughout the village for his enormous strength and for his kindness and warmth. He became, for his young grandson, not only a surrogate father but also a genuine hero. He was so successful as a carpenter, making baroque furniture for a pope of the Orthodox church, that he eventually had half a dozen men working for him and therefore could spend all the time he wanted entertaining Ben. He did this with great love and enthusiasm. He constantly made things for the boy, carving out a little cart with a goat and any number of other toys, as well as teaching Ben how to carve objects himself—most memorably, a multiple-link chain, out of a single piece of wood. Wolf-Lion was always kind to Ben, even while disciplining him, which he did with tenderness.

Ben's maternal grandmother, a tiny woman, was also unfailingly sweet to him. Her husband, however, Ben's first teacher, was a red-headed tyrant, who was luckily soon replaced by a somewhat more understanding instructor. And despite the tyrant's brief reign, for the most part Ben, the oldest grandchild, was spoiled, so much so that his mother summoned help from her own brother, a rigid disciplinarian. According to Ben, he resembled a bearded Protestant minister with his black coat and white collar, and he had no influence on him whatsoever.

One of Ben's childhood memories was of a powerful fire that destroyed most of Vilkomir in 1902. Terrified, he walked through the charred town with his grandfather, whose five or six houses, since they were on the outskirts, were among the few not damaged. It was frightening: the fire bursting out everywhere, hundreds of people standing in the shallow river, carrying chests of drawers and bedding, in an effort to save themselves and their belongings. Lines of men formed a bucket brigade from the river, and in the background the blinding light of flames illuminated the burning town. This devastating fire left an indelible impression on him. Raging flames became a symbol of destructive power in many of his paintings and drawings.

Most important, in Vilkomir Ben learned to draw. Drawing came naturally to him; and he was always encouraged to draw whatever he could not explain in words. Because very little paper was available, he made most of these drawings on the flyleaves and inside covers of books. In *Love and Joy About Letters*, published in 1963, Ben described his first drawing, a portrait of his uncle Lieber, a member of the Russian cavalry, who, Ben was told, rode a horse and was very far away. Though he had never seen or met him, the boy was certain that his uncle was famous, because his family spoke of him so often and with so much respect. He wrote of this portrait:

"Since the only military installation that I had ever known was the striped sentinel box at the *caserne* at the end of our street, I drew my uncle sitting on his horse in front of that. The stripes were nice, but the horse troubled me because it looked like a cow—at least it looked more like a cow than a horse." To make sure that no one mistook the horse for a cow, he placed a caption, "Uncle Lieber Sitting on His Horse," beneath the drawing.

Ben's early formal education consisted almost exclusively of Bible and Talmudic studies. A precocious child, he was placed in a class with older students. They worked diligently for nine hours a day, studying the Bible, putting letters together to make its words, and studying its prayers and psalms. Discipline was severe; students who arrived late were whipped. Ben learned one important lesson at school: to despise injustice and fight it vigorously whenever and wherever he found it. He was enraged, for instance, by his teacher's practice of punishing the entire class for something that only one student had done. He hadn't done it, he would insist, and he wouldn't tell who had (if he knew). He categorically refused to pay for something for which he was not responsible. "I hate injustice," he told an interviewer in 1944. "I guess that's about the only thing that I really do hate. I've hated injustice ever since I read a story in school."

He repeated that story throughout his lifetime. It was a part of his Bible studies, and it concerned the building of Solomon's temple and the carrying of the Ark of the Covenant into that temple. According to the story, the Ark was to be brought in by two oxen; it rested precariously on a pole laced between them. The Lord warned that the pole would inevitably totter, but demanded that no one touch it since it was God's Ark, and He would take care of it. This was a test of faith. Of course, the Ark did totter, and one man did touch it, instinctively, in order to stop it from falling. Immediately, as he had been warned, the well-intentioned man was struck dead.

Young Ben, enraged, began to argue with his teacher. God was unjust, he insisted, and he refused to return to school until this injustice was officially admitted. After a week or ten days, and endless discussions between his teacher and his grandfather, Ben returned to school. "I must have compromised," he told an interviewer many years later, "probably my first compromise."

At this early age, Ben began to challenge the fundamental beliefs of Judaism. In the course of a Saturday class, reserved for questions, he boldly asked the rabbi, "Who made God?"—and the response was a slap in the face. He also tested the laws of his religion. According to those laws, it was forbidden to touch the candlesticks or have anything to do with fire on the Sabbath. At a large Sabbath dinner, however, Ben did touch the lighted candles, just as they were about to fall. Certain that something awful would happen to him because of his defiant act, he was puzzled when he was not punished. He was not chastised, either, when, on another occasion, he defied the laws of his religion by keeping a coin in his pocket throughout the Sabbath. He was, he noted later in his life, being brought up with values that were unacceptable to him.

CHAPTER TWO

Becoming an American

WHEN BEN'S FATHER WAS EXILED TO SIBERIA, HIS PARENTS believed that the family would someday be reunited in Russia. Actually, Hessel stayed in Siberia for only a short time; he soon escaped and made his way to Sweden, then to England, and finally to South Africa, where, in the booming post–Boer war period, he had no difficulty finding work as a carpenter. By 1906, he had been away for four years, and it was obvious that he would not, in the foreseeable future, be able to return to his home. The political climate in Russia was now even more hostile to his socialist ideals than it had been when he was sent away. Furthermore, life for all the Jews of Russia had become both difficult and dangerous as violent pogroms swept the country and increasingly harsh anti-Semitic laws were enacted. For a large number of Jews, emigration was the only solution, and the country most hospitable to them was far away, across the ocean, in the New World. For this reason, Hessel and Gittel Shahn made plans to meet and make their new home in New York.

In spite of the problems and hardships they would face—the need to learn a new language, to find work, and to adapt to a very different way of life—they were determined to uproot themselves in search of a better future than their homeland could offer them.

Ben's memories of his last days in Russia are—because he was older at the time—undoubtedly more reliable than those of his earlier years. He remembered the final preparations for the journey, his mother's hysteria when she learned that the many jars of preserves she had prepared to take to America had been stolen, and her relief when his grandfather found out who the thieves were and assured her that the jars would be given back to her if she paid a few rubles—and they were. And then there were the packers, stuffing enormous burlap bags with feather bedding and down pillows and even the brass and copper pieces of the beds themselves, as well as those jars of preserves.

The departure itself was poignant. His mother and her three children began the journey by stagecoach, his grandfather following alongside, holding on to Ben's hand as long as he could as the coach began to move slowly away. Ben's sadness was overwhelming—if only Wolf-Lion could accompany them, he would have been happy, but this, he knew, was impossible. After a short while, Ben told Edwin Rosskam many years later, "The coachman said he would have to start driving now and said something to my grandfather, and he was going to speed it up, and my grandfather handed me a little nutcracker that he had carved for me, a screw that you could turn in the face when the two jaws came together, and I screamed as I was drawn away from him, and that was the end for me."

The stagecoach took them to the train station, where they boarded a train for Latvia, which seemed to be part of another world. Ben was astounded by the sharp corners of the sidewalks, and of the buildings themselves. There had been no such things in Vilkomir, where everything had been worn down by age. He was also impressed by doorknobs, which he now saw for the first time; in Vilkomir, there were only latches.

From Latvia, they took the boat to London where, upon arrival, Ben was introduced to square white bread. That strange bread and a box of sardines were given to the new immigrants by some ladies whose job it was to look after them. Then they were taken to Liverpool, where he was introduced to traditional English cooking and to spices he had never before tasted. Though he didn't much like the food, he coveted a pair of shoes with heels as high as those worn by the English, and he badly wanted binoculars and a sailor suit—all of which he asked for, but none of which his mother could afford to buy.

On the crossing to America, Ben enthusiastically explored every corner of the ship. For his mother, however, the voyage was a disaster: unwilling to eat any of the nonkosher food that was served on the ship, she had prepared her own. But the trunk that contained her food had been mislabeled; it ended up in the hold, and she was forced to live on tea alone. (This was just as well, since she was seasick all the time.) Her children found their way to the kitchen where they were given snacks—cookies and hard-boiled eggs.

After arriving in Boston, the family was transferred to still another ship. This one took them to New York, their final destination, the gateway through which hundreds of thousands of Jews passed in search of a better life. That year alone, more than 150,000 Eastern European Jews emigrated.

Everything that happened that first day was a revelation to young Ben. Immediately following the arrival at Ellis Island and the completion of formalities there, the family, along with the hordes of other immigrants, was served breakfast. The breakfast included one more discovery for Ben: rolls, the first he had ever seen. At that first breakfast, too, the young boy was astounded to see for the first time people whose mouths were filled with golden teeth.

From Ellis Island, Ben and his family joined the other immigrants on the short boat ride to Manhattan. His first look at the great city must have overwhelmed the young boy as it had the forty-year-old H. G. Wells, who visited New York in that same year and recorded his impressions in his book *The Future in America*:

> Against the broad and level gray contours of Liverpool one found the ocean liner portentously tall, but here one steams into the middle of a town that dwarfs the ocean liner. The skyscrapers that are the New-Yorker's perpetual boast and pride rise up to greet one as one comes through the Narrows into the Upper Bay, stand out, in a clustering group of tall irregular crenellations, the strangest crown that ever a city wore.

Gittel and the children were greeted in New York by Hessel Shahn, who had arrived in America from Cape Town on May 20, several weeks earlier. Ben barely recognized this handsome man who, wearing a huge hat, an elegant chain, and carrying a cane, looked like a wealthy prospector. He even found it difficult to address Hessel in the familiar second person *du,* using instead the more formal third person *ir.* It would take him some time to think of Hessel as his father.

Hessel had prospered in South Africa, earning so much that he had managed to send money regularly to his family in Russia. When he and Gittel were reunited in New York, however, his wife proudly returned all that money to him. A strong-willed, ambitious woman, she had wanted to prove her independence by earning enough herself to support her children by smuggling tea and shawls from nearby Prussia, just across the border from Lithuania.

Hessel, Gittel, and their children were not the first Shahns to come to the United States; Hessel's brothers had emigrated there twenty-five years earlier, in the 1880s. Because of this, they were already "Americanized"—and very proud of it. Their children had gone to college in America, and one child even became a concert pianist. They wanted as little as possible to do with Hessel's family: Gittel's peasant background made her unacceptable, and Hessel himself was dismissed as lower-class because his language was Yiddish. To disguise their origins Russian immigrants were considered inferior to their German counterparts Hessel's American family had even changed their name to the Germanic "Sohn." (Hessel, Gittel, and their children were given the name "Shan" at immigration; the extra "h" in Ben's name was added sometime later.) Though the Sohns formally welcomed their relatives to the United States, for the most part they had little to do with them after their arrival.

Members of Gittel's family, who had also preceded the Shahns, offered them a far warmer welcome. It was to the Liebermans' home in Brooklyn that they went on their first day in America, and there they were to remain until they found a home of their own.

In order to reach Brooklyn, the Shahns boarded the electrically propelled elevated train in Manhattan. This ride, another dazzling experience for Ben, came to an end with the awesome sight of a huge cloth being lifted from a statue; he later learned that a statue of George Washington was being unveiled that day on the Williamsburg Bridge Plaza, just over the bridge to Brooklyn. On that first day, too, Ben observed people chewing gum, a habit he quickly adopted so that he would look more American. For the same reason, he soon began to eat tomatoes, which he had never before seen. He hated them and could bear to eat them only peeled, in sandwiches.

Brooklyn was to be the family's home for many years, as it was for a large number of Jewish immigrants who had overflowed Manhattan's Lower East Side, where the earlier newcomers had settled, and found homes across the river. The city's Jewish population was growing rapidly, and Manhattan could no longer contain them. Only about eighty thousand Jews had lived in New York City in 1880; that number would increase to approximately one and a half million by 1910.

For Ben, moving to Brooklyn was like going to a new planet. He had to accustom himself not only to tomatoes and chewing gum, but to rocking chairs—he almost fell over backward the first time he sat in one—and the use of gas for both cooking and illumination, unheard of in his former home. Even more startling were the enormous concrete buildings, the hurrying crowds, the horseless carriages, and the subway. He was desperately homesick at first, above all for his grandfather; his only consolation was that the moon he looked at in Brooklyn was the same moon that Wolf-Lion saw in Vilkomir.

In *Love and Joy About Letters,* Ben described the "cataclysmic change" that resulted from his immigration:

> All the secure and settled things were not settled at all. I learned that there was a history quite apart from the intimate Biblical legends; there was an American history and a world history that were remote and unreal and concerned people who were strange to me and had nothing to do with my family or with Abraham, Isaac, and Jacob. Time was moving toward me, and time was passing away. It seemed as though there wasn't enough of it for anyone—and of all the new friends that I made who were my own age, none could make letters or draw or carve.

Ben's major concern was to Americanize himself, to make himself an integral part of this marvelous new world and put his birthplace behind him. He wanted to set aside the languages and customs of his past and absorb every aspect of American culture. Before too long, he even dreamed of becoming a baseball player, and tried to learn the batting average of every professional player.

The most important step in this direction was, of course, his education: he had to start school and master English, his new language.

With his keen intelligence he managed to accomplish this in a remarkably short time, but his beginning was not a promising one. Discipline at his American school, P.S. 122, was strict. Both his teacher and the school principal smacked a ruler across the knuckles of students who showed dirty hands or wrists during morning inspection. His teacher, Miss Johnson, had black skin; since he had never seen a black person in Russia, the puzzled boy assumed she was a Gypsy.

His first run-in with Miss Johnson came shortly after the beginning of the school year when his English, though improving, was not yet perfect. An uncle whom his parents had not seen for twenty-five years had visited the Shahn family and had bought Ben a xylophone. Ben, proud of his gift, brought it to school to show to the class. When Miss Johnson asked where the instrument came from, Ben replied that it was a gift from an uncle, adding: "I didn't see him for twenty-five years." Miss Johnson was dismissive. What did he mean by that? Baffled by this strange response, she assumed that Ben had learning difficulties and immediately sent him out of her class, first to one where he learned only basket weaving and then to a special class for backward students. It was not long, however, before the school principal realized a serious mistake had been made. Ben's knowledge of arithmetic was advanced, and his enthusiasm as well as capacity to learn were far above average. He was clearly not a backward student. He was moved to another class; in a very short time, the boy who had been put in first grade at the age of eight and a half caught up with the children of his own age.

Ben himself spoke and wrote little about his time in P.S. 122, and most of what is known about that period comes from an unpublished manuscript by his closest childhood friend, Willy Snow. Ben was, Snow wrote, a brilliant student, with a thirst for knowledge and an extraordinary intellectual curiosity. Willy's parents, like Ben's, insisted that their sons be well educated. A fortune, if made, could easily be lost, the boys were told, but a good education was indestructible; it would always serve as the basis for any endeavor they undertook.

As a part of that education, Ben further developed his special interest in art, largely under the influence of his fifth-grade teacher, Miss Quick, who recognized that the young boy possessed a natural ability to draw. She bought him watercolors and crayons and encouraged him to work. She was so impressed that shortly before Christmas she excused him from his regular assignments and asked him, instead, to draw a head of Santa Claus on the blackboard. Delighted with the result, Miss Quick enthusiastically praised Ben's work and recommended him to other teachers who had him draw for their classes as well. For the first time, he seriously thought of himself as an artist.

The following year, his talent was nourished by his drawing instructor, Miss Turner. Though not as warm and exuberant as Miss Quick, Miss Turner earned the respect of Ben and the rest of the class because of her knowledge of art and her ability to convey that knowledge to the students. She drilled them in the essentials: an understanding of perspective and the mixing of colors. She had them draw cylinders, cones, boxes, vases, and flowers, and she taught them lettering—or, as they used to say, how to print.

It was Miss Turner who gave Ben his first "professional" assignment, when she asked the school principal to allow him to write the names of the graduates on their diplomas, a job previously entrusted to adults. Ben took great pride in this work, which gave him a chance to put into practice his growing interest in lettering. And the small sum he was paid became a source of badly needed income for his family.

Willy Snow also singled out Mr. King, Ben's teacher in the seventh and eighth grades, who was known for having established the first elementary school bank in the United States. Children could deposit and withdraw money in multiples of five cents; since Willy and Ben were the best students in the class, they were chosen to be assistant tellers. To their delight, they became bankers at the age of eleven.

The two boys also loved to make things outside of class. They worked together to make a wagon using wheels from a discarded baby carriage, a wooden box from the grocer, and scrap board from the local lumberyard. Separately, each built a telegraph system, which they proudly brought to class. According to Willy, Mr. King preferred his system to Ben's; this, to Willy's surprise and dismay, made his friend sullen with jealousy. Willy even became afraid that Ben might sever their friendship because of this. So strong was Ben's fear of competition that it made him bitter, which undermined his usual uninhibited enthusiasm for living.

Ben and Willy often hiked to the Brooklyn Museum, fascinated by the exhibitions displaying examples of human creativity throughout the ages. They learned one important lesson: "new" did not necessarily mean better. In later years, Ben particularly enjoyed telling of an excursion beyond the museum, when, eager to find green grass, he led a group of eight or ten friends across the Williamsburg Bridge into Manhattan in search of Central Park. Knowing little about Manhattan, they walked miles up Park Avenue: surely, they believed, a street called *Park* Avenue would lead to the famous park, so there was no need to ask—until about Ninetieth Street. There, not realizing that the park itself was only two blocks west, they gave up and, ravenously hungry, began the long walk home. During their adventure they had been sustained only by orange peels and crusts of bread, refuse left behind by families who had used the small grassy area at one end of the bridge as a picnic ground.

Not long after this excursion, which ended with a spanking and a warning never to undertake any similar trips again, Ben and Willy discovered a park closer to home. Prospect Park was (and is) a huge expanse of greenery, which offered the pleasures of sitting in a rowboat on a Sunday afternoon or playing tennis. There was also the tranquility of the splendid Botanic Garden, next to the museum, and the exotic Japanese Garden.

Although Ben enjoyed the process of becoming an American, life in Brooklyn also had ugly, disturbing aspects. The gangs of angry young people who roamed the streets of Williamsburg frightened him, and he was profoundly upset by the all too frequent displays of anti-Semitism. It was, he soon learned, best not to walk through certain sections of Brooklyn, since there was always the danger of being attacked and of having one's books taken away and thrown down the sewer. This seemed somehow even more threatening and more violent than the anti-Semitism he had experienced in Vilkomir.

In spite of these problems, Ben flourished during his early years in America. His enthusiasm for learning intensified. His precocious skills as an artist were encouraged not only by his teachers but above all by his father, who had asked him to draw a portrait of Abraham Lincoln when he was little more than ten years old. His talent was even recognized by the normally hostile gang members, who urged him to draw on the sidewalks of Williamsburg.

CHAPTER THREE

A Lithographer: From Apprentice to Journeyman

HESSEL SHAHN HAD ALWAYS BELIEVED IN THE POWER OF HARD work, and of all laborers he most respected those who worked with their hands. He was proud of his young son Ben, who—as an artist and letterer—would be among these, and he encouraged him, as Wolf-Lion had, to express himself through both written words and images.

Because of the importance he placed upon work, it was therefore most surprising that after only a few years in America, Hessel announced that he wanted to retire. He could afford to. The family had the money he had managed to save in South Africa, as well as all the money he had sent to Gittel, which she had not touched. They could live well—if modestly—and Hessel could spend his time quietly reading as well as writing occasional articles for New York's Yiddish newspapers. Gittel, however, would have none of it. She was furious at the very thought of Hessel retiring, appalled at the thought of his sitting in the house doing nothing. They were no longer in Russia, where everything seemed hopeless and there was little incentive to work. They were in America, the land of endless opportunity, where the small amount they had could be invested and therefore multiply. Unfortunately, both Gittel and Hessel were amateurs when it came to finance. Everything they did was wrong.

First, they put a large amount of money in what seemed to be a promising real estate deal, but, because of their ignorance, this investment lost them all but a few thousand dollars of their capital. Next, they became involved with a group of Polish weavers who convinced them that Hessel, though he knew nothing at all about weaving, should not only invest his money but also be in charge of hiring workers for the company. He did not even have enough time to show his incompetence, however. The Polish weavers suddenly abandoned the company, taking the looms and other equipment with them. Now most of the family's savings were gone; Hessel had barely enough to participate in one more business venture. This one ended not only unprofitably, but tragically.

With only $500 left, the couple, now desperate, were somehow convinced by two of Hessel's cousins that they should begin manufacturing washing soda. Hessel diligently studied the process, and, to facilitate his work, moved his family from their home on Moore Street into a small building next to the stables where his cousins were constructing the washing-soda plant.

It was there that the tragedy occurred. One evening, when Ben's parents were out, flames swept through the small apartment in which the Shahn children—by then there were five, including Eva, born in 1908, and Hyman, born in 1909—slept. When Hessel returned home, the entire building was in flames. Climbing up a ladder, the distraught father courageously took his young children out of the house one by one and dropped them into the arms of a friend who waited below. The family's home and all of their belongings were destroyed; and though the children were unharmed, Hessel was badly disfigured by the flames. He looked, Ben remembered, as if he were suffering from some terrible disease. His skin was scarred, his hair completely burned off. Ben never forgot that fire, which reminded him of the one that almost destroyed Vilkomir.

Hessel, a shy, sweet, and gentle man, was resigned to his fate; apart from his exceptional good fortune in South Africa, he had been accustomed to making no more than a modest living. Willy Snow remembers him saying, "When a poor man finds out how to make shoelaces into gold, they throw him into jail. When a rich man sneezes, it is put to music." Gittel, more aggressive and ambitious, remained angry for the rest of her life. After the fire, the family was poorer than ever before. There were bitter quarrels. When Hessel announced that he had found work making bakers' trowels in a nearby bakery for three dollars a day, Gittel contemptuously told her weary husband that he should have asked for four dollars, or three and a half, or three and a quarter. . . . (This reminded Ben of the embarrassment he felt when his mother bargained for the clothes she bought him.) Eventually, the Shahns' fortunes improved, though periods of poverty continued to alternate with periods of relative comfort.

Since there was far less demand for woodcarving in America than there had been in Russia, Hessel had to seek other work that made some use of his skills. It wasn't easy, however. A perfectionist unwilling to compromise, he generally set his job bids far too high; he insisted upon doing the best possible work, and therefore the most costly. Nonetheless, he did manage, sporadically, to find employment. Once, he worked diligently for six months on the renovation of an elegant Madison Avenue Oriental rug shop, delicate work that involved carving and gilding. At another time, he was entrusted with the renovation of three synagogues. From time to time there was other work, such as carving gilt-dabbed baroque curlicues and miniature columns for saloon and barbershop mirrors in Brooklyn.

During these years in Brooklyn, the Shahn family moved several times, but always within the poor section of Williamsburg. Whether on Moore Street, on Lorimer Street, or at any of several addresses on Walton Street, the apartments in which Ben grew up differed from one another very little. They were all railroad flats, so called because the rooms are lined up one after another, as on a train, with no corridor. The kitchen, which also served as the dining room, was usually at the end of the flat that faced the backyard. The coal stove, which heated the entire apartment, was also located there, as were the sink and sometimes a small washtub. The toilet was either in the backyard (never more than a small plot of grass) or in the hallway separating two apartments. It served the occupants of both. Each of the Shahns' apartments included two or three small bedrooms, and there was a small front room or parlor facing the street.

Summers were hot and sleeping indoors was difficult. Families slept on fire escapes, on the roof, and sometimes even on sidewalks. For the children, this was an adventure; for the adults, it was a hardship. During the harsh winters, both children and adults stayed indoors, huddled near the coal stove in the kitchen.

The Shahn children, accustomed to poverty, complained little. They had more than enough to occupy them: household chores, reading, doing their homework. Nonetheless, the family's financial situation was so precarious that in 1913 Gittel made a decision that would eventually lead to a complete estrangement between her and her eldest son: she insisted that Ben go to work instead of attending high school. It was the only way, she believed, that their economic situation could be improved. As the oldest child, she maintained, Ben had to be sacrificed for the benefit of the rest of the family.

Ben, who had enthusiastically looked forward to high school, was deeply hurt. Willy Snow tried to convince him that there was no need to go to high school in order to become an artist. Art wasn't even taught there, Willy told him, and Ben could just as well study history and literature on his own. In spite of this, Ben remained angry and bitter at what he felt was proof of his mother's preference for his younger brother Phil—who, of course, would be able to go to high school because of Ben's sacrifice. Phil was, in every way, a devoted, dutiful son, unfailingly gentle and kind and eager to please. Ben, on the other hand, was independent, argumentative, and outspoken. Gittel, equally outspoken, made no effort to hide her feelings toward her sons. She had always criticized and picked on Ben, while never having anything but praise for Phil, who was uncomfortably caught between two adversaries both of whom he loved.

The bitter conflict between Gittel and Ben was the inevitable clash of two strong, forceful personalities. Gittel, however, did have her gentle side, though she seldom showed it to her eldest son. Two of the Shahns' neighbors in Brooklyn think of her with affection. One, Sophie Rosenbaum, characterized her as "a wonderful, kind lady." Another, Gertrude Flax Gold, thought Gittel was "the best-natured, motherly type of person"; Gittel took Gertrude in when the young girl's mother was in the hospital, and was always willing to give the Flax family a few dollars to tide them over during hard times. And Mrs. Gold affectionately remembers Gittel leaning out of her window and calling down to the iceman, half in Yiddish and half in English, to bring to the Shahn apartment ten cents' worth of ice for their small wooden icebox.

Ben had no such affectionate memories of his mother. In his eyes, she was a tyrant, who, by denying him a chance to go to high school and failing to encourage his desire to become an artist, had come close to ruining his life. According to Willy, who understood his friend, it was Ben's struggle with his own unhappiness, caused by his mother's emotional abuse, that often made him contrary, quarrelsome, aggressive, and angry for much of his life.

Though Ben undoubtedly suffered profound psychological damage at this point, there was nonetheless a professional and artistic advantage in going to work. He was a born student—away from school as well as at school—and had little need for professional guidance. His love and respect for learning, and his intellectual curiosity, were guarantees of a substantial, if informal, education.

Hessel, who had at first opposed Gittel's decision to take Ben out of school, had finally agreed on two conditions: that Ben find work as a craftsman, and that this first job would be one that could lead to a solid career. Through a relative who worked at *The New York Times*, Hessel found what he believed to be the perfect job for his son—an apprenticeship in Hessenberg's lithography workshop at 101 Beekman Street in downtown Manhattan. Mr. Hessenberg was indeed an ideal employer, a gentle soft-spoken man who allowed his workers, highly skilled lithographers, to run the firm by themselves. As a result, they took great pride in what they did, paying no attention to the time clock. They worked six long days, from eight in the morning until at least six in the evening, except during the month of August when the shop closed at two on Saturday afternoons. This was considered their annual summer vacation.

At first Ben spent most of his time running errands and doing menial work in the shop. He brought lunch in for other employees and went out twice a day to get them beer. He swept the floors and mixed acid. After a while, he was allowed to sharpen chisels and to "grain," or prepare, the stones, lugging them to the lithographers' workbenches. Though they required no special skills, these duties

Ben worked as a lithographer in New York in 1918–20.

gave him an opportunity to observe and study the actual process of lithography.

Reflecting on this job many years later, Ben confessed: "If learning a craft was my ostensible reason and purpose, my private one was to learn to draw—and to draw always better and better." Before he had a chance to practice his drawing, however, he had to serve his apprenticeship. He also learned that there were two kinds of lithographers, those who executed the drawings and designs of others and those who did their own drawings and designs and then put them onto stone. He wanted to be one of the latter, but first he had to master the basic elements of the craft; he had to learn to make letters—"thousands and thousands of letters until I should know to perfection every curve, every serif, every thick element of a letter and every thin one, where it belonged and how it related to the form of the letter to which it belonged." It was an exciting phase of Ben's love affair with and mastery of the art of lettering, which began when he was a child and which he lovingly described at length in *Love and Joy About Letters:*

> I discovered the Roman alphabet in all its elegance and its austere dignity, and I fell in love all over again with letters. To make a perfect Roman letter—I suppose that I spent months just on the A alone; and then when I felt that I was ready to move on to B, the foreman of the shop, my boss and my teacher, would not accept that A, but condemned me to more work and more making of A's.
>
> As I learned the alphabet, and then many alphabets and many styles of alphabet and ornamentation and embellishment of letters without end, I found here too the wonderful interrelationships, the rhythm of line as letter moves into letter. There is the growing insight—there are, after all, only two basic kinds of letter, the severe unornamented Gothic without serifs and the Roman with serifs. . . .
>
> And then there is spacing. When I had begun to achieve assurance and mastery over the letters themselves, there was still something missing. Even to me, the line seemed awkward and glaringly imperfect. And again the foreman criticized my work with that inexorable perfectionism of the true letterer. He made me look past the letters at the spaces around them—a minor theme, one might call it, of shapes and patterns carved out of the background by the letters themselves. How to determine these spaces? I tried measuring, I tried allowing for curves and angles, but no formula that I could devise provided for every shape, so that all the letters might emerge into a perfect line.
>
> Then he shared with me the secret of the glass of water. "Imagine," he said, "that you have a small measuring glass. It holds, of course, just so much water. Now, you have to pour the water out of the glass into the spaces between the letters, and every one has to contain exactly the same amount—whatever its shape. Now try!"
>
> That was it; letters are quantities, and spaces are quantities, and only the eye and the hand can measure them. As in the ear and the sensibilities of the poet, sounds and syllables and pauses

are quantities, so in both cases are the balancing and forward movement of these quantities only a matter of skill and feeling and art.

As a lithographic engraver, I had learned to work in a precise way, literally to cut the lines that I made, working always against the resistant material of the stone. Then, when I studied art more formally and drew extensively, I found that this chiseled sort of line had become a necessity, a sort of temperamental fixture, so that even when I drew with a brush the line retained that style. Again, in my painting, I found the influence of my early experience very strong, for I loved—and still love—the clear patterning of forms, the balance and movement of shapes and the sense of major and minor themes of which I had become so conscious during my early youth.

When Ben was nineteen, he rose from the rank of apprentice to that of journeyman lithographer, "master" of his trade. This not only assured him a respectable future as a professional but also enabled him to undertake work that called for creativity on his part. Complicated assignments were entrusted to him, such as designing and executing posters and billboards. Before long, he was overjoyed to see his work appear in subway advertisements, evidence that he was able to communicate effectively through his art and could tell a story through the use of images.

During these years at the workshop, Ben continued to paint and to study literature and history. Before he had started working he went to the Division Street Library, where he complained that he had been forced to leave school and asked a librarian for a reading list that would enable him to educate himself. The librarian worked out a lengthy reading program, emphasizing the classics, that would last him for several years. On the top of the list was Homer's *Iliad*, which so fascinated him that he read it in three different translations, memorizing sections of it while traveling to and from work each day. He was thrilled by Shakespeare, too, reciting his verses while grinding down lithographic stones.

His hunger for knowledge was not limited to the classics. He wanted to read everything that had ever been written. In time, he became aware of contemporary literature. He was especially impressed by one novel, Ernest Poole's *The Harbor*, set in Brooklyn, which depicted in terms he understood the experiences of an immigrant. He knew the sights and the sounds that Poole described and wrote to the author, praising him while at the same time correcting what he felt were certain errors concerning Brooklyn. Surprisingly, Poole responded, informing his critical reader that he was not an expert on Brooklyn and had spent only one day of his life there. This, according to Ben, was the first time he realized that it was possible to write about places one had never seen or visited.

The list of books Ben read during these years was a long one, including both European and American literature. He felt a special affinity for Emerson, "a man putting into words all the things that I have been feeling," and he discovered Thoreau and Mark Twain, among many other American authors.

He didn't, however, want to limit himself to self-education, and attended the Eastern Evening High School in Williamsburg and the Eron Preparatory School on Manhattan's Lower East Side at night while working during the daytime, in order to prepare himself for college. He took courses in a number of subjects; English, math, chemistry, Latin, and Greek among them. In addition, during the academic year 1916–1917, he attended anatomy classes given by a noted teacher, George B. Bridgman, at the conservative Art Students League on West Fifty-seventh Street in Manhattan. There Ben hoped to study all the muscles of the body. He spoke with passion to Willy Snow of his fascination with hands—gnarled hands and strong workers' hands, the hands his father worked with as a woodcarver, the hands he would use in his art to express both strength and anger.

CHAPTER FOUR

Education
and the
National Academy

BY 1918, BEN WAS MAKING A RESPECTABLE $60 A WEEK AS A lithographer, with the prospect of making considerably more. Since his father was working only sporadically, Ben was the most reliable source of income for the family. Nonetheless, he was tired of his job, and also came to believe that its health risks were too great. He had heard that lithographers often went blind after a while, and he had even seen a lithographer keel over on his stone and die without warning. Taking note of the pale, sickly complexions of the workers around him, he decided it was time to get out of New York City and go into the countryside to look for work. This would be his first time away from home, and he looked forward to it eagerly.

He spent the summer working with an Italian truck driver on a farm near Westport, Connecticut. When fall came and there was no more work to be done on the farm, he was hired by the New Haven Railroad to work on the tracks. After a few weeks at this manual labor, his boss found out that he could read and write and promoted him to clerical work as a checker.

After several months of this, Ben had proven to himself that country life was not for him. He would be better off returning to Brooklyn and his job as a lithographer, so he could earn enough money to go to college full-time. He meant to show his parents that he could pay for his college education and help them at the same time.

When he thought he had earned enough money at Hessenberg's, he applied to Columbia University, but he soon learned that the tuition there was beyond his means and instead entered the Washington Square College at New York University for the academic year beginning in September 1919. His schedule was a heavy one—"Trigonometry and Solid Geometry," "Composition and Rhetoric," "Medieval and Modern Europe," "General Principles of Zoology," and a course called "Intermediate Art." Apparently he excelled in zoology: at the end of the academic year he was awarded a scholarship to study at the highly respected Marine Biological Laboratory at Woods Hole, on Cape Cod, Massachusetts, during the summer of 1920. He hated waiting tables, which he was obliged to do in exchange for the scholarship, but he delighted in the social aspects of his stay there—the hikes, swimming, boating, and dancing, and above all a trip to a neighboring island where he was fascinated by the twisted windswept trees, which reminded him of the weatherbeaten gnarled hands that had long fascinated him.

When Ben returned home after the summer, he realized that even the tuition at NYU was too high for him. Still determined to attend college, he registered as a full-time student at the tuition-free College of the City of New York. CCNY was far more suited to his needs and temperament than NYU had been. Started in the middle of the nineteenth century, when it was known as the Free Academy, the college had developed into one of the most vibrant and vital institutions of learning in the country. Selective in its admissions, it attracted some of the most intellectually curious and creative students in the New York area. Among the distinguished speakers who addressed the students during the academic year Ben spent there were Franklin D. Roosevelt, then candidate for vice president of the United States; Albert Einstein, who made the college his New York headquarters while visiting the States; and Rabindranath Tagore, the Nobel Prize–winning Indian poet.

Even though Ben signed up for an astounding twenty credits during his first semester at CCNY, he also found time to work for the school's monthly magazine, the *College Mercury*, contributing a cover drawing, a view of the college's newly built Lewisohn Stadium, portraits of four unidentified professors, and a sketch of Tagore, which so pleased the poet that he autographed it to the artist. All of these were published in the issue of December 1920. Benjamin H. Shahn was also credited with three rather amateurish drawings that appeared in January 1921.

During his second semester, Ben reduced his workload drastically, to two courses. His first-semester grades had been poor, and he was growing restless and bored. He found his fellow students spoiled and immature; they had little in common with him. Increasingly, he felt the need to study his art seriously, and he decided to give up his dream of earning a college degree so that he could devote all of his energies to acquiring the skills that would make him a great artist.

Ben applied to New York's National Academy of Design, a venerable institution then considered the best fine-arts school in the country. Because of its reputation and the fact that it charged no tuition, a large number of students applied for admission each year; all of them had to submit drawings, which were judged by an especially severe jury. Because of a shortage of space that year, all but the most gifted students were rejected. Ben remained. Somehow he had made considerable progress since the days of his clumsy City College drawings.

He registered at the academy on January 21, 1921. Among his fellow students were Raphael Soyer, who became a close friend, and Meyer Schapiro. One of his teachers was Charles L. Hinton, well known for his classes in both Antique and Life Drawing.

Unfortunately, Ben's experience was a disappointing one. The academy was conservative and rigid. Students had to follow the rules and were strongly discouraged from displaying any signs of individuality. They were, it was said, poured into a mold like the plaster casts from which they all worked. Though he believed it was wisest to conform to the rules and he was, with effort, able to do so, Ben was uncomfortable with them. He was especially troubled by the kinds of subject matter that apparently satisfied the teachers: the Buddha against a piece of Chinese drapery; barns; girls with windblown hair; boats of all kinds; tranquil scenes of country life. Ben far preferred to paint scenes of everyday life, things he himself had observed. He would have liked, for example, to paint a group of Italian workers who had stopped for lunch and were eating gigantic sandwiches. He was intrigued when one of the workers spat into a pile of fresh clean sand and left a mark on it. He was, he told a fellow student, determined to paint scenes like that, even if his teachers complained that they were not "artistic."

If nothing else, he did manage to learn just what he *didn't* want to do as an artist. In an interview with the critic and art historian Katherine Kuh, he summarized his experiences:

> I underwent a multiplicity of influences—from my teachers at the Academy, one of whom told me very directly, "When in doubt, use purple." I tried to do that. Others told me I must draw with bravery; I tried to do that, too. I came to a point where I began to question myself, who I was, what my antecedents were, what my interests were, and the answers to all these questions did not square with my strongest influence at that time— Cézanne. Cézanne's father, I've read, was a banker; my father was a woodcarver. Cézanne's school was classical—Greek, Latin; mine was the Bible and the Talmud. Cézanne's surroundings had remnants of Roman architecture; mine had just pathetic little rundown homes. I don't know whether Cézanne loved to tell stories, but I always did. However, I learned very quickly in my art education that art does not tell stories.
>
> Art, as I saw it one day when I helped to hang a National Academy show while I was a student there, was about cows. In those days, early in the twenties, there were many cow paintings. More than that, the cows always stood knee-deep in purple shadows. For the life of me I never learned to see purple where there was no purple—and I detested cows. I was frankly distressed at the prospects for me as an artist. But there came a time when I stopped painting, stopped in order to evaluate all these doubts. If I couldn't see purple where there was no purple—I wouldn't use it. If I didn't like cows, I wouldn't paint them. What then was I to paint? Slowly I found that I must paint those things that were meaningful to me—that I could honestly paint in the shapes and colors I felt belonged to them.

CHAPTER FIVE

First Love

BEN SHAHN WROTE NOTHING ABOUT HIS SOCIAL LIFE DURING this period. Willy Snow's manuscript describing Ben's boyhood in Brooklyn is also the only important source of information concerning his early manhood, during which Ben fell in love for the first time. The object of his love was Tillie Goldstein, and his courtship of her might be described as casual and cautious.

They had met at Eron Prep, and through Tillie Ben came to know a group of girls, most of whom were schoolteachers. Ben became a member of the group, and at first was its only male. They all shared cultural interests as well as an enthusiasm for outdoor sports, especially tennis. Ben often invited Willy to join the group, but his friend usually refused: he was too busy with his medical studies at Columbia, and, even more important, he was afraid to play tennis with Ben, who grew sullen whenever he was bested in a competition—a real possibility in this case, since Willy was at least as good a tennis player as he.

The girls liked Ben. He was tall and handsome, with blue eyes and an animated, expressive face. He was capable of playing cruel, insensitive pranks on his friends, but he was quickly forgiven. Intelligent and witty, he charmed them with his colorful tales and

anecdotes. Among them, he was, as he demanded to be, the center
of attention. Though it could be said that all of these young women
vied for his affection at first, the number of admirers gradually
dwindled to two. One of these was Yetta, a tall, thin young woman,
witty and attractive but with a sharp tongue. Ben enjoyed her stimulating company, but Willy knew that she was not the girl for Ben:
he would soon tire of her sarcasm. Far more suited to Ben, Willy
decided, was Tillie, the second girl. Tillie was also attractive, with
deep black hair and blue eyes, of medium height and, in Willy's
words, "pleasingly plump," with skin of "peaches and cream."
Tillie, unlike Yetta, was warm and gentle, kind and affectionate.
Most important, she was obviously devoted to Ben and hung on his
every word. Soon the "dating" began—Ben saw Tillie alone. He
also saw Yetta alone, but he spoke more enthusiastically about
Tillie. He liked her and he liked her home, considerably more lux-
urious than his own. He was also impressed by her family's telephone and phonograph, and by their piles of classical records. It
was not the home of very rich people, but the Goldsteins were
obviously better off than the Shahns.

During the summers, Ben, Willy, Bill Burston (who had been
the editor of CCNY's *College Mercury*), Yetta, Tillie, and other
members of their group, which now included several men, often
spent weekends at what Willy liked to call his "Camp Olympus," at
the foot of the Palisades opposite Yonkers, on the western side of
the Hudson. There they hiked, swam, canoed, and sailed. There
were two tents, one for the girls and one for the boys. The girls
were in charge of cooking and cleaning up, while Willy was in
charge of water activities and Ben led the hikes. Harriette Erdos,
who was part of the gang, remembers them all sitting around a
campfire, singing songs like "Blow Ye Winds," which Ben had
taught them. Saturday nights were special: the campers from the
city often went to Twombly Landing, where they improvised
humorous skits. There was, Willy said, "no off-color fun," or
uncouth sexual behavior. He and Ben were in charge of the girls,
and they took this responsibility seriously.

In spite of these rules, apparently strictly enforced, Ben and
Tillie did not hide the fact that they were becoming more than just
casual friends. For that reason, Willy was astonished when one

night Ben, with great seriousness, generously offered to step aside
if his friend Willy wanted to marry Tillie. Willy was dumbfounded.
He was fond of Tillie; he thought of her as a sensitive young
woman who was deeply in love with Ben, certainly not with Willy
or anyone else. Willy could only guess that this was Ben's awkward
attempt to escape the responsibilities of marriage. He speculated
that Ben's bitter relationship with his mother might have made
him afraid of a lasting relationship with any woman.

Whatever his fears might have been, Ben overcame them; on
August 8, 1922, he and Tillie were married. There was no large
party, just a simple ceremony. Tillie continued her work as a book-
keeper-accountant, and Ben returned to his old job at the lithography workshop. Their goal was to save enough money to be able to
spend a whole year in Europe. In every way, their prospects for
happiness seemed bright. Tillie, too, had come to America in 1906.
She was the last of twelve children—her mother had died while
giving birth to her—and her father, a merchant and Hebraic
scholar, was the undisputed head of the family. While in Europe,
Tillie had studied in a convent school—the only education available—but she had attended public school in America until the age
of thirteen, when she went to work as a secretary. She later studied
for two years at Cornell and at NYU.

Tillie and Ben moved to 120 Columbia Heights in Brooklyn
Heights, across the East River from Manhattan. For Ben, it was a
significant escape from the Jewish working-class section where he
had been raised. Now he found himself in a markedly different
world, ethnically diverse, intellectually and socially far from
Williamsburg. Their apartment, a fourth-floor studio in a building
once owned by the Squibb family, was modest, but the neighborhood was one of the most vital and colorful in Brooklyn, populated
largely by writers, artists, and musicians drawn to it by its delightful tree-lined streets, its charming brownstones, and its low rents.

In Brooklyn Heights, with Tillie's help, Ben became a changed
man. Exposed to a new and far more stimulating ambiance, he
gained confidence and sought to broaden his horizons. Each Friday night, he and Tillie held open house, attended by friends and
neighbors, as well as strangers; here Ben, king in his own home,
delighted in holding court with his stories and his strong opinions.

Tillie, in a portrait painted by Ben in the mid-twenties and in a photo taken at Truro during the same period.

Shahn at play, with a scarecrow, at Truro.

During this period, though they kept in touch, Willy Snow saw far less of Ben and Tillie than he had before. In his memoir, Willy relates two anecdotes that do not show his childhood friend in a very favorable light. The first episode took place in 1923. Willy, having graduated from Columbia's College of Physicians and Surgeons, was interning at what was then called New York City Hospital. As part of the holiday celebration, interns were permitted to bring guests to their dining room for Christmas dinner; Willy invited Ben and Tillie. After dinner, the interns and their guests retired to the lounge, where some played pool, a few played the piano, and most sat around the huge fireplace, chatting. Ben, in an effort to entertain his hosts and amuse himself, began to make quick sketches of the men. Some of the likenesses were remarkable, but some were offensive and insensitive. The artist all too frequently exaggerated the unattractive features of his subjects: those with long noses were given gigantic ones; flat-nosed physicians were depicted as pigs. There was mild laughter as Ben showed his works, but many of those present felt they had been ridiculed. According to Willy, Ben had thoughtlessly hurt the feelings of his hosts.

The second incident is considerably more disturbing. Ben had regaled Willy with stories of Woods Hole and other areas on Cape Cod, and in the winter of 1924, just after Christmas, he convinced Willy, his fiancée, Amy, and her friend Marie to join him and Tillie on a holiday there. Instead of going by train, they made a leisurely journey to the Cape by boat. Once they arrived, Willy quickly understood Ben's enthusiasm for Woods Hole: it was, as he had promised, the ideal place for a vacation. Their holiday, however, came to an abrupt end. A few days after their arrival, two men arrived in a car; without any explanation, Ben and Tillie joined them, saying only that they would return in a day or so. The "day or so" became a week, but Willy was not disturbed. There was more than enough to be enjoyed without them. Immediately after their return from this mysterious absence, however, they once again left, this time for good reason: a telegram informed them that Tillie's father had just died. They hurried to catch a train to New York, but not until Ben had borrowed all but a dollar and a half of Willy's money, promising to repay him by wiring the money as soon as he arrived in New York.

Willy, Amy, and Marie waited in vain for a week, living on nothing but bread and chocolate. Unable to reach Ben and unwilling to wire his own family for money—he wanted to conceal Ben's inconsiderate behavior—Willy and his friends left for home, using the boat tickets they had fortunately purchased in advance.

When Willy went to pay a condolence call to Ben and Tillie, he asked why the borrowed money had never been sent. Ben did nothing more than mumble that he had just forgotten. There were no regrets or apologies.

CHAPTER SIX

"Pictures Will Be My Manifesto"

BY THE FALL OF 1924, BEN AND TILLIE HAD SAVED ENOUGH money to enable them to plan what they hoped would be an extended trip through Europe.

At that time in his life, Ben, like so many artists in America, felt an acute need to leave home, primarily to study European art of the past and present and to absorb the fruits of different civilizations. He looked forward most to staying in Paris; virtually every man and woman of importance in American art and letters had settled—for a short time, at least—in what was then the artistic capital of the world, making the capital of France also the capital of American intellectual life.

As was the custom of the time, their passport was issued in his name alone; Tillie was merely noted in that official document as his wife, who would accompany him. Only Ben is described: twenty-six years old, six feet tall, with blue eyes, brown hair, and a fair complexion. The couple's passport photo reveals Ben to be curly-haired, mustached, with full lips and a high forehead. He appears both friendly and self-assured. Tillie, an attractive young woman, also seems sure of herself, yet far more reserved than her husband. She wears glasses, as does Ben, and her straight hair is bobbed. According to their passport, the purpose of the trip was to be "study and travel."

Though Paris was Ben's ultimate goal, the couple first traveled throughout North Africa and Europe. Their trip began in March 1925, and the experience proved to be as stimulating as Ben had anticipated. He was enchanted by North Africa. Having been lured there by his reading of Delacroix's notebooks, he saw the land and its people through the eyes of the French master.

The couple spent a month in Italy—from the middle of May until the middle of June—visiting Florence and Venice. In Venice, Ben came to understand that he had been taught to paint in the manner of the Venetian school of painting, with soft, tentative lines, and what he felt were "vague and amorphous colors." Neither the landscapes of Tintoretto, nor any other landscape painting appealed to him very much; he was far more concerned with human figures. In Venice, however, he did learn one very important lesson. Many hours spent studying Gentile Bellini's *A Procession of Relics in the Piazza San Marco* showed that, contrary to what he had been taught in art school, a painting could effectively tell the story of something that had happened, that a work of art could "celebrate an actuality."

He discovered he far preferred the precision of design and the colors of the Florentine school. In the art of the Florentine masters, he found none of the vagueness that he discerned in the art of the Venetians. The colors of the Florentines were bold rather than muted. A yellow robe was, decisively, yellow, and a blue sky was unmistakably a blue sky. He understood for the first time that there was no compelling reason for him to follow the restrictive rules of the academies he had attended in New York.

A short stay in Vienna, which they visited following Italy, was also significant, for there Ben saw for the first time and bought a copy of George Grosz's collection of sardonic drawings and watercolors, *Ecce Homo*. "I almost dropped dead in excitement over it," he told the art historian Morris Dorsky, speaking of Grosz's work. Later he came to consider Grosz the finest draftsman of the twentieth century, one whose work profoundly influenced his own.

Ben and Tillie reached Paris sometime in June. The French capital, Gertrude Stein had written, "was where the twentieth century was . . . the place that suited those of us that were to create twentieth century art and literature." Writers, among them Stein, Joyce, and Hemingway, came to Paris for the freedom of expression it offered, since France was not burdened by rigid censorship laws. They also came for the opportunity to work in a community of writers who were accepted and respected as they had not been at home. Musicians, too, flourished in Paris, where they had a greater chance of having their compositions played than anywhere else in the world. For example, during the season of 1925–1926, 3,394 musical performances were given in the French capital, compared to 1,156 in New York during the same period. Artists, too, were drawn to the city from all over the world: Picasso and Miró from Spain; Chagall from Russia; Brancusi from Romania; and Modigliani from Italy. Paris was unique in welcoming new and sometimes revolutionary ideas and forms of expression. "Paris with its twenty-five to fifty thousand artists," Ben told his first biographer, Selden Rodman, "could exist in the illusion that the world is a world of artists, just as Detroit thinks that the world is made up of motor-makers and people who drive cars."

Ben, of course, was an outsider. He was young and unknown, not a part of any group or movement. His personal contact with the Parisian art world was nonexistent; he was merely a distant, though fascinated, observer. Years later, he joked about this to an interviewer: "I remember how thrilled I was one day when Picasso and Derain came into a café where I was sitting. After about a half an hour I'd slyly eased my way from table to table towards them until I was close enough to hear their conversation. Now, I thought, I'm going to learn something. Now I'll get the low-down. I held my breath so as not to miss a word they were saying. They were saying:

" 'Dites, tu as mangé?'

" 'Non. Je n'ai pas mangé. Où est-ce qu'on peut manger par ici?'

" 'Je ne sais pas.' "

During his four months in Paris, Ben studied either at the Académie Julian, where Matisse, Léger, and Derain had worked, or at the Grande Chaumière. In a catalogue edited by Dorothy C. Miller and Alfred H. Barr, Jr., in 1943, Ben wrote that he was not accepted by the Académie Julian and instead studied at the less costly Grande Chaumière (but his brother Philip said that Ben sketched at the Julian with Jack Lewis, an American friend, and worked in the style of Léger and Braque). Ben was also enormously interested in the work of Picasso. In addition, he studied the French language assiduously, filling his notebook with a list of words he wanted to remember.

Though Ben undoubtedly profited from his formal studies in Paris, he benefited even more from his daily life in the city itself. (He complained that his friend the painter Moses Soyer, who was there at the same time, spent far too much time in his studio and far too little on the streets of the splendid city.) The artist's Paris, in the 1920s, was a series of small villages, each with its own character, a city of narrow streets lined with colorful bakeries, their sweets tantalizingly displayed; butcher shops with huge pieces of meat hanging from hooks; and fruit and vegetable stalls whose arrangements were works of art in themselves. Ben wandered through the city, from Montparnasse to the Sacré-Coeur in Montmartre, looking about him attentively, absorbing the sights and sounds of this most human of cities. He came to know each street and each square, and he developed a special affection for the splendid symmetrical Place des Vosges, Paris's oldest square, which became his own private retreat.

Paris's museums, too, offered him more than any art academy possibly could. They were proof of his conviction that the best art school was one that could be reached only by passing through a museum. He was fascinated by Gustave Moreau's Egyptian academic work at the museum devoted to the artist, and he came to think of the Musée Carnavalet, devoted to the history of Paris, as his "personal" museum. He was greatly affected by Le Corbusier's controversial Pavillon de l'Esprit Nouveau at the 1925 Paris Exposition Internationale des Arts Decoratifs, and by much of the work of the younger painters whose art could be found in the city's many galleries. Wherever he went, he drew copies of paintings and drawings that had attracted his interest.

Paris's famous cafés showed Ben another side of the artist's life. He sketched at the three most famous cafés of the period, all of them located on the wide, tree-lined boulevard Montparnasse: the Rotonde, which Rivera, Modigliani, Soutine, and Picasso had frequented; the Sélect, which set up its first tables in 1924 and played host throughout the twenties to both American and Central European painters, presided over with stern efficiency by Madame Sélect, a formidable, large-bosomed woman with shrewd eyes who wore fingerless mittens as she worked away behind her cashier's desk while her husband, sporting a long drooping mustache, made Welsh rarebits; and the Dôme, the favorite of Americans, like those depicted in Hemingway's *The Sun Also Rises,* which was as crowded at two in the morning as at seven in the evening. These cafés gave Ben the opportunity to draw and to talk, his two favorite occupations. "I argued art and politics," he wrote, "as everyone did. Political views then often incurred high feeling, but not ostracism." Among the topics discussed most heatedly was the case of the two Italian-American anarchists, Nicola Sacco and Bartolomeo Vanzetti, alleged murderers whose trial, conviction, and appeals had infuriated much of the French population—not only intellectuals but also members of the French working classes—to such an extent that children were being named Sacco and Vanzetti, as were many of the tugboats that wound their way up and down the Seine.

On October 15, 1925, Ben and Tillie left Cherbourg for New York. Ben's stay had been an exhilarating one, but it was only a beginning. He knew that upon his return to his home in Brooklyn, he would again have to save money, this time for a second trip abroad. By the end of his stay there, he had begun to formulate his role in the world of art, and his personal mission within it. He wrote many years later:

> Like every young artist under the sun, I was intent upon finding the deep and abiding way of things. I read the constantly proliferating art literature of the late Twenties in Paris—the manifestos, the tracts, the declarations, the testaments, the confessions, the diaries, the autobiographies, the monographs, always seeking the clue, the magic key to what was what, the elusive ingredient that made art, art, and not just more paint upon canvas, more filled-up space.
>
> There must be something, I thought—as young artists still think, and that they still seek—some knowledge that must be

possessed by the elect, that must endow them with those especial powers not possessed by ordinary persons.

But however avid my reading, my looking, seeking, pondering, I did not find any such clue at all. The tracts and the manifestos said too much the same thing. Oh, certainly, line, form, color, texture were the stuff of the images of art—no denying that. But one had to be honest with himself; this was all rudimentary. Essential, indeed, but there was more. There was something further that infused an image that gave it life. I agreed with the manifesto-writers that art should not be burdened by a mission to uplift, nor should it be loaded with academic rules and principles. I was as ready as anyone to throw off the traces and be free.

But I wanted to be free also of the new academy that was already moving in, already setting up its cast-iron rules for the new generation of painters. Indeed it did create them, and indeed the artists of today are still tyrannized over by its grim ethic of disengagement. (When will they free themselves? Who knows?)

Alone now in my thinking, I began to believe that art did, after all, have a mission—certainly not the Beaux-Arts kind of mission, but another one. Its mission was to tell what I felt, to say what I thought, to be my own declaration. I could not accept the current ones; they expressed some other fellow's beliefs and intentions, not mine. Pictures would be my manifesto.

CHAPTER SEVEN

Obeying the Inner Critic

BEN RETURNED FROM EUROPE SEEMINGLY CHANGED, ALMOST comically pretentious. He often wore what Willy called a trick vest, and a large signet ring on his left index finger. He would frequently take a small vial of perfume out of his pocket, remove a glass rod from the vial, and draw it along the length of a cigarette before starting to smoke it. After a while, however, Ben dropped what Willy considered "superficial props" and became his old self again.

Ben enthusiastically showed dinner guests stacks of a French magazine, *Le Petit Pain et Beurre*, filled with caricatures in the style of Daumier, which they perused together. He also displayed examples of African wood sculptures, which he had acquired abroad. He had been enchanted by their magical and bizarre qualities, as had so many European artists during the first decades of the century.

Although Ben told Morris Dorsky that he didn't feel he was sufficiently productive during this first trip to Europe, he had worked—especially in Paris. His paintings and drawings reflect the influence of Cézanne, Soutine, Matisse, and especially Rouault. He experimented with Cubism and with German Expressionism. "My first discontent with art—by no means my last—arose during the mid-twenties," he wrote many years later. "I began to be aware, then, that my pieces and those of my contemporaries were continually a re-statement of the product of earlier artists; that much of their work was, in its turn, a reiteration of what had gone before."

In spite of his own reservations about his early work, Ben was included in a group exhibition held at the Jewish Art Center in New York in the winter of 1926–27. The center had been founded in Greenwich Village in 1925; Chaim Gross and Raphael Soyer were among the painters who first exhibited in its small private space. Not only was Ben's work shown; it was even reviewed in the February 1927 issue of *The Menorah Journal,* which also carried articles by Louis Fischer, Maurice Samuel, Maurice G. Hindus, and Clifton Fadiman. There was, in addition, a roundup by Louis Lozowick, a Russian-born artist, of midwinter exhibitions in New York, which contained the first published comment about Ben's art. "Ben Shahn," Lozowick wrote, "is admittedly competent in many directions, which is perhaps the reason he is so difficult to characterize."

More important, Frank Crowninshield, the urbane editor of the sophisticated monthly *Vanity Fair,* as well as a founder of the Museum of Modern Art, saw one of Ben's paintings and proposed to arrange a one-man show for the young artist at the prestigious Montross Gallery.

Ben was flattered, but he was wise enough to realize that it would be a mistake to accept the offer at this point in his career. His work, he believed, was still far too derivative; he was seeing through the eyes of painters of the past, not through his own. Years later, he wrote in *The Biography of a Painting:*

> During the early French-influenced part of my artistic career, I painted landscapes in a Post-Impressionist vein, pleasantly peopled with bathers, or I painted nudes, or studies of my friends. The work had a nice professional look about it, and it rested, I think, on a fairly solid academic training. It was during those years that the inner critic first began to play Hara-Kari with my insides. With such ironic words as, "It has a nice professional look about it," my inward demon was prone to ridicule or tear down my work in just those terms in which I was wont to admire it.

The questions, "Is that enough? Is that all?" began to plague me. Or, "This may be art, but is it my own art?" And then I began to realize that however original it might be, it still did not contain the central person which for good or ill, was myself. . . .

It was thus under the pressure of such inner rejections that I first began to ask myself what sort of person I really was, and what kind of art could truly coincide with that person. And to bring into this question the matter of taste I felt—or the inner critic felt—that it was both tawdry and trivial to wear the airs and the artistic dress of a society to which I did not belong.

Ben realized that, paradoxically, he could best carry on his search for identity as an artist— an American artist—in Europe rather than in America. In America art was an isolated activity, something exotic and foreign to the mainstream of life. It was still several years before experimentation and new ideas would find acceptance there. For this reason, after his first trip to Europe Ben spent much time preparing for a second one, which he hoped would be longer and more fruitful.

Though he lacked enough money to embark on this expensive trip very soon, the prospects were good that he and Tillie could in time accumulate it. Ben easily found work in New York as a professional lithographer—and that paid well. He also sought and found employment as a commercial artist. He believed it was in no way demeaning to do so. Toulouse-Lautrec had executed posters for commercial purposes, and Daumier's drawings, published regularly for a wide public, were equally "commercial." So Ben painted signs at Coney Island, executing lifelike reproductions of huge frankfurters with mustard and relish, or enormous waffles with half-melted ice cream running down their sides. Each in its way was art . . . and would be taken quite seriously a few decades later.

CHAPTER EIGHT

The Death
of Hymie

EVEN AFTER HIS MARRIAGE TO TILLIE, WHO WAS WELCOMED enthusiastically by the entire Shahn family, including Gittel, the relationship between Ben and his mother remained hostile. Her behavior to him in his youth was something he found impossible to forgive. Friends, as well as her grandchildren, remember her as a warm friend and a loving grandmother, but she and Ben emphatically did not get along.

Ben's relationships with his two sisters—Hattie, who had been born in Russia, and Eva, who was born in Brooklyn—weren't much better. In a conversation with Selden Rodman, both sisters criticized their brother for having always avoided family chores and responsibilities. Hattie specifically recalled Ben's selfishness even on the voyage from Lithuania, when his seasick mother sent him to get tea from the kitchen and he returned, having stuffed himself, but having completely forgotten to bring back anything for her.

Ben did remain close to the male members of his family. From early childhood he had shared with his father a passion for drawing and craftsmanship, as well as storytelling, that created a strong bond between them. He had also become increasingly close to his kind, affectionate, and generous brother, Philip, who remained steadfastly loyal to him. Throughout his life, Phil willingly sublimated his own creative interests to the hero-worship of his brother. Ben, for his part, unfailingly permitted Phil to disagree and challenge him—a privilege he granted very rarely to others.

Ben, too, felt nothing but love for his other brother, Hyman, eleven years younger than he. Described by those who knew him as highly sensitive and of angelic temperament, Hymie was the adored baby of the family. Although the Shahns often fought with one another, they were unanimous in their great love for Hymie. Though he united the family when alive, his premature death tore that family irrevocably apart.

This terrible tragedy occurred during the summer of 1926. Two years earlier, before leaving on their first trip to Europe, Ben and Tillie, using money Tillie had received as a bonus on her job as a bookkeeper, had bought two broken-down houses, without electricity or plumbing, at Truro, near the tip of Cape Cod. They immediately sold one of the houses to a painter who, in turn, sold it almost at once to Iago Galdston, an extraordinary character they had met in Brooklyn. (His original name had been Isadore Abraham Goldstein. He combined the first letters of his first and second names with the first two letters of his original last name, which he then changed to Galdston. According to many who knew him, in inventing his name he also reinvented his character and became the villain whose name he had taken.) Ben and Tillie intended to restore the house themselves, with occasional help from Ben's father, whose skill would be especially useful.

On August 22, 1926, Hessel arrived in Truro, accompanied by young Hymie, who had come at the special invitation of Ben and Tillie. The following day, the three of them went bathing at an inlet of the Pamet River. As the tide started to go out, Hymie was swept rapidly away by the current. Unable to swim, he was submerged.

Victor Wolfson, Iago Galdston's brother-in-law, who was later to become a well-known playwright, witnessed Ben and Tillie desperately trying to rescue Hymie. Wolfson never forgot the sight of the boy's body, alone and motionless on the bottom of the clear deep water of the inlet's arm. Tillie and Ben, speechless with grief, dragged the body out and carried it up the hill to the small cottage and, finally, down the long dusty road to the railroad station, for the final journey to Brooklyn.

Hymie's death marked conclusively the end of Ben's relationship with his mother. Gittel, hysterical at the news of her youngest child's death, immediately blamed it on Ben and, to a somewhat lesser degree, on Hessel: against her wishes, they had persuaded the seventeen-year-old boy to go to the country with them. Her anger never abated.

After Hymie's funeral, Willy Snow went to the Shahn home at 111 Walton Street, where he found the grief-stricken mother screaming at Ben, who stood by ashen, and at an equally grief-stricken Hessel, hurling accusations that they had killed her Hymie. Afterward, Hessel withdrew, distancing himself from all those around him, speaking even less than he had before. According to those who knew him best, Ben, too, was permanently damaged, haunted by this tragedy until the end of his life. It caused him to reject his own family (with the exception of Phil), his old friends, and even, in a few years, his devoted wife, Tillie.

Ben rarely spoke of Hymie or of his death, as if the memory of the tragedy that had befallen his young brother was too much to bear. Tillie, on the other hand, spoke frequently of Hymie to their daughter Judy, who remembers that her mother, normally a relaxed parent, became tense and unnaturally vigilant whenever the young girl wanted to play on the shore near the site of the boy's drowning.

CHAPTER NINE

A
Turning
Point

BY EARLY 1928, BEN AND TILLIE HAD EARNED ENOUGH MONEY to embark on their second trip abroad. They sailed from New York on March 7, and stopped briefly in France before arriving, at the end of the month, in Tunisia. They planned to spend several months on the island of Djerba, off the southeastern coast. Djerba offered everything that Ben felt he needed. His resources were limited, but the cost of living was low; the language, French, was one he understood; and the island could offer him the isolation he felt he needed in order to concentrate on his work. He hoped that he might develop his own voice, his own style, in a completely foreign land, away from the influence and competition of Paris or New York.

He remained on Djerba for more than a year, drawing and painting, his work still influenced, above all, by Cézanne and Matisse. His memories of this period are anecdotal. They include visiting a harem in a small town, and being called Harold Lloyd by many Tunisians because of the eyeglasses he wore. He was fascinated by a colony of Jewish goldsmiths, whose work with ancient Hebrew symbols and designs he studied for hours on end. He made portraits of Jewish prostitutes, surprised that in spite of their profes-

Siesta at Djerba, *a pen-and-ink sketch drawn by Shahn on the Tunisian island in 1929.*

THE MUSEUM OF MODERN ART, NEW YORK. GIFT OF MONROE WHEELER

sion, they still lit candles on the Sabbath, and he painted portraits of affluent Tunisians whenever he was asked to do so.

In early 1929, Ben and Tillie, who was then pregnant, left Tunisia for Paris. A letter to a friend and Brooklyn Heights neighbor, Philip Van Doren Stern, expresses the artist's mood at the time and gives a rare insight into both his doubts and his basic strength during this period.

Dear Phil:

Well Philip today is exactly one year since we left. One year—there's magic in the word. You remember how often and how longingly I expressed the desire to stay away at least one year. And now that the year is up I feel—well it's hard to say how I feel. But I know how I felt. I felt it was necessary to be away at least a year. In a year one has time to forget his background—to forget a lot of undesirable friendships—and especially a lot of false ideas and ideals. And the falseness of all these ideals were [*sic*] impressed all the more on me when I glanced thru the art section of the *N.Y. Times* (for which David has been subscribing here in order not to forget his English). I saw what it is that moves New York artistically. And Phil it made me sick to vomiting. And when I think about it and try to reason it out I feel more and more that it isn't the artist of N.Y. who is at fault but N.Y. itself. For the talent, the understanding is very much alive everywhere. It is the background that varies—or rather the ideals of this background. The notes on the exhibitions that were going on at that moment made me feel as if I were suddenly back in N.Y. You know that sick in the heart feeling the first few weeks when you're back. I could stand it no longer and with a hearty bullshit I threw the paper aside and fled America again. The *N.Y. Times* is a marvelous cure for homesickness. But one of these days I suppose I must come back to reality and no amount of papers thrown aside and no amount of yelling bullshit will bring me back half as quickly. Therefore I felt I had to fortify myself, as it were, to keep my vision clear even when I'm surrounded by such bunk as the *N.Y. Times* and other papers and almost all the people around me are constantly shooting off. And now that this year is up I feel strong. Strong enough to see thru all this hairsplitting and nonexistent nuances.

But again one of these days I must come back—and I will. But it won't be much before July and I don't look forward to it with any great fear for the urge to work—to work is what counts—and the place matters little to me now.

That we're still here isn't due to any careful nursing of money but rather to the fact that we've had a furnished apartment and have been eating in. What with that and working every day and almost all day, very little time is left for spending money. Otherwise we couldn't have done it for the cost of living has almost doubled since we were here last time (and the same holds true for France). . . .

By the time they reached Spain, where they planned to spend a month before going to Paris, Ben and Tillie were almost penniless. They were forced once to walk out of a café without leaving a tip, and only a hundred dollars remained for their entire time in Spain.

Fortunately, they could look forward to receiving money that Ben's brother had sent to Paris, enough to enable them to stay in Europe for a few more months.

They reached Paris in the middle of May, but there is little detailed information about their stay in the French capital. Ben spent most of his time painting, visiting museums, and attending lectures at the Louvre on the arts of Egypt, Greece, Persia, Chaldea, and Italy. He also heard lectures on Cubism given by the noted art dealer Léonce Rosenberg.

Among Ben's American friends in Paris were the painters Moses Soyer and William Gropper; he painted a portrait of the latter seated at a café table. Gropper, a gentle, even-tempered man and a brilliant critic of modern society, could tell a story as well as Ben could; he and his wife, Sophie, became good friends of Ben.

On July 14, Ben and Tillie's first child was born at Neuilly-sur-Seine, a suburb of Paris. Their daughter was named Judith Hermine Shahn, the middle name an homage to the memory of Ben's brother Hyman. A few months later, they returned home, reluctantly but out of necessity, for they were again running out of money. Their stay abroad—especially the time spent in Djerba—had been productive for Ben. The more than two hundred drawings and watercolors he produced bear witness to his growth as an artist. According to Morris Dorsky, who saw much of the work Ben did in Djerba, he developed for the first time an "individualistically identifiable artistic line, with sweep, taste and verve, repeating again and again proof of his successful ease and control." Before these works he could show little that in subject and style was undeniably his own. "This was the proof he needed and here was the turning point which he could accept," Dorsky added. Even many years later, in 1952, when Ben showed Dorsky these early works, he expressed satisfaction with the drawings, most of them rapid sketches, of Arab faces and figures in various positions and costumes. They were to become the basis for his first one-man exhibition.

CHAPTER TEN

Edith Halpert's Gallery, Mrs. Rockefeller's Horse, and De Quincey's "Levana"

BEN AND TILLIE RETURNED TO BROOKLYN HEIGHTS ONLY A FEW weeks before the stock-market crash that ushered in the Great Depression. Ben managed to find some freelance work as a lithographer, but not nearly as much as he had hoped. He had been away from the country for too long and had been replaced by others. Advertising jobs had become even more scarce. Ironically, he was now forced to try to make his living as a painter; there was no alternative. However, in order to do so he would have to find a gallery to show his paintings and represent him.

The New York art scene was far different in 1929 from what it is today. There were art galleries, but only a handful of them would even attempt to sell the works of contemporary American artists. So it was extraordinary good fortune that led Shahn to the daring, innovative gallery of a courageous and temperamental woman, Edith Halpert.

Her background resembled Shahn's. Born Edith Gregoryeva Fivoosiovitch on April 25, 1900, she arrived in New York from Odessa with her impoverished, widowed mother on May 6, 1906, the same year as Ben. She was brought up in Manhattan and worked in a candy store where, at a very early age, she learned the

essentials of business and merchandising. At sixteen, she began to
show a more than casual interest in art. Lying about her age to gain
admittance, she attended the National Academy of Design and the
Art Students League; like Shahn, she took George Bridgman's
class in anatomy and life drawing. There was no question of her
pursuing a career as a painter, however. Edith had to make money,
and because there seemed to be no place for her in the world of
art, she decided to develop her considerable skills in the world of
business. She worked in the advertising departments of two stores,
Macy's and Stern's, and later as personnel manager, head of the
correspondence department, and systematizer for an investment
banking firm.

She was only eighteen when she married Samuel Halpert, a
painter sixteen years her senior. In the summer of 1925, they spent
several months in Paris. There she was astounded, and delighted,
to learn the esteem in which painters were held.

Back in New York, her love of art rekindled by her Parisian visit,
and her bank account replenished by a bonus from the investment
banking firm, she opened an art gallery at 113 West Thirteenth
Street in Greenwich Village. It was called simply Our Gallery, a
name that was soon changed to Downtown Gallery. Its first exhibit,
on November 6, 1926, fulfilled Mrs. Halpert's desire to show paintings and sculptures by modern American artists: she hung works
by Max Weber, John Sloan, Elie Nadelman, and Marguerite and
William Zorach.

From the very beginning, Edith Halpert's approach was somewhat unusual. She strongly believed that she could best serve her
artists (and herself) by charging low prices, so that the works of her
artists might be hung and admired in as many homes as possible.
She also strove to place work in public museums—or to sell it to
clients who might eventually donate it to a museum—thereby
enhancing the artist's reputation. And she energetically sought
commercial commissions for her artists, which would enable them
to continue with their painting without wasteful financial stress.

A small, attractive woman with lively blue eyes, she was often
shrewd, tough, and strong-willed. As a female art dealer in a world
dominated by men, she needed exceptional strength and determination in order to make her gallery succeed. She generally treated

her artists well. Accepting their work on a consignment basis, she charged them a commission of 30 or 33⅓ percent on all sales. In return she paid all costs—including the printing of catalogues—of each exhibition (an uncommon practice at the time), fought hard for royalties and generous payments for reproduction rights, aggressively publicized her artists' work, and, in many cases, offered her emotional support. However, as one of her artists noted tactfully, she was "not always fun to be with." According to the art historian Avis Berman, she was

> a difficult woman, but she was difficult for just causes. For years she had to insist that whom she loved was important, and her habit of disregarding others was not easily broken. Moreover, her virtues and faults sprang from the same roots. It was point-less to criticize her obstinacy, because when wedded to her unerring instinct for quality, her obstinacy was both justifiable and necessary. Her excesses were more than balanced by the contributions she made. An old acquaintance explained, "There was a black side to Edith, but the good was so good. And the bad? Well, what of it?"

There are two versions of how Shahn was introduced to Edith Halpert. According to her, Shahn's good friend Philip Wittenberg asked her to look at the artist's work. She had, of course, never heard of him, but she agreed because Wittenberg was a friend of her husband. When Shahn came to the gallery with his portfolio (Mrs. Halpert had refused to go to his studio), he was very shy. He became less so when, after looking through his work, Halpert announced to his astonishment that she would give him a one-man show.

Ben himself gave a different version. He decided in late 1929 that he would have to begin a search for a gallery. He found out which ones sold American art, began at the top, and finally reached the Downtown Gallery at the bottom. Halpert dismissed him summarily, asking that he leave his work at the gallery, since she looked at paintings by new artists only on Fridays and this was not a Friday. When he returned the next week, she confessed that she had not yet had the time to look at his work. Then, to his sur-prise, he received a telegram from her a few days later, asking him to bring in more of his paintings. Apparently Mrs. John D. Rocke-feller, Jr., had seen his portfolio and bought a few works on the spot. Ben eagerly returned to the gallery with more paintings, and an exhibit was planned for the following spring.

Whichever version is true, there is no doubt that Mrs. Rocke-feller's enthusiasm for Shahn's work early in his career fueled Edith Halpert's interest. Abby Aldrich Rockefeller was no dilet-tante; her interest in and knowledge of art were considerable. A charming, witty, and vivacious woman with impeccable taste, she was an astute collector and a founder of the Museum of Modern Art. She was also a patron and friend of Edith Halpert, whose gallery she had chanced upon in 1927, and who became her art adviser between 1928 and 1935. Mrs. Rockefeller bought at least one of Shahn's paintings, *Girl in Kimono,* an oil on paper, before the opening of his first Downtown exhibition, and she certainly used her powerful position to help Halpert in her efforts to stir up interest in Shahn before that.

Suddenly, as Morris Dorsky has noted, "for an unknown all the doors miraculously opened." Shahn's work was included in a group show held at the Newark (N.J.) Museum early in 1930, and Mrs. Halpert herself showed some of his work in her own exhibition "33 Moderns." That exhibition—in full, its name was "Paintings, Sculpture and Watercolors, Drawings and Prints by 33 American Contemporary Artists"—held not at her own gallery but at the uptown Grand Central Galleries, included an oil, a watercolor, and a drawing by Shahn. Most important, three of Ben's works were included in the fifth exhibition at New York's Museum of Modern Art, then located at 730 Fifth Avenue. "An Exhibition of the Work of 46 Painters and Sculptors Under 35 Years of Age" ran for only two weeks in April and was the worst-attended MOMA exhibition that spring, but it was valuable as a showcase for young and rela-tively unknown American artists. The method of selecting the artists whose work was represented has never been revealed, though there was a strong suspicion that most, if not all, were rep-resented in the collections of the museum's trustees. It was reported that when one of these trustees was discussing the exhi-bition with Alfred Stieglitz, the latter asked if the museum wanted the best Marsden Hartleys, to which the trustee answered that the museum wanted to show only painters whose works were owned by the trustees. "That's the only way we can run this museum," the trustee added.

No matter how and why they were chosen, the exhibition did include the works of a number of artists still remembered today, as well as several by artists who have been forgotten. Among the former were Isamu Noguchi, Peggy Bacon, Peter Blume, Miguel Covarrubias, Arshile Gorky, Alexander Brook, Pavel Tchelitchew, Reginald Marsh, Franklin Watkins, Reuben Nakian . . . and Ben Shahn, who was represented by two oils, *Baby* (1929), *Anna* (1930), and *Arabs*, an undated watercolor.

Whether by design or by coincidence, Ben's show at the Downtown Gallery opened only a few days before MOMA's. During the same period, Mrs. Halpert opened the Daylight Gallery, built in the backyard of the brownstone that housed her original gallery. The MOMA show plus the inauguration of the new gallery only added to the attention given Shahn's exhibition, which opened on April 8 and lasted three weeks.

The catalogue listed three oils on paper, two priced at $50 and one at $40, and seventeen watercolors selling for from between $25 and $50. In addition, a separate group of watercolors at $25 each is listed as a "Special series of Watercolors based on mythological and biblical subjects." The titles of these works suggest that all or most were done in Djerba, though a few might have been executed in Europe.

According to Halpert, all the listed works were sold. She wrote to James Thrall Soby: "I think it is an important note that during the depression a one-man show was completely sold out—by an artist completely new to the public." Shahn, however, said only that the pictures sold "fairly well," and he remembered that Mrs. Rockefeller, Alfred H. Barr, Jr., Mrs. Cornelius N. Bliss, and a Mrs. Bethune purchased works. Mrs. Halpert confirmed this to Morris Dorsky, adding that Duncan Chandler, an architect to the Rockefeller family, was also among the buyers. Dorsky believes that members of Shahn's family also purchased some of his works.

For the most part, the critics responded well to Ben's first one-man exhibition. Two of them are worth noting. The anonymous reviewer for *The New York Times* wrote:

Ben Shawn [*sic*] is exhibiting at the Downtown Gallery mascu-
line drawings and watercolors that assert their sex in bold
strokes, in straightforward red and blue and in qualities more
deep-seated than those of obviously strong line and color. . . .

. . . Grotesque heads under striped turbans, or flowers sky-
rocketing out of a blue vase. The special series of watercolors
(without titles) based on mythical and biblical subjects are great
fun and a little difficult to follow. Certainly you can be sure
enough of Adam and Eve, but is that winged horse Pegasus, and
does that scrawny bull carry Europa on his back? However, the
Near Eastern setting that seems to fit the mood of this artist is
also the proper setting for these stories, which makes for a special fitness about it all.

The reviewer for the New York *American* noted:

Ben Shahn bears watching. He possesses a creative sensibility
which if brought intelligently to maturity should carry him far.
What he has already accomplished may be observed in the
watercolors and drawings of his first one-man show. . . . What he
is further to accomplish seems fairly indicated.

Shahn's works show a rare gift for strong line and a keen
appreciation of strong color. He can usually articulate his
thoughts and emotions. He has already achieved a rather individual style, though this will probably undergo radical alteration
in time.

If it is not presumptuous, one would wish to suggest to him
that he need further concern himself but little with contemporary painting in Paris, and concern himself no more with studying Rouault. He should have complete regard for his own
creative self and in that regard increase his range of meaning,
especially in line and color.

Several years later, Shahn rather surprisingly complained to
Morris Dorsky that he had already been hardened to a lack of
recognition and that at the age of thirty-two(!) he had found success too late. In addition, he felt regret that he had not yet
achieved a style of his own, a fact noted by some of his critics and
borne out by the work he did at Truro the summer following the

exhibition. Those paintings and drawings, though competent and professional, were still marked by the influence of modern European artists.

Of more concern, however, in spite of the recognition his work had received, was the fact that it was not selling. Though his faithful brother Philip bought at least two watercolors, and his work was included in group shows at the Chicago Art Institute, the Cincinnati Museum, and the Buffalo Museum during 1930, Shahn was not close to reaching his goal of being able to make his living as a painter. He was still largely dependent on Tillie's earnings as a bookkeeper and on the generosity of friends and admirers.

One of these was Abby Aldrich Rockefeller, who, sometime in 1931, invited him to spend time at the 3,000-acre Rockefeller estate at Pocantico in upstate New York. She so admired what she called the "Shahn brown" that she wanted the artist to paint a portrait of her favorite horse, who was of the same color. Bernarda Bryson Shahn, Ben's second wife, wrote John Carlisle in 1972 that Ben "did a few watercolor pieces—very reluctant-looking—of a horse that the Rockefellers were proud of. Otherwise he spent his time trying to get enough to eat because the meals there were famous for being on the skimpy side." In a letter to his brother Philip, Ben confided that the horse was not even brown. It was gray.

Mrs. Rockefeller's commission was somewhat frivolous, but a more serious source of help was Philip Van Doren Stern, one of the first friends Ben had made in Brooklyn Heights, who offered him a chance to use his serious art for potentially profitable commercial purposes. Stern was a truly remarkable man; according to Willy Snow, he was "a scholar, an aesthete, a perfectionist, and a man of high principle." In addition, he was a good and generous friend to Ben.

Born in 1900, Stern had graduated from Rutgers in 1924 and immediately entered the worlds of business and advertising. By 1930, however, realizing that he could never be intellectually satisfied by commerce, he turned to his real interest, literature. At first, he worked as a designer and then as an editor for a number of book publishing houses, but before long he set out on his own as a writer and scholar. His interests and tastes were varied. He wrote novels and short stories (one of his stories was to become the movie classic *It's a Wonderful Life*); he wrote a book on typography, one on the history of the automobile, and several on the Civil War, and he edited collections of the writings of Abraham Lincoln, Edgar Allan Poe, and Thomas De Quincey. It was because of his enthusiasm for the works of the author of *Confessions of an English Opium Eater*, as well as his sincere desire to help his friend, that he proposed that Ben undertake to illustrate an edition of one of De Quincey's lesser-known works, "Levana, and Our Ladies of Sorrow," from *Suspiria de Profundis*, a sequel or appendage to the well-known *Confessions*. The sequel itself was never completed, and De Quincey wove some of the completed essays into other parts of his work in the collected edition of his writings. Four essays were left, among them "Levana," considered by the eminent De Quincey scholar, David Masson, to be "one of the most magnificent pieces of prose in English or any other language."

In his proposal to Shahn, Stern specified that the artist execute ten lithographs to illustrate the text. As part of their agreement, it was stipulated that Stern pay for the paper, printing, binding, and promotional material. After those initial expenses were recovered through the sales of the portfolio, the entire profits would go to Shahn. "Levana," which its author characterized as a "dream-legend," essential to an understanding of the *Confessions*, is a powerful and often enormously beautiful evocation of De Quincey's vision. However, it is unlikely that Ben himself would have chosen to illustrate a subject of this nature. Furthermore, he had developed a strong aversion to the medium of lithography. After his many years in a lithographer's workshop, he had come to hate the very smell of tusche, the black liquid lithographers use for drawing. But he needed money almost desperately and never considered rejecting Stern's generous offer.

Two hundred and twelve portfolios were published in early 1931. Each contained De Quincey's text, a note by Stern, and a suite of ten original lithographs. According to a flyer that accompanied the portfolio, each lithograph, measuring ten inches by thirteen inches, was "printed in sepia on Canson & Montgolfier's *papier ancien*. Portfolios 1–12 (of which numbers 1 and 2 are not for sale) contain a suite of mounted and signed lithographs." These deluxe portfolios sold for $25 each, while the regular edition was priced at $10. In spite of the elegant presentation and a note that certified Ben's importance by mentioning that his pictures had been exhibited in the Chicago Art Institute, the Buffalo Museum, the Newark Museum, and New York's Museum of Modern Art, "Levana" found few buyers.

There was little notice in the press, either; the only significant review was by E. A. Jewell of *The New York Times,* who preferred De Quincey to Shahn, lavishing praise on the writer's "haunting fragment," which "rises to superb heights of beauty and tenderness." "One reluctantly confesses that Mr. Shahn, in his often grotesque and clumsy lithographic annotations, seems to have missed the spirit of this rare document," Jewell wrote.

Ben estimated that no more than ten copies of "Levana" were sold. Stern recovered little more than half of his investment, and the artist was therefore not paid for his work. Not very long after its publication, Ben, out of frustration and anger, destroyed the unsold copies.

The lithographs do not, in fact, give much indication of the strength that Ben would display in his later works. He must have felt uncomfortable with the subject since it reflected Stern's taste and not his own. In addition, his work was still imitative, influenced by Gauguin, Chagall, Cézanne, and African art. Yet "Levana" remains important: it was the first narrative Shahn ever illustrated, and the first time that lettering—there were one or two lines of script beneath each image—became an integral part of his work. There was no hint of the original lettering and alphabet he would later create, but his own handwriting, utilized here, was clear, elegant, and strikingly beautiful.

CHAPTER ELEVEN

The Summer of 1931

WHEN BEN AND TILLIE ARRIVED IN TRURO, WHERE THEY planned to spend the summer of 1931, their financial situation seemed hopeless. Tillie had found work sporadically as a secretary, office manager, or bookkeeper, but no steady employment which would assure them of an income. As for Ben, Mrs. Rockefeller had paid him $500 for the sketches of her horse; Halpert took $150 as commission, leaving Ben with $350, which he characterized as "a veritable windfall and comparative affluence for the summer of 1931," but only that long. In addition, Ben had done freelance jobs for a friend, Izzy Steinberg, who owned a commercial art studio; his brother Philip had purchased some of his paintings; and he was given occasional commissions, which he rarely enjoyed. Once, he was asked to paint a portrait of a spoiled brat who stubbornly refused to stand on a spot that Ben had marked on the floor. After many attempts to get the child to cooperate, Ben had an idea. He asked Judy, who had accompanied him, to stand on the spot. As he had hoped, the brat pushed her away so he could stand there himself.

Despite the pressure of poverty, the summer was an immensely productive one. It marked Ben's emergence as an independent artist; he no longer imitated artists of the past and no longer limited himself to styles and subject matters essentially foreign to his own nature. His work began to reflect his own personality. This burst of creativity resulted in three projects, his finest and most original work to date.

The first of these was an illustrated Passover Haggadah for which he wrote the text by hand, after which he placed it on the center of each page, with "decorative color illustrations on all sides."

The word "haggadah" means literally "what is said" or "narration"—in broader terms, the telling of tales. And the tale Ben wished to illustrate, which is told in the Passover Haggadah and recited during the seder, is the magnificent one of the deliverance of the Jews from slavery in Egypt and their emergence as a free people. Ben's inspiration for such an ambitious undertaking undoubtedly stemmed from his childhood, when the seder was a joyous celebration and an illustrated Haggadah the most cherished of books. The form that Ben's *Haggadah* was to take—the Hebrew text surrounded by color illustration, in the style of medieval manuscripts—derived from his childhood practice of drawing in the empty margins of Hebrew books when no paper was available.

A later source of inspiration for Ben's *Haggadah* was his observation of the turbaned Jews he lived among on Djerba. They are the people of his *Haggadah,* recognizable by their headdresses, their kneeling body positions, and their dark faces. According to the Judaic scholar Stephen J. Kayser, these Tunisian Jews, for Shahn, became living illustrations of Biblical scenes.

Apart from some highlights in gouache, Ben's paintings were executed in watercolor, the traditional medium used for centuries to decorate Haggadahs. The illustrations are, for the most part, dreamy, vibrant works depicting the traditional elements of the seder service as well as the story of the Exodus. The religion Shahn depicts is a joyful one, consistent with the celebration of a liberation. Some of these illustrations are especially powerful; noteworthy is his use of strong arms and expressive hands. In the first, *The Bread of Affliction,* Moses leads the Israelites out of bondage under the protection of the outstretched arm and hand of God. In the third illustration, *Our Fathers Worshiped Images,* Shahn uses the forceful image of the arm and hand of Abraham. In the fourth, *In Every Generation Men Rise Up Against Us,* arms and hands, including the hand of God, again surround the text. In the sixth illustration, *And We Cried unto the Lord,* God's redeeming might is represented by his powerful hand, and God's mighty arm dominates the page from above the seventh illustration. Four large hands appear on the bottom of the eighth illustration, *The Reckoning of the Miracles,* and a bearded, turbaned patriarch is depicted gesticulating around the top of the text. Finally, kneeling figures, hands clasped in prayer, dominate the tenth illustration, *Bondage and Prayer.*

After finishing eleven of a projected twelve pages, Ben showed the work to a publisher who had expressed interest in it, but he refused to publish these illustrations in color. Disappointed and disheartened, Ben stopped work on the *Haggadah,* leaving the last plate undone. The completed plates were soon sold to Mrs. Frieda Warburg, who gave them to her son Edward M. M. Warburg, who in turn donated them to the Jewish Theological Seminary of America, in New York City. When, in 1947, Mrs. Warburg presented her Fifth Avenue mansion to the seminary to be used as the Jewish Museum, the Shahn illustrations became part of the museum's permanent collection.

That summer was significant, too, because during it Ben reinforced his friendship with Walker Evans, which led to an exhibition and the artist's second important project of the period. Ben had met Evans, then at the beginning of his career as a photographer, two years earlier in Brooklyn Heights. Theirs was an unlikely friendship. Ben, an immigrant and a Jew, was outgoing, passionate, vital, and intense, with a need to dominate and control. Evans, born in a small midwestern town and educated in the East, was a middle-class Christian American, reserved and soft-spoken, with courtly manners and the accent of a cultured gentleman. He found Ben an overpowering figure: "All he had to do was come into the room and you felt tired," he once said. Knowing Ben was an education, however, he added, since the little boy from the Midwest had never seen anyone like him. Beyond their differences, and most significant, Evans noted that they had the same kind of eye.

Shahn enjoyed the company of Cookie, a Scottish terrier belonging to a Truro neighbor. He used the shack in the background as a studio during the early thirties.

Shahn and his daughter Judy on Cape Cod in 1930 or 1931.

Evans spent most of the summer following their first meeting at the Shahn home in Truro. He provided transportation around the Cape in his Model T Ford and, with little success, gave Ben driving lessons. In return, he was treated like a member of the Shahn family. There was little to eat, but Ben and Tillie and Judy generously shared with their guest the soured milk that dairy farmers gave them, the vegetables and fruits Ben diligently gathered as they fell from delivery trucks, and the clams, always abundant on Cape Cod.

The following summer, Evans again visited the Shahns, and it was then that the idea of the exhibition was born. The exhibition was initially conceived as an angry response to the establishment artists who lived and worked in the area. Though Ben had joined the official Provincetown Art Association and shown his work at their group exhibitions, he had soon become disenchanted by their pretensions. But their worst crime was their unpardonable behavior towards the De Luze family, black-skinned Cape Verdean Portuguese who lived fifty yards down the hill from the Shahns and had become their friends. The warm and generous De Luzes, parents of more than ten children, served as caretakers for many summer visitors, working for them during the summer and looking after their homes during the winter. Though members of the family were on good terms with many of the local intelligentsia and had known both John Reed and Eugene O'Neill, they were ignored by the "white" community, neither asked to participate in their cultural activities nor invited to their art exhibitions. An outsider himself, an immigrant from Russia, Ben felt a kinship with this unpretentious, warm-hearted family.

Eager to right the wrong that had been done to them, he sought revenge by joining Evans in mounting a two-man show in the De Luzes' newly whitewashed barn. The exhibition was to consist of a number of photos Evans had taken of the family and their colorful home, and a series of Shahn watercolors.

Although at first Ben planned to hang his newly completed illustrations for the *Haggadah,* he suddenly changed his mind, deciding on a new work that might serve to define him as an artist. "What had been undertaken lightly," he wrote in *The Biography of a Painting,* "became very significant in my eyes."

At the time, Ben was reading an illustrated book he had bought in France that recounted the history of the notorious Dreyfus case. He immediately realized that he had found by chance the subject for which he was searching: the theme of injustice challenged, of a wrong uncovered and brought to light after a long, arduous struggle.

The story of the infamous Dreyfus case, which shook France and the rest of the western world at the end of the nineteenth century, began in September 1894, when a French spy at the German embassy came across an unsigned letter, with an appended memorandum (*le bordereau*), listing secret documents that revealed French military secrets. The *bordereau* was obviously meant for the German military attaché. An intense search for the traitor followed, and the army finally accused Captain Alfred Dreyfus, a wealthy Alsatian Jewish officer with a spotless record, who worked at the War Office. Though he vigorously protested his innocence, Dreyfus was court-martialed in December 1894 and sent to Devil's Island, to spend the rest of his life in solitary confinement. Few doubted that his religion accounted for the verdict.

The story did not end there, however. In March 1896, Colonel Georges Picquart, head of the Information Branch of the Secret Service, discovered conclusive evidence that Major Marie-Charles-Ferdinand-Walsin Esterhazy was in German pay, and that it was his handwriting, not Dreyfus's, on the *bordereau*. Picquart was silenced by the War Office, but in March 1897 Mathieu Dreyfus, Alfred's brother, also discovered evidence incriminating Esterhazy and exonerating his brother. As a result, there was a court-martial at which Esterhazy, in spite of the overwhelming evidence against him, was acquitted in only a few minutes. Two days later, the newspaper *L'Aurore* published "J'accuse," an open letter from Emile Zola to the president of the French republic, Félix Faure. Zola accused the judges of having followed the orders of the War Office by covering up material evidence, and this led to Esterhazy's acquittal. Zola was prosecuted for libel and sentenced to prison, a fate he avoided only by escaping to England.

France was sharply divided into two camps; the case became a major political issue, until, in the summer of 1898, it was conclusively proven that the evidence against Dreyfus had been forged.

Incredibly, after a new court-martial in 1899, the verdict was still "guilty." This time Dreyfus was sentenced to ten years in prison, but a few weeks later he was officially pardoned. Finally, in 1906, an appeals court completely exonerated Dreyfus; he was reinstated in the army and awarded the Legion of Honor.

Instead of depicting the shameful events of the story, Ben decided to paint watercolors of the protagonists in the case, both heroes and villains. He stated his goal:

> Within the Dreyfus pictures I could see a new avenue of expression opening up before me, a means by which I could unfold a great deal of my most personal thinking and feeling without loss of simplicity. I felt that the very directness of statement of these pictures was a great virtue in itself. And I further felt, and perhaps hoped a little, that such simplicity would prove irritating to that artistic elite who had already—even at the end of the twenties—begun to hold forth "disengagement" as the first law of creation. As artists of a decade or so earlier had delighted to *épater le bourgeois,* so I found it pleasant, to borrow a line from Leonard Baskin, to *épater l'avant-garde.*"

Underneath each gouache, Shahn had put the name of the person or persons depicted (one caption appears above the portrait), in variations of what he called "my best lithographic script." There are five single portraits (either busts or full-length figures) and three groups of two or three standing figures. As a private joke, or just to confuse those who studied the gouaches, the names of four handwriting experts are given under a group portrait of only three of them.

Painted for the most part in blacks, blues, and grays, these figures are distinguished by their facial expressions (above all, their eyes), their costumes, and the way they hold themselves and stand. Obviously based on illustrations—probably the photographs in the book Shahn was reading (since he executed them in a few days, there was no time to do research)—they are reminiscent of the French "Imagerie Populaire." Though they have been criticized as too light-hearted for their serious subject (Ben himself called them semi-serious), they are skillfully executed, effectively if not profoundly delineating the characters depicted. They constitute a large step forward in the artist's development, especially as his first attempt to lodge a social protest through his art.

Shahn and Evans had worked to make the opening night a festive occasion. They cleared the barn, sent out formal invitations, and served tea and cookies (ordered from New York) to the assembled guests.

The exhibition lasted only two days, but it was not the end of Shahn's Dreyfus series. After returning to New York in the fall, he learned that a new film based on the Dreyfus case and starring Cedric Hardwicke as the captain had opened in the Warner Theatre on Broadway, to great success. Shahn went to Warner Bros. and asked if his watercolors could be exhibited in the lobby of the theater. Warners agreed to exhibit the pictures during the last two weeks of the film's run and to pay Shahn $50 a week. At the end of the run, Ben went to the theater to take the pictures back but was told that they had disappeared. Rather than being upset, he was delighted: the watercolors had been insured as part of a floater policy, at $1,000 each, which meant that he would be paid $10,000 for the set. About to become rich, he was, he said, "walking on clouds"—until one day he was informed that the precious gouaches had been found in a safe-deposit box. They had never even been exhibited, because the manager of the theater was afraid they would be lost or stolen.

CHAPTER TWELVE

The Passion of Sacco and Vanzetti

BEN'S THIRD PROJECT THAT SUMMER, *THE PASSION OF SACCO and Vanzetti,* marked the start of a new chapter in his life as an artist and led to his recognition as the most passionate socially committed painter in America. The *Haggadah* and the Dreyfus series were historical, but the conviction of the two Italian immigrants, still heatedly disputed, was a contemporary example of what he felt was injustice. From that time on, Ben would be a vigilant observer of America, seeking out injustice wherever he found it, and fighting it through his art.

The idea of illustrating the story of these two men had come to him at least two years before he actually began work on the project. Referring to his return to America from Europe in 1929, he told John D. Morse in a 1944 interview:

> I had seen all the right pictures and read all the right books—Vollard, Meier-Graefe, David Hume. But still it didn't add up to anything. Here I am, I said to myself, [thirty-one] years old, the son of a carpenter. I like stories and people. The French school is not for me. Vollard is wrong for me. If I am to be a painter I must show the world how it looks through my eyes, not theirs.

Then I got to thinking about the Sacco-Vanzetti case. They'd been electrocuted in 1927, and in Europe of course I'd seen all the demonstrations against the trial—a lot more than there were over here. Ever since I could remember I'd wished that I'd been lucky enough to be alive at a great time—when something big was going on, like the Crucifixion. And suddenly realized I was! Here I was living through another crucifixion. Here was something to paint!

Though not another crucifixion, the case of the two Italian immigrants, one a shoemaker and one a fish peddler, who were accused of killing a paymaster and a guard in an attempted holdup in South Braintree, Massachusetts, had become a cause célèbre throughout Europe and the United States. Their arrest, conviction, and failure to receive a new trial in the face of substantial evidence showing that their first trial had been riddled with procedural errors and questionable decisions by a racist, anti-immigrant judge were vigorously protested by academics, intellectuals, civil libertarians, and literary figures from 1921 until 1927, when Sacco and Vanzetti were executed. Following their deaths, riots broke out in the United States as well as Europe, led by angry crowds who maintained that the men were sentenced to death because they were admitted anarchists, draft evaders, and radicals, and not because they were murderers.

Ben had closely followed the case and in Paris, on his first trip to Europe, had witnessed a demonstration by more than 20,000 protesters. Back in the United States, he had twice gone to Boston to join futile demonstrations on the defendants' behalf. Protests from abroad intensified. Alfred Dreyfus offered to help the men, and Benito Mussolini entered a plea on their behalf. On the day Sacco and Vanzetti were sent to the electric chair, Ben wandered the streets of Brooklyn Heights in tears. "I hate injustice; I guess that's about the only thing I really do hate," he often said. For this reason, he was ideally suited to tell with compassion and sensitivity the story of these two immigrants whom he believed to be victims of a cruel injustice.

In *The Biography of a Painting* he notes that he "set about revealing the acts and the persons involved with as rigorous a simplicity as I could command. I was not unmindful of Giotto, and of the simplicity with which he had been able to treat connected events—each complete in itself, yet all recreating the religious drama, so living a thing to him.''

Before working on the gouaches, Ben had done intensive research, largely at the Main, Forty-second Street branch of the New York Public Library, in search of photographs on which to base his images. The task was a difficult one: he spent months going through newspapers, magazines, pamphlets, and books (foreign as well as American). Several years later, he admitted that he felt guilty about this procedure, all the more so because of objections raised by two men he respected, Walker Evans and Moses Soyer, to the use of photographs as the models for his own art. Nonetheless, he persisted in this method—necessary, he believed, since he had never actually seen any of the protagonists in the drama he was to depict.

Ben worked on the Sacco-Vanzetti watercolors under enormous pressure. He had found a night job preparing advertisements for a department store in Newark, New Jersey. At the same time, his father suffered a heart attack and was hospitalized; and Ben was the only visitor he wanted. So his schedule was an exhausting one. During Hessel's three months in the hospital, Ben visited him every day between two and four in the afternoon. At six o'clock in the evening, he would begin work on his Newark job, preparing drawings for the advertisements until two in the morning. When they were completed he delivered them to an engraver in Manhattan, then went home to Brooklyn Heights, where he slept for five or six hours, awakening to work on the Sacco-Vanzetti series for three or four hours. Despite this arduous schedule, Ben was happy: he was too stimulated by his work on the series to suffer from the fatigue that would ordinarily have overcome him.

For a while he worked in secret, afraid any negative reactions to the watercolors might discourage him. When he finally had the courage and confidence to show them, first to friends and then to a number of painters and writers, the response was unanimously enthusiastic. He could now exhibit them with confidence.

The obvious site for that exhibition was the Downtown Gallery. According to Ben, Edith Halpert was cool at first. For one thing, she objected to the long captions that accompanied some of the watercolors—e.g., "Enrico Bastoni, Baker Who Bought Eels from Vanzetti on the Morning of December 24, 1919." Nonetheless, at the urging of Holger Cahill, the influential curator who advised Abby Aldrich Rockefeller on her growing collection of American folk art, Mrs. Halpert finally agreed to hold the exhibition in April 1932—with Ben's captions. (Mrs. Halpert's version of the story differs. According to her, she went to Shahn's studio to see the series and liked them at once. She hesitated only when some of her friends tried to talk her out of showing them for fear that the gallery might be raided for exhibiting subversive art.)

The *Passion*'s twenty-three gouaches are organized in three parts: before the trial, during the trial, and after the trial, more or less chronologically. First, there are portraits of the two principals, manacled to each other, their faces sad but resigned. It is, as are a number of others, an exact copy of a photo. Next, there is a view of Villa Felletto, Vanzetti's hometown, followed by a portrait of Vanzetti alone. After this, Sacco's parents, nieces, and nephews are shown in Torremaggiore, Sacco's hometown, followed by a portrait of Sacco with his wife and young son.

Trial scenes follow. The two defendants are depicted enmeshed in a courtroom cage. Next, portraits of the presiding judge, Webster Thayer, stone-faced and haughty; the four stiff, cold prosecutors, and then of Benjamin J. Bowles, a witness for the prosecution who identified Vanzetti. Then four works depict the attorney for the defense, the eel-buying baker, three unidentified witnesses, and six additional witnesses who also bought eels from Vanzetti.

There follow two scenes, which take place after the verdict of guilty has been announced: one shows the defendants handcuffed to their solemn, brass-buttoned guards, and the other Sacco's family following the verdict. Next, there is a portrait of Sacco's wife, with the words, "Be of Good Courage, Victory is Surely Ours." There follow a head of Judge Thayer, presiding over the second trial as he had over the first, a scene of Mrs. Sacco with an organizer of the defense, and one of Alvan T. Fuller, the governor of Massachusetts, to whom the defendants issued a final appeal.

Scenes of demonstrations, one at New York's Union Square and one in Paris, are followed by a portrait of the members of the Lowell Committee, which included the presidents of Harvard and MIT, who had been appointed to judge the appeal. It is a scathing, satiric portrait of these pompous, overbearing men, shown bust length, standing before a decrepit courtroom. The series concludes with a painting the artist captions "That Agony is Our Triumph"—Vanzetti's last words to the court.

Mrs. Halpert's rather cautious press release emphasized art rather than politics. It read in part:

> He [Shahn] has based his new group of twenty-three pictures on an issue which held the public attention for a long period— the Sacco-Vanzetti trial. What his sympathies were in this much discussed episode is not relevant—no more than Rivera's in his paintings of "A Day in Moscow." It is of significance, however, that he interpreted the major events with passion, keen understanding, and a careful study of the material on hand, giving us a contemporary picture of a historical topic in American life. He has portrayed the main actors—Sacco, Vanzetti, Judge Thayer, the committee of three, the courtroom, and many more intimate details of the life of Vanzetti—interpreting the spirit of each act in a personal, decisive manner.
>
> The accent of "art for art's sake" is slowly being lessened and many artists are turning to theme painting again. The painting lesson has been learned, and the artists are bringing this knowledge to "story-telling" pictures without fear or scorn.

The press gave an extraordinary amount of coverage to the exhibition, considering that the artist was still little known. Both Mrs. Halpert, an expert at attracting attention to the work of her gallery's artists, and the influential collectors who bought from her were unusually effective in promoting Shahn. Furthermore, the idea itself—that of telling a story by means of paintings—as well as the strong political aspects of the exhibition appealed to the critics. Most reviews were enthusiastic. Ben was compared to Picasso, Cocteau, Daumier, Hogarth, Pascin, and Grosz. His future seemed to be most promising. "Shahn's first show," wrote the reviewer for *The New York Times,* "caused a mild tremor in artistic circles; the seismograph now suggests greater excitement." The critic for *Art News* predicted that Shahn "is henceforth someone to be reckoned with." Curiously, the most negative comments came from the radical weekly *The Nation*, although they might have been predicted given the hostile reaction of the members of the Communist John Reed Club, who vigorously protested the artist's use of the word "Passion" because of its religious connotation.

From the left came another opinion, however, this time an enthusiastic endorsement by the great Mexican muralist Diego Rivera, who wrote in the autumn 1932 issue of *Modern Quarterly*:

> I saw yesterday the work of a lad—formerly a painter of abstract art [*sic*]—who has just completed a series of paintings on the life and death of Sacco and Vanzetti which are as moving as anything of the kind I have ever seen. The Sacco and Vanzetti paintings are technically within the school of modernistic painting, but they possess the necessary qualities, accessibility, and power to make then important to the proletariat.

Edith Halpert understandably called the exhibition "a fabulous success." The gallery was crowded throughout the two weeks the paintings were shown. The people who came were not those who usually frequented New York galleries. "They behave before the drawings as though they were in church," noted the art critic Henry McBride, "and when, on the occasion of my visit, I indulged in a little light conversation with Mrs. Halpert over the desk, some of the visitors turned upon us reproachfully as though we were misbehaving in a sacred edifice."

Commercially, too, the show was a success. A large number of the gouaches were sold immediately: to the playwright Elmer Rice; to John Dunbar, a member of MOMA's advisory committee, who purchased three at the insistence of his friend Diego Rivera; and to Abby Rockefeller. According to Philip Wittenberg, Mrs. Rockefeller originally wanted to buy the entire series and when asked why replied, "Comes the Revolution, I can fill the windows with these, and the House of Rockefeller may survive." Instead, she settled for a portrait of Sacco and Vanzetti, which later became a part of the collection of the Museum of Modern Art.

In spite of this, Halpert was, in a way, dismayed. In order to make the gouaches accessible to the general public and not only to the usual affluent collectors, she priced each at only one hundred dollars. It was a useless gesture, however, as she explained to Selden Rodman:

> "I thought workers would dash for those pictures," she recalled, "but all the buyers, from the Rockefellers on down, were from the other side of the tracks—or, politically speaking, fence. I got in touch with the Sacco-Vanzetti Club in Little Italy and offered to pay ninety dollars myself so that the Club could own one of the pictures, each of the members to pay ten cents to make up the remaining ten dollars. They came to the show. They thought the pictures were grotesque. Their answer was a decisive NO. I was *so* anxious to be able to tell Ben that he had reached the right audience! But it was the rich—whether because of a guilty conscience or a more perceptive taste, who knows?—who bought the pictures."

The artist was not, however, as distressed as his dealer had anticipated. Several years later he informed an interviewer that his works were intended for "Park Avenue, rather than Thirteenth Street." As a human being eager to fight injustice, he meant to make his protest known to the general public. As an artist who needed to support himself and his family through his art, he understood that his paintings had to appeal to the "Park Avenue" collectors, his patrons.

Shahn was, of course, gratified at the critical and popular response to the *Passion*. However, he joked about his commercial success, suggesting that the real reason these gouaches sold so well was that they would fit into the small apartments that were a part of modern life. Whatever the reason, he had achieved a considerable measure of recognition, as well as enough money to build a new kitchen extension to their Truro home, naming it "The Passion of———."

Ben must have been even more satisfied upon learning of his father's rarely articulated interest in his art, since he often repeated with obvious pleasure this anecdote about him. By the time of the Sacco-Vanzetti show, Hessel Shahn had returned home from the hospital. Among his visitors was a woman who frequently came to read to him. She kept asking him if he had read this or that review of Ben's show, and Hessel unfailingly answered that he hadn't. The woman was distressed at his complete indifference to his son's work; but while she was reading, Hessel fell asleep, and in turning his back to her, he displaced his pillow. Under it was a pile of clippings about Ben's exhibition. The old man's feigned ignorance of Ben's successes can be explained by the fact that he was one of the misnagid, a Jewish sect whose members believe they should never publicly exhibit pride or joy.

The humorist Robert Benchley had no such compunctions. He sent Ben a book about the case which he inscribed, "To Ben Shahn without whom this crime could never have been committed."

The Passion of Sacco and Vanzetti was shown again as a series (along with the Dreyfus watercolors) by the Harvard Society of Contemporary Art at the Harvard Co-Operative building in Cambridge. The reception was somewhat more reserved than it had been in New York. This was to be expected. Cambridge was close to the scene of the crime and the trial, and one of the primary targets of Ben's anger was the president of Harvard, A. Lawrence Lowell, who appears standing, sanctimonious and stiff under his mortarboard, over the coffins of Sacco and Vanzetti. A self-appointed censor, Captain Charles A. Apted of the Harvard Yard police, tried to have the exhibition canceled. His charge that it was improperly promoted at Harvard, that it would renew agitation over the execution of the two anarchists, and that the works were caricatures and not art were clumsy, almost laughable attempts at censorship, and were rejected as such.

It could be said that this series "made" Ben Shahn, that—with apologies to Benchley—there would have been no Ben Shahn without Sacco and Vanzetti. Certainly the *Passion,* justly or not, has remained Ben's most widely known achievement, the one for which he has gained lasting fame.

CHAPTER THIRTEEN

Hang Shahn!

THE BRUSH WITH (PRESUMABLY UNOFFICIAL) CENSORSHIP AT Harvard was Ben's first such experience. A far more serious threat came unexpectedly from, of all people, the trustees of New York's Museum of Modern Art. The cause of the controversy was an exhibition called "Murals by American Painters and Photographers," which was to be shown at the museum's new headquarters at 11 West Fifty-third Street. It was the brainchild of a man Ben had met in Brooklyn Heights, Lincoln Kirstein, an intense, energetic, and difficult twenty-five-year-old, who had been the driving force behind the Harvard Society of Contemporary Art, and of young Nelson Rockefeller, the son of Abby and John D. Rockefeller, Jr., chairman of the museum's junior advisory committee.

Sixty-five American painters and photographers, selected by Kirstein, were invited to show samples of their work. Each was asked to submit sketches for a proposed three-part mural, twenty-one inches high by four feet wide. In addition, each artist was asked to complete one section of this proposed mural on a large panel, seven feet high by four feet wide. Any practicable medium was allowed, and the subject was to be some aspect of the postwar world. Kirstein was determined to avoid those symbolic figures

The artist contemplates the right-hand section of a study for the Sacco and Vanzetti mural, to which members of the Museum of Modern Art's board of trustees objected.

representing Industry, Science, Education, or similar clichés, which were then popular. In the foreword to the catalogue of the exhibition, he wrote: "No other restrictions were placed upon the artist. The subject matter, its interpretation and the technique used are entirely the artist's own choice."

Unfortunately, the intentions of Kirstein and the other members of the junior advisory committee did not take into account the views of the museum's affluent trustees. Most of them were deeply offended when they saw photos of three of the works to be shown. One of these was Hugo Gellert's *Us Fellas Gotta Stick Together,* and another was William Gropper's *The Writing on the Wall.* Both contained unflattering, satirical representations of some of the richest and most powerful men in America, among them Henry Ford, J. P. Morgan, John D. Rockefeller, Jr., and Andrew W. Mellon. The third work the trustees wanted to eliminate was Ben's.

When he learned that he had been selected to contribute to the mural exhibition, Ben decided to contribute a three-part composition based on his Sacco and Vanzetti gouaches. Using elements from this already completed series, his panels included figures at a protest demonstration, portraits of Sacco and Vanzetti themselves, and an image of Governor Fuller. Finally, on the larger panel, on the right, Ben showed the pompous members of the Lowell Committee as seen in the original gouache, two of them hovering, daylilies in hand, over the coffins of Sacco and Vanzetti. In the background is a portrait of Judge Thayer, in his legal robes, looking out of a window of the courthouse at Dedham.

It was this last grouping that, perhaps predictably, disturbed the board. All three members of the Lowell Committee were friends of the trustees. Ben had "portrayed them so faithfully there was no danger of them not being recognized," he admitted. And these men, like Ford, Morgan, and Mellon, were either generous donors or potentially generous donors to the new museum.

Some of the trustees advocated canceling the entire exhibition at once. One of them, Sam Lewisohn, who usually slept through the meetings until something of special interest came up, reportedly opened one eye and murmured sarcastically, "I thought this museum needed money." Even Alfred H. Barr, Jr., the museum's brilliant twenty-seven-year-old director, objected to Hugo Gellert's contribution. His protest, however, was a halfhearted one and, though drafted, it seems never to have been sent. In it, he informed Gellert that the museum's executive committee had a policy forbidding any representation of a living person that showed any "malicious" intent. Asserting that the museum had no objection to any depiction of the class struggle, he objected to the lampooning of any persons "who may be indirectly responsible for the future of the museum."

Finally, members of the board of trustees made a formal protest to Kirstein, who stood firm. If the museum didn't show all of the paintings, he would hold an independent show, publicizing the museum's refusal to exhibit the work. Some of the trustees wanted Kirstein fired at once, but Nelson Rockefeller, after consulting his father as well as J. P. Morgan and the Rockefellers' attorney, Thomas M. Debevoise, backed Kirstein wholeheartedly.

The artists themselves adopted an uncompromising position, announcing that they would not allow their paintings to be shown at all if any of the works submitted were removed. In the end, many of the trustees resigned. The new board, loyal to Kirstein and wanting to avoid damaging publicity, finally agreed to hang all of the paintings.

Ben, hospitalized with a serious throat infection, had at first been silent, unable to speak. When told that his work had been chosen for the exhibition and that Alfred Barr had expressed enthusiasm for it, however, he recovered rapidly, certain that this good news had speeded that recovery.

Shortly afterward, Ben received more good news: a wealthy collector, probably Mrs. Rockefeller, wanted to buy his large panel and was willing to pay $2,000 for it—an enormous sum at the time. He had never received anywhere near that much for any of his works.

Shahn immediately started planning to return to France where he would buy not only a château but also a vineyard. His euphoria was short-lived, however: he learned that the buyer would purchase the work only on the condition that she could take possession immediately. That meant, of course, that it could not be hung in the museum's show. With bitterness, Ben quickly understood that the mystery buyer did not really want to buy his painting, but only to prevent it from being hung in the show. Sadly, but without hesitation, he rejected the offer. Though profoundly disappointed, he consoled himself with the thought that the brush could be indeed an immensely effective and powerful instrument. When he arrived home, he received a phone call from Kirstein: the news now was that the painting simply could not be hung because of the opposition of many of the museum's trustees; there was no word about any offer.

Desperate, he turned to Horace Kallen, a founder of New York's New School for Social Research and a noted civil libertarian. Kallen's advice was that the power of the trustees was so great that it would be senseless to do battle with them. If Ben fought their decision, no painting of his would ever hang in any museum. Ben disagreed; he was determined to fight. Whereupon Kallen is said to have suggested that a "Hang Shahn" committee be organized.

According to Ben, he heard nothing further from anyone, including the officials of the museum. Finally, after the show had opened, he summoned up his courage and headed for the room where the paintings were hung. Half fearing that his way would be barred, he found instead, for reasons never explained, that not only was his painting hung with all the others; it was also reproduced in the catalogue.

The trustees' reservations were in one way justified: the exhibition was greeted with contempt by most members of the press. Edward Alden Jewell's comments in the *Times* were typical: "The exhibition is so bad as to give America something to think about for a long time. The class struggle orgies may be dismissed as harmless trifles—not because of their theme, but because of the childish or generally uninspired way in which they are handled." As for Shahn's work, he added that it was "a violation of even the most catholic conception of good taste."

Once the exhibition was over, Ben offered to sell his painting for $25 in order to avoid paying the two-dollar taxi fare necessary to take it back to Brooklyn. There were no takers. Nonetheless, he was far from dismayed. He had reached the pinnacle of his career, he told his early biographer Selden Rodman: "I was in my glory. The big money had wheeled out its heavy artillery, and then wheeled it back without firing a shot. I had won my first battle."

CHAPTER FOURTEEN

The Tom Mooney Series

IMMEDIATELY FOLLOWING THE MOMA EXHIBITION, BEN LEFT for Truro, where he felt he could gain back the thirty pounds he had lost during his illness. This was not to be a holiday, however. Barely a week after his arrival there, he began work on his next narrative series. In it, he chose once again to register a protest. This time it focused on the case of the militant labor leader Tom Mooney, who was arrested in 1916 in connection with a bombing during a San Francisco Preparedness Day Parade. The bombing resulted in the deaths of ten people. Mooney was tried, convicted, and sentenced to death, in spite of numerous protests from all over the world similar to those following the Sacco-Vanzetti verdict. A year later, a thorough investigation by a committee appointed by President Wilson found that much of the evidence against Mooney had been perjured. The sentence was commuted to life imprisonment, hardly a just fate for a man who had been unfairly judged. Despite several calls—by the judge, all the living jurors, and all those who had been connected with the prosecution—for a full pardon, Mooney was not released from prison until 1939.

Throughout the spring and summer of 1932, Ben worked on the Mooney series much as he had on the Sacco-Vanzetti narrative, basing his gouaches on photos found in books and newspapers

from the New York Public Library. As he had not done for the earlier series, however, Ben now made preparatory drawings. These
were not to be used in the series, but were, instead, drawings of
many people involved in the case who would not be portrayed in
the final work. His intention, he told Evans and Kirstein, was to do
a thousand of these; he completed only thirty or forty.

The final series consists of fifteen small gouaches and one large
tempera. There are studies of Mooney, his wife, and his mother; of
the defendants (three others were accused along with Mooney);
lawyers for the defense; witnesses, including the perjured prosecution witnesses Mellie Edeau and her daughter Sadie; the judge and
the jurors; members of the Supreme Court of California, which
reviewed the conviction; Jimmy Walker, the mayor of New York,
who acted as a defense lawyer at a public hearing held by California's governor, James Rolph, Jr. (former mayor of San Francisco
and among those in the parade at the time of the explosion), who
is himself portrayed by the artist; Mooney and his warden; and a
group of demonstrators. There are striking and moving portraits
and scenes: Mooney's determined mother, a band across her chest,
boldly proclaiming, "My son is innocent"; Governor Rolph, a huge
white flower in his lapel, one hand clutching a pair of gloves and
the other holding a top hat on high; and Mooney himself, shown
as an ordinary man, a victim who has been handcuffed. The colors
of these images are bolder than those of the earlier series, and
more attention is paid to architectural detail—a wall, bricks, and
cement blocks. (Shahn's interest in the latter was first apparent in
the Sacco-Vanzetti series, and became increasingly important in
his early paintings.) These works are understated; the details—
facial expressions, clothing—carefully define each characteriza-
tion.

After the success of the Sacco-Vanzetti series, expectations were
high. The Mooney series, however, proved a disappointment. Most
reviews of the exhibition—held at the Downtown Gallery in May
1933—were poor. The same critics who had praised the Sacco-
Vanzetti series were unenthusiastic this time. Henry McBride of
the *Sun*, who had also disapproved of Ben's sketches for the
MOMA mural, characterized the new series as stodgy, repetitious,
mannered, and self-conscious. Others found Shahn's color

"scrubby," and the entire series derivative, pseudo-primitive, and cliché-ridden.

Some critics, however, disagreed with these negative assessments. Diego Rivera, in a foreword he had volunteered to write for the exhibition's catalogue, argued that the Mooney gouaches were superior to the *Passion:*

> Ben Shahn has discovered the just note for his work now that his subject matter is the struggle of the proletarianized American petit-bourgeois intellectual against the degeneration of the European bourgeoisie translated on this continent. His ability and his aesthetic qualities are magnificent, as witness the fact that he is accepted by the most sophisticated connoisseurs of art as well as by the masses of workers.
>
> Also, the case of Ben Shahn demonstrates that when contemporary art is revolutionary in content, it becomes stronger and imposes itself by the conjunction of its aesthetic quality and its human expression. To the extent that it answers the demands of the collective spirit, the collectivity will respond by according success to the painter. It demonstrates as well that once art is set in this road, it acquires a progressive rhythm identical with that of its epoch. Hence, Ben Shahn's series on the Mooney Case is even stronger and of finer quality than his Sacco-Vanzetti paintings.

James Thrall Soby, an early supporter of Shahn's work and an official at the Museum of Modern Art, writing several years later, also noted an improvement in the artist's style:

> The didactic force of the series is no greater than that of the Sacco-Vanzetti panels, but there is an evident advance in technical assurance. The color, mostly muted and solemn the previous year, now became brilliant and light; yellows, pinks and fresh greens replaced the browns and blacks of the Sacco-Vanzetti gouaches. At the same time, the forms grew bolder, the use of contrasting motifs more skilled.

A perceptive assessment of Shahn's position in the world of American art in the early 1930s was expressed by Jean Charlot in the July–September 1933 issue of *Hound and Horn:*

We can safely look at Ben Shahn as a most valuable witness to our epoch. Both his language and subject matter are unmistakably contemporary. . . .

Much of Shahn's plastic is explainable by his aims. Being a story-teller, his source material consists mainly of newspaper reports, his models being the photographs of rotogravure sections and tabloid sheets. Degas also used photographs, but depurated, stylized, lifted to the plane of his art. Shahn, on the contrary, delights in what is peculiarly accidental, cynical, and ungentlemanly in camera work.

In any case, the Mooney series did not do as well as *The Passion of Sacco and Vanzetti* had, critically or commercially. Perhaps the subject matter was of less interest, and perhaps, as Edith Halpert remembered, the series was in a way repetitious. Ben, however, seems to have been undismayed. At the time of the exhibition, he was involved—personally this time—in what he considered another shameful case of injustice.

CHAPTER FIFTEEN

Rivera and the Scandal at Rockefeller Center

UNLIKE MOST PAINTERS, WHO WERE UNABLE TO SELL THEIR work or find jobs during the early years of the Depression, Ben had been, for the months preceding the Tom Mooney exhibition, steadily employed at the relatively generous salary of thirty dollars a week. His job was as one of several assistants to Diego Rivera in the execution of a large mural in the lobby of the newly built RCA Building in New York's Rockefeller Center. The job not only gave him a source of income; it also afforded him the opportunity to learn from a master muralist the art of the fresco, a technique that had interested him since his two trips to Europe. There could be no better teacher than Rivera, one of the most distinguished of the Mexican artists responsible for the revival of this centuries-old method of creating images on walls.

Rivera's enthusiasm for Ben's work had begun with the Sacco and Vanzetti series; hence his offer to write the introduction to the catalogue of the Mooney show. Rivera also wrote Ben to ask if he could help with the Rockefeller Center project, suggesting that they discuss it when he visited New York during the winter of 1932–1933. (He was in the United States working on a mural commission for the Detroit Institute of Fine Arts.) They arranged to meet at the Barbizon Plaza Hotel, where Rivera was staying with his wife, Frida Kahlo. Inexplicably, Rivera told Shahn to come at four o'clock in the morning. Ben dutifully arrived on time, but Rivera didn't show up until seven hours later. He offered no apology. They then got down to work; Ben was given an idea of the shape, size, and theme of the mural and shown a rough sketch of it.

Rivera had negotiated for several months before agreeing to work on the Rockefeller Center project. Originally, there was to be a competition among Matisse, Picasso, and Rivera, but Matisse had replied that he was not interested and Picasso failed to reply at all. Rivera said that he would be interested but announced he was beyond competitions. He should either be offered the assignment or not, on the basis of his past achievements. At Nelson Rockefeller's urging—this was *Rockefeller* Center, after all—Rivera was given the commission and entered into discussions with a representative of the building's developmental managers in the fall of 1932. There were two conditions that the artist refused to meet. The architect, Raymond Hood, wanted only black, gray, and white used, to be in harmony with the colors of the interior of the lobby; and he wanted the work to be done on canvas and not as a fresco. Rivera insisted on using color and on working in true fresco. Once again at Rockefeller's insistence, he got his way.

The theme of the mural was to be lofty: "Man at the Crossroads Looking with Hope and High Vision to the Choosing of a New and Better Future." Rivera interpreted the "crossroads" as a choice between economic capitalism (and along with it all evils such as war, unemployment, and gambling), placed on the viewer's left, and socialism on the right (with workers holding banners on high, singing and smiling as they marched down the road). The sketch, according to Ben's friend Lou Block, an artist and a photographer, was "pure socialism," yet Hood accepted it without any reservations.

The mural was to be enormous, sixty-three feet wide by seventeen feet high, and Rivera hired several artists and craftsmen, in addition to Shahn, to collaborate with him. Among these were Block; Lucienne Bloch, also a painter and photographer, who had studied in Paris and had worked for Rivera in Detroit; Stephen Dimitroff, a Bulgarian, who had also worked for Rivera in Detroit; Hideo Noda, a Japanese student; Arthur Neindorff, a Texan; and

Andrés Sánchez Flores, a chemist. Since the *buon fresco* (also known as true fresco) technique, used by Giotto, Masaccio, and Michelangelo, required lengthy preparation of the plaster base, the assistants began to work on the walls and grind the colors while Rivera was still in Detroit.

The Mexican artist arrived in New York at the end of March. He was tired, not only because of the strenuous schedule he had followed in Detroit but also because the political and social content of the mural there had caused a stressful controversy. It was important, however, that the Rockefeller Plaza mural be completed in time for the official opening of the seventy-two-story building on May 1, 1933, and he was asked to begin work as soon as the basic plastering could be finished.

It was a complex and exhausting process. First, Rivera himself drew the outline, or cartoon, on paper. Then his assistants, having enlarged it to the scale of the wall, transferred the cartoon onto large sheets of onionskin tracing paper. They then poked holes in the tracing paper along the lines of the drawing, creating a series of perforations.

Dimitroff's job was to mix the final layer of fresh plaster, the *intonaco*, which Neindorff then applied over an area large enough for one day's work. This mixing and plastering alone took from four to six hours. Black dust, or pounce, was then pushed, or pounced, through the perforations of the cartoon onto the fresh *intonaco*, so that a dotted line remained on the plaster. Rivera, or sometimes one of his assistants, then recreated the cartoon by connecting the dots, after which he applied the pigments, which had been mixed with lime water. Because in fresco both the paint and the plaster are wet, the pigment becomes part of the plaster wall itself. The finished work is therefore virtually indestructible.

Since the plaster was drying at the same time as the pigment was being applied, work had to proceed rapidly. The crew usually worked about eighteen hours before reaching the end of the freshly plastered area. Any corrections had to be made immediately; once the crew was forced to paint for thirty hours without stopping. Most of the time Shahn, Block, Noda, and Bloch ground colors, washed brushes, and climbed up and down the scaffold so that Rivera could spend all of his time painting. There were, occasionally, other odd jobs to be done. In her diary, Lucienne Bloch noted that one day Ben and Block brought Rivera medical books to follow when painting representations of various microbes—syphilis, gonorrhea, and tuberculosis among them—that were to cover a huge expanse of wall. To speed up the work, the two assistants tried to help by painting some of the germs themselves. This was reportedly the only time Rivera allowed anyone else to paint; predictably, he found the results totally unsatisfactory and had the section ripped off and the wall replastered.

On another occasion, Rivera sent Shahn and Block out to look for a red-haired woman he could use as a model for a figure in the mural. Ben and Lou were lucky. At a subway entrance they spotted two young women on their way to Grand Central Station to catch a train for Vassar, where they were studying. When told that Rivera might want to use one of them, they eagerly changed their plans and went to the RCA building.

Block recorded an occasion on which Ben independently came up with a solution to one of Rivera's potential problems. Just when the artist was about to paint a scene symbolically depicting unemployment, Block wrote, "a violent demonstration took place on Wall Street in desperate response to the conditions of the Depression. Ben brought in newspaper photos showing the commotion, and Diego painted the scene directly from those clippings, with the police on their horses, ready to strike."

Work on the mural became an event of great interest. Spectators filled the lobby at all hours, some of them initiating political discussions with Rivera, who frequently responded from the scaffolding. Walker Evans came by frequently, as did friends of Lou Block. "Lou . . . always brings friends to view the work so that it is always full of elegantly dressed females when he is around," Lucienne Bloch wrote in her diary. Nelson Rockefeller, too, was a frequent visitor, repeatedly expressing his enthusiasm to Rivera.

By April 24, 1933, enough of the actual painting was done to enable the viewer to understand Rivera's interpretation of the mural's theme. It was clearly apparent to Joseph Lilly, a writer for the New York *World Telegram*, whose indignant article headlined "Rivera Paints Scenes of Communist Activity for RCA Walls—and Rockefeller, Jr. Foots the Bill," appeared that day. Why, Lilly wanted to know, was a piece of Communist propaganda adorning the wall of one of America's proudest symbols of capitalism? The article had a great impact on the Rockefellers and on public opinion, but Ben felt it was he himself who inadvertently had been the cause of the scandal that followed. Noticing that drops of greasy oil paint from the brushes of workmen painting the lobby's ceiling were hitting the fresco, he summoned Hood, the architect, to see the damage being done to Rivera's work. While examining it, Hood casually asked if one of the figures depicted was Trotsky. No, said Ben, just as casually, it was Lenin.

Nobody knows how word of this exchange reached Nelson Rockefeller. Now, though he had obviously noticed the appearance of Lenin in the mural before then, Rockefeller could no longer remain silent. Long a supporter of Rivera's, he must have been pained at writing the following letter to the painter on May 4 (in spite of all the work, the May 1 deadline had not been met):

> While I was in the No. 1 building at Rockefeller Center yesterday viewing the progress of your thrilling mural, I noticed that in the most recent portion of the painting you had included a portrait of Lenin. This piece is beautifully painted but it seems to me that his portrait, appearing in this mural, might very easily seriously offend a great many people. If it were in a private house it would be one thing but this mural is in a public building and the situation is therefore quite different. As much as I dislike to do so I am afraid we must ask you to substitute the face of some unknown man where Lenin's face now appears.
>
> You know how enthusiastic I am about the work which you have been doing and that to date we have in no way restricted you in either subject or treatment. I am sure you will understand our feeling in this situation and we will greatly appreciate your making the suggested substitution.
>
> > With best wishes, I remain sincerely,
> > Nelson A. Rockefeller

Two days later, Rivera answered:

> In reply to your kind letter of May 4, 1933, I wish to tell you my actual feelings on the matters you raise, after I have given considerable reflection to them.
>
> The head of Lenin was included in the original sketch, now in the hands of Mr. Raymond Hood, and in the drawings in line

made on the wall at the beginning of my work. Each time it appeared as a general and abstract representation of the concept of leader, an indispensable human figure. Now, I have merely changed the place in which the figure appears, giving it a less real physical place as if projected by a television apparatus. Moreover, I understand quite thoroughly the point of view concerning the business affairs of a commercial public building, although I am sure that that class of person who is capable of being offended by the portrait of a deceased great man, would feel offended, given such a mentality, by the entire conception of my painting. Therefore, rather than mutilate the conception, I should prefer the physical destruction of the conception in its entirety, but preserving, at least, its integrity.

In speaking of the integrity of the conception, I do not refer only to the logical structure of the painting, but also to its plastic structure.

I should like, as far as possible, to find an acceptable solution to the problem you raise, and suggest that I could change the sector which shows society people playing bridge and dancing, and put in its place, in perfect balance with the Lenin portion, a figure of some great American historical leader, such as Lincoln, who symbolizes the unification of the country and the abolition of slavery, surrounded by John Brown, Nat Turner, William Lloyd Garrison or Wendell Phillips and Harriet Beecher Stowe, and perhaps some scientific figure like McCormick, inventor of the McCormick reaper, which aided in the victory of the anti-slavery forces by providing sufficient wheat to sustain the Northern armies.

I am sure that the solution I propose will entirely clarify the historical meaning of the figure of leader as represented by Lenin and Lincoln, and no one will be able to object to them without objecting to the most fundamental feelings of human love and solidarity and the constructive social force represented by such men. Also it will clarify the general meaning of the painting.

This compromise was not acceptable to Rivera's assistants. Ben wrote a note of protest, signed by all except Neindorff, deploring

Rivera's offer to modify the mural and charging that any changes would diminish the importance of the artist as well as the value of his art. The note ended by threatening a strike if even one modification were made.

As Rivera and his crew awaited Rockefeller's response, the atmosphere in the lobby of the building changed from one of dedicated enthusiasm to one of tension. In her diary Lucienne Bloch wrote that Frida Kahlo "told me not to lose a minute and make photos of the frescos since rash things might happen any time now." Bloch, who had from the beginning assumed the role of unofficial photographer for the project, now had a critical task: to find a way to photograph the mural without the knowledge of those in charge of the building's security. Ben, also anticipating problems, had already asked the building superintendent, who had previously befriended him, if he could invite Evans to take photos of the murals, and had received a firm and none too warm negative response. Knowing the difficulties she would face, Bloch managed to take her photos only by hiding her small 1927 Leica in her blouse.

By May 9, there had still been no reply to Rivera's letter of compromise. Though very much aware that the situation might become explosive, the crew continued to work. Journalists, too, realized that something was about to happen; one of them, a *New York Times* reporter named Lind, showed up every quarter-hour to check on what was happening. By evening, the worst fears of Rivera and his staff were confirmed.

Shahn and Lou Block have somewhat different versions of what happened. According to Shahn, who places himself at center stage, he and Rivera were alone together on the scaffold when two unidentified men arrived, pulled the scaffold away from the mural (it was partially portable), and informed Rivera that he was to stop working on the fresco. According to Block, he and Ben were having supper that evening when Noda arrived, shouting that Rivera was off the scaffold and that the lobby was full of policemen. Both agree that Hugh Robertson, from the development manager's office, accompanied by at least a dozen uniformed guards, approached Rivera and handed him a check for $14,000 as final payment for the mural (he had been paid $7,000 in advance), informed him that he was not to continue work, and ordered the scaffold to be moved away from the wall. Immediately afterward, according to Ben, "about thirty or forty men rushed in—it had obviously all been planned—with big planks of lumber and began building a barrier in front of the mural." Within half an hour, the RCA Building was surrounded by mounted police.

Lou Block went to the toolshed, which also served as an office for the crew, to call Lind, but the phone went dead in the midst of their conversation; the line had been cut. All communications with the outside world were suspended. Guards carrying revolvers stood at the RCA Building's entrances, and all visitors were ordered to leave. Workmen hastily covered the mural with canvas sheeting.

Within two hours, between seventy-five and one hundred men and women were already marching around the building, voicing their indignation. This was only the beginning. For two or three days, the incident was front-page news in the United States and Mexico. Committees were formed to fight for the preservation of the mural, and countless letters—from, among others, John Sloan, Lewis Mumford, Alfred Stieglitz, and Van Wyck Brooks—poured in supporting Rivera. Many letter writers compared the Rockefeller Center incident to the censorship being practiced by the Nazis.

On the night of May 14, four hundred sympathizers assembled in Irving Plaza in New York to form a "United Front" committee to protest the veiling of the mural. A near riot broke out when the various factions—among them the official Communists and dissidents like the Trotskyites and the Lovestoneites—noisily attacked one another. Ben assumed the leadership of the protesters, restoring peace with an announcement that representatives from the fifteen organizations that made up the United Front would picket Radio City between six and eight the following evening. This was to be followed by an open-air meeting in Columbus Circle. The best that the protesters could hope for was an official statement promising that the mural would not be destroyed or in any way mutilated. It was a concession worth fighting for, and Rockefeller Center officials agreed, pledging that the mural would not be harmed but merely covered up.

The following day, Ben once again assumed the position of leader and announced that Rivera had not given up. In spite of the cancellation of projects that had been scheduled for Chicago and for Minnesota, he still planned to create a mural for the United States. In order to do it, he would, with great pleasure, use the $7,000 of Rockefeller money that remained to him after the covering of his Radio City mural. (Of the total of $21,000 paid him, 30 percent had gone to his agent, and some $8,000 had been used for supplies and salaries for his assistants.)

For the site of this new mural, Rivera chose the New Workers School, whose director was Bertram D. Wolfe, Rivera's good friend and biographer. Wolfe was a leader of the Lovestoneites, a small anti-Stalinist leftist group, no longer officially affiliated with the Communist Party. Since Rivera himself had been expelled from the party three years earlier and had been sharply criticized as a renegade by American party leaders for even deigning to work for the capitalist Rockefellers, it was an appropriate choice. There was, however, one serious problem. The New Workers School was located in an old building on Fourteenth Street between Fifth and Sixth Avenues that was scheduled for demolition in the near future. In order to make certain that his new mural would not be destroyed along with the building, Rivera decided to do several smaller panels, set in huge wooden frames that could sustain the weight of the plaster so the mural could be moved when the time came.

To assist him in the execution of these twenty-one panels—which depicted, not surprisingly, the exploitation of workers by bankers and industrialists and the hope of escape through socialism—Rivera hired the same people who had worked with him at Rockefeller Center. Each had a specific job, and all served, at times, as dishwashers, sweepers, and general handymen and handywomen. Both Ben and Lou Block, who built the huge solid frames, hated their work; they disliked the mural's didacticism and found the work excessively caustic and negative. They were also frustrated because Rivera once again would give them little opportunity to paint. But no one, especially not an artist, could reject a steady job, especially one lasting several months at $30 a week.

At the end of the year, Rivera, his work completed and his Rockefeller money spent, returned to Mexico. Soon afterward he received the news that, in spite of the pledge that had been made, his work had been destroyed. On the night of February 4, 1934, the mural was uncovered and smashed to pieces with chisels and sledgehammers. The pieces were thrown in the garbage and the wall replastered. The official excuse was that structural changes in the building were about to be made, necessitating the removal of Rivera's masterpiece.

Shahn heard the news at two o'clock in the morning, when a reporter phoned to ask for a comment. "That's when I first opened my mouth and stuck my foot in and it's been there ever since," Shahn later commented. "I said, 'This is typical Rockefeller vandalism.' That was all. I went back to sleep." But Ben's foot was not really stuck in his mouth. He remained on good terms with the Rockefeller family and was especially proud of his warm relationship with Nelson.

Nevertheless, Ben continued to protest the mural's destruction. He was among the leaders of demonstrations in Irving Plaza as well as of a meeting held at the New Workers School. In addition, he (along with other artists) withdrew from an eagerly anticipated Municipal Art Show because it was to be held in Rockefeller Center; he also signed a letter urging Mayor Fiorello La Guardia to either cancel that exhibition or transfer it to other quarters not connected with the Rockefellers. (Presumably, he did not learn until later that Nelson Rockefeller had privately stated that he had known nothing about the plans to destroy the mural, and regretted it. He had, however, been forced to remain loyal to the corporation that owned the building and feared that the presence of the disputed mural might scare away potential tenants.)

Ben also remained personally supportive of Rivera. Following the covering up of the mural, Rivera and Kahlo moved into the Shahns' spacious (though unheated) home for a while. Judy Shahn, then four years old, remembers telling the burly painter that he was the ugliest man she had ever met in her whole life. The child must have redeemed herself in Rivera's eyes a few weeks later, however, at the time Harry Bakwin, a doctor and a close friend who built a fabulous art collection with the help of Ben's advice, commissioned Rivera to paint a portrait of his son, Robert. When the artist showed Bakwin the completed portrait, the doctor was stunned: it was a Cubist painting, and he was unable to find Robert among the cubes. Judy, however, saved the day for Rivera.

Called in and asked what she thought the painting was meant to be, she answered without hesitation that it was obviously a portrait of Bakwin's son.

Ben argued with Rivera frequently, particularly about art. He made no secret of his belief that Rivera's work was too cluttered with images and that his message would be stronger if his design were simplified. Unlike Rivera, he believed in the power of empty space. When he asked Rivera why he crowded so many figures into the same space, the Mexican artist angrily replied: "Look around you. Do you see any space at all?" Ben also disagreed with his colleague's vision of his subjects, complaining that "his workmen always have heavy wrists and that kind of nonsense."

Nonetheless, Ben admitted that Rivera was a brilliant man. A microbiologist Ben had introduced to him was so impressed with Rivera's knowledge that he was convinced that he was a scientist rather than a painter. By the same token, Rivera's understanding of Judaism was so extensive that when Ben introduced him to his father, Hessel was certain that Rivera was not only a Jew but a Talmudic scholar. In spite of these extraordinary qualities, Ben was able, in the end, to dismiss Rivera with a few words—"I didn't share his painting ideas or anything else"—though he added that he had "always honored his integrity."

Still, Ben gained a great deal from his time with Rivera. He had wanted to learn the art of the fresco, and had done this. He learned another lesson from Rivera: no matter how long and hard the Mexican artist had worked on something, he would have it erased if it didn't meet his expectations. Shahn also came to appreciate the mural as a uniquely effective art form, by which an artist could tell a story or make a moral point to a large audience in a public place instead of in the privacy of a home or the limited space of a museum.

Equally important, the experience with the Rockefeller Center mural further politicized Shahn. He had taken political stands in the past through his art, as in the Sacco and Vanzetti and the Tom Mooney paintings, but he had not been directly involved. During the battle of Rockefeller Center, however, he was able to participate personally in protesting the injustice of political censorship.

CHAPTER SIXTEEN

Prohibition and Prisons

AFTER RIVERA'S RETURN TO MEXICO, BEN FOUND HIMSELF IN the same position as most American artists of the time.

Works of art were impossible to sell in a depressed economy that considered art a luxury meant only for the very rich. There being no collectors, galleries first suffered tremendous losses and then failed, leaving painters and sculptors with no place to show their work. With more than six million people out of jobs by the end of 1930, these artists had little hope of finding alternative employment. Local relief organizations, largely in New York, were able to offer some work—but only for a very small number.

With the election of Franklin Delano Roosevelt in 1932, however, direct governmental intervention in creating jobs for artists became a possibility. The artist George Biddle, an old friend of the president, is generally credited with initiating the movement for government aid. Biddle wrote FDR a letter that read, in part:

> There is a matter which I have long considered and which some day might interest your administration. The Mexican artists have produced the greatest national school of mural painting since the Italian Renaissance. Diego Rivera tells me that it was only

possible because [Alvaro] Obregón [the president of Mexico from 1920 to 1924] allowed Mexican artists to work at plumbers' wages in order to express on the walls of the government buildings the social ideals of the Mexican Revolution.

The younger artists of America are conscious as they have never been of the social revolution that our country and civilization are going through; and they would be eager to express these ideals in a permanent art form if they were given the government's cooperation. They would be contributing to and expressing in living monuments the social ideals that you are struggling to achieve. And I am convinced that our mural art with a little impetus can soon result, for the first time in our history, in a vital national expression.

In December 1933, the first of four government aid programs, the Public Works of Art Project (PWAP), was started. It was followed by the Section of Painting and Sculpture (known as the Section), the Federal Art Project (FAP) of the Works Progress Administration, and the Treasure Relief Arts Projects. Each tried, with some success, to ease the suffering of the American artist.

That same year Ben received a letter from Lloyd Goodrich, an art historian and critic and a curator of the Whitney Museum (which had shown Ben's *Bathers, Truro* of 1931 in its first Biennial in 1932—which exhibited only paintings—as well as a watercolor in 1933's Biennial for sculpture, watercolors, and prints). Goodrich was writing him as a member of the recently established PWAP, whose purpose was to help needy artists by giving them work. Ben remembered little of the exact contents of the letter that made him so happy and could only tell an interviewer, "Suddenly they set up a project called the Public Works of Art Project. . . . I was on salary two weeks before I knew why." That salary, he remembered, was $44 a week; Shahn's assignment was to come up with an idea for a mural to be placed in a public space in New York City.

The idea came to him quickly. The election of Roosevelt, who opposed Prohibition, signaled the end of the constitutional amendment which had prohibited the sale, manufacture, and distribution of alcoholic beverages in the United States. Meant to improve the morals of the American people, the amendment had

instead established a new and dangerous criminal world of boot-
legging and speakeasies. After Roosevelt took office in March
1933, his first step toward the abolition of Prohibition was to support and eventually sign a bill before Congress that made the manufacture and sale of low-alcohol (3.2 percent) beer and wine legal.
Immediately afterward, New York's new mayor, Fiorello La
Guardia, announced plans for the establishment of beer gardens
throughout the city—at Riverside Park, Carl Schurz Park, and
Jones Beach, and one large one in the Casino at Central Park, in
mid-Manhattan. These new beer gardens would need to be deco-
rated, and Ben proposed to design and execute a large mural for
the Central Park Casino, commemorating the end of the age of
prohibition.

He was excited, eager for the opportunity to put to practical use
all he had learned from Rivera. In early January he sent a letter to
Goodrich enclosing an article from *The New York Times* in which
the term "beer garden" appeared no fewer than six times. He
underlined "beer garden" each time it appeared to emphasize his
enthusiasm: "I enclose a clipping from the *Times,* which has sent
my hopes for a wall to fever heights. Please tell me there are
prospects. Yours for an endless wall . . ."

On January 8, 1934, he sent an architectural sketch to Juliana
Force, director of the Whitney Museum and chairwoman of the
PWAP, showing the wall behind the musicians' platform (presumably the wall to be used for his mural). To Force, he described
some of his ideas:

> I want to show Federal destruction of liquor. Thousands of
> bottles being broken. Endless numbers of barrels of beer being
> emptied into sewers. Raiding of otherwise respectable and
> renowned hotels. The beginning of the hideaway speakeasy and
> later elegantly gowned ladies and gentlemen being scrutinized
> through peep holes before being permitted to drink. Rum ships
> transferring cargoes at night—beer running trucks. Capone and
> his car, driving his armored car with bullet proof glass. A shop
> window selling malt and hops and utensils necessary for illicit
> stills. Home brew, Bathtub gin. . . . In short, a frank but amus-
> ing statement of a great error.

Ben envisioned eight separate panels; he prepared a study for each. One showed a parade of solemn, drably dressed women, members of the Women's Christian Temperance Union, which fought tenaciously for Prohibition, standing in front of a saloon. Another panel was to depict a number of prosperous-looking, flag-waving businessmen in suits carrying placards. A third sketch shows a group of men in front of a closed speakeasy. The stores surrounding the speakeasy are identified by lettering on their awnings: "Chop Suey," "Glass and Picture Frames," and "Malt, Hops, and Caps," the ingredients used for bootleg beer. Two policemen, nightsticks in hand, stand near a sign that reads "For Bethune Street Only," which places the scene near a studio Ben shared for a while with Walker Evans and Lou Block, and the apartment, across the street, to which he and his family had moved. In these studies, Ben used architectural design and lettering to a far greater extent than he had in the past, and to good

Parade for Repeal (c. 1934) is one of the studies for a projected—and rejected—mural on the subject of Prohibition for New York's Central Park Casino.

MUSEUM OF THE CITY OF NEW YORK

effect. These panels display a different side of the artist. Instead of the bitterness and indignation of the Sacco and Vanzetti and Mooney series, he shows a sharp eye for satire and irony. Rather than railing against Prohibition, he ridicules it.

For no stated reason, the sketches were rejected and the project abandoned. Most probably, the serious judges who selected the projects found these biting and often witty sketches too frivolous a response to what had been a complete failure and a misreading of the social attitudes of the American people.

Ben's enthusiasm was not dampened. Even before the sketches were rejected, he and Lou Block considered the possibility of executing another mural, one which would depict the history of penology for the walls of the hospital at Sing Sing Prison. Block, whose idea this first was, had proposed it to Webster Thayer, Jr., the New York State commissioner of corrections; Thayer had expressed interest. He agreed that Sing Sing might be an appropriate site but also mentioned the possibility of Wallkill Prison, north of Ossining. Nothing, however, came of this initiative.

A few months later, however, Block arranged a meeting with Audrey McMahon, executive secretary of the College Art Association, which was supervising the works division of the Department of Public Welfare. The timing was perfect: the New York City Department of Corrections had just decided to rebuild the prison at Rikers Island. It had been recommended that as part of the multimillion-dollar reconstruction some of the walls be covered with murals.

At Mrs. McMahon's suggestion, Lou and Ben got in touch with the New York City commissioner of corrections, Austin MacCormick, who expressed serious interest, as did Mayor La Guardia.

According to Ben, Lou's proposal was so brilliant that there was no chance of it being rejected. Shortly thereafter, the two men were hired for a period of one year, to conduct research and prepare three sketches, at $27 a week each. They were also permitted to employ two assistants, Joseph Vogel and Lydia Nadejena. The mural's theme was to be the contrast between the cruel prison policies of the past and the more humane and enlightened modern methods of rehabilitation; the purpose was to depict for visitors, prison officials, and students of sociology the history of penology in the United States.

The technical problems involved presented Block and Shahn with a complicated challenge. The site for the mural was a hundred-foot-long corridor, which led to a large room. Once a week, this room was partitioned to make three separate chapels for different denominations. During the rest of the week, the walls of the partition were raised, leaving a tremendous space that could be used for recreation and social gatherings. The artists agreed to a division of labor. Ben would be in charge of the corridor, while Lou was responsible for the chapels–recreation rooms.

Ben's was by far the more difficult assignment. The corridor was only twenty feet wide, too narrow to allow a spectator to back up and see much of it at one time. To make matters even more complex, there were no breaks in the long walls—just one continuing windowless surface. To solve this problem, Ben adapted a method

Morris Kantor, David Smith, Harry Knight (director of the Public Works of Art Project), and Shahn en route to Rikers Island in 1934.

he had learned from Rivera. He divided the long wall into a number of scenes, indoor and outdoor ones alternating. These separations were marked by broken brick walls like those Ben had used in some of his paintings.

Before beginning work on the sketches for their murals, Ben and Block wanted to know more about prisons, past and present. Armed with letters of recommendation from Audrey McMahon and Commissioner MacCormick, the two artists traveled extensively through New York State. They interviewed trained penologists and saw firsthand how prisoners were treated and how they lived and worked. They consulted the wardens at the medium-security prison at Blackwells Island, the reformatory at Warwick, the prison at New Hampden, and a women's prison, among others. They also had a long talk with Lewis E. Lawes, the celebrated warden of Sing Sing. Lawes did not impress them. His best-selling book, *Twenty Thousand Years in Sing Sing*, they believed, was ghostwritten, and Lawes himself was, they felt, "as phony as a twelve-dollar bill."

Wherever he went, Ben took copious notes and drew small sketches, well over a hundred of them. At one point between trips, he complained to his friend Evans, already becoming known as a photographer, that his notebook was too cumbersome to carry and that the sketches were inadequate for his purposes. Evans suggested that Ben take photos with a Leica camera instead. Unfortunately, Shahn didn't have a Leica—a small 35-millimeter hand-held camera that would have been well suited to his purpose. Besides, although he had taken a number of family photos and a number of informal pictures in New York (many of which he used as subjects for his paintings) he wouldn't have known how to use a Leica if he had one. He asked his brother Phil, then making a good living as an accountant, to buy him a Leica, promising to return it if he was unable to get at least one photo from the first roll published in a magazine. This was, Ben knew, a bold promise.

Evans had often told Shahn that he would teach him how to use the camera, but he had never done so. Finally, desperate for advice, Ben confronted Evans: how did one use the Leica? The answer was simple: "Well, it's very easy, Ben. F/9 on the sunny side of the street, f/4.5 on the shady side of the street. For a twentieth of a second hold your camera steady." This was the only lesson Ben had, but it was enough to enable him to take photos of sidewalk theater groups, which he had published in the 1934 issue of *New Theatre*. After that, the Leica became his. All he needed to add was a right-angle viewfinder, which he attached to the camera, enabling him to catch his subjects unawares—he could face straight ahead and unobtrusively take photos of a subject on his left. Shahn had used photographs taken by others for the Sacco and Vanzetti and Tom Mooney series. In the future he would have his own photos as points of reference.

Ben's notebooks and sketchbooks of this period survive and bear witness to the thoroughness with which he applied himself. He made lists of books to be read and studies to be made. Among the books: Oscar Wilde's "Ballad of Reading Gaol," Warden Lawes's *Twenty Thousand Years in Sing Sing*, *The Underground Railroad from Slavery to Freedom* by W. H. Siebert, *The Slave States of America* by James S. Buckingham, *American Prisons of Today*, *The Pageant of America* by Ralph H. Gabriel, Alice Earle's *Curious Punishments of Bygone Days*, William Bradford's *Punishments in Pennsylvania*, *Three Criminal Law Reforms* by Philipson Coleman, Mendelsohn's *Criminal Jurisprudence of the Ancient Hebrews*, published in Baltimore in 1891, Herbert's *Chinese Testament*, and Lincoln's *Ecce Homo*.

His notes were equally wide-ranging: Georgia chain gang, Prison library, Prison fire, Hopelessness of getting employment when freed, Copies of USSR prison works, Guards who can only order but have forgotten to listen, clipped hair of new prisoner, flogging in Delaware, execution by hanging, public execution of Newgate, Pillory in Delaware, Treadmill England, Abnormal sexuality, Beginning of Elmira Reformatory, Similarity of filing cabinet of records to cell block, Roots of crime in tenements and poverty, Crimes now not crimes twenty years ago . . .

Once their research was completed, Lou and Ben began work in their studio on the sketches for the panels. Ben was not pleased with this arrangement. He felt that he and Lou shouldn't have been working in the same room because his energy and Lou's lethargy were mutually destructive. Though he admitted the idea for the mural was Lou's, as were its promotion and sale, Ben was disturbed that Lou never managed to complete even one panel. Furthermore, he was angry that Lou was "having an affair in the daylight" (presumably in their studio) because daylight, he believed, was for painting. Though he didn't think much of Block as a painter, Ben insisted that he liked him as a man—this in spite of his often expressed belief that he could never like an artist whose work he did not admire.

In February 1935, when the sketches were finished, they were submitted to Commissioner MacCormick, who approved them. So did Mayor La Guardia, who called them a "swell job" and said the mural would be a credit to his administration. Both officials even came to the Bethune Street studio to express their enthusiasm personally.

In spite of these endorsements, the Municipal Art Commission rejected the sketches on the grounds of "psychological unfitness." The members of the commission also charged that the work contained "antisocial" propaganda.

Furthermore, a poll of forty Rikers Island prisoners had been taken to confirm the commission's judgment concerning the suitability of the sketches. Those polled had been chosen at random by Commissioner MacCormick, and the questions asked had been devised by a criminal psychologist who was the head of the Hawthorne School for Boys.

There was a short introductory explanation: "Here is a set of pictures showing the good and bad sides of prison life. The small ones are sketches and the large ones will give you an idea of how it will look on the wall. This is planned for a mural in one of the halls of a brand new and modern prison building. The artist would like to know what you think of these pictures." The prisoners were also asked how they felt about having the murals on the walls of a new prison, what other prisoners would think of them, and whether visitors would have any interest in them.

About a fifth of the questions were left unanswered and almost as many responses were considered indifferent. Ten responses were deemed unfavorable—for instance: "They prove only a novelty. See today. Forget tomorrow" and "As a prisoner I wouldn't care to see them; we see enough tragedy without them."

An overwhelming number, however—ninety-seven—were categorized as favorable: "I believe that these pictures very ably point

the way that we should follow if we desire to be really civilized";
"They will certainly brighten the place up a bit and also give the
inmates something to concentrate on besides the walls"; "To me
they prove that there has been a wonderful improvement in which
a criminal is treated morally, physically, as well as educationally."

For some reason, much of the press misrepresented or ignored
the results of the poll. The New York *Herald-Tribune* reported that
the commission turned down the murals because it was felt that
"their gloomy subject matter might have a bad psychological effect
on the prisoners." *The New York Times* noted that "the general dis-
approval registered by the prisoners, it was said, was an important
factor in bringing about the rejection." And the *New York Post* simply stated that the mural was rejected because "the prisoners didn't
like it."

The reason given by MacCormick, who had enthusiastically
supported the project from the beginning, was equally puzzling. "It
is a matter of deep regret to me now that we feel it necessary to
abandon the project. Although a number of prisoners submitted
written opinions that were favorable to the sketches, we found
afterwards that many of them expressed approval because they
thought they were expected to do so."

Immediately after the announcement, both Juliana Force and
Audrey McMahon protested to the Municipal Art Commission,
arguing that the murals were of high artistic merit and would,
when executed, constitute a distinguished contribution. "I fail to
see by what principle the City Art Commission finds itself empow-
ered to dictate, on purely psychological or sociological grounds,
what is or is not acceptable for installation in a municipal building—the Commission's function being, as I understand, purely
aesthetic in character," Mrs. Force wrote.

Others joined in the protest. Edward Alden Jewell of *The New
York Times,* who had first seen some of the sketches at the Downtown Gallery in December, visited Ben's studio to examine all of
them. "This visit," he wrote, "has resulted in increased enthusiasm. The sketches . . . leave little doubt in my mind that the project, had it not been vetoed, would have been carried through to a
very striking conclusion. These artists have worked, it seems to me,
with deep understanding. It is not possible, on the basis of
sketches alone, to determine exactly what a finished mural will be.

There is everything to indicate, in this instance, however, that a mural sequence of really fine quality and of profound human significance would have resulted."

Philippa Whiting, in a long article in *American Magazine of Art,* reviewed the case and came to the conclusion that the poll, since its results carried no weight, was meaningless to the arts commission. "The murals," she wrote, "are, potentially, one of the most important mural achievements of a period which is using the mural as never before in this country. They have proved themselves in every possible way, and they will be carried out on twentieth-century New York walls when the New York City administration decides to accept the cooperation of its artists and its prisoners in building a finer social order."

It remained for the painter Stuart Davis, however, to place the blame for the rejection squarely on the shoulders of commission member Jonas Lie, a painter who was also the president of the National Academy of Design. Lie was a conservative both artistically and politically, and Ben had never attempted to hide his contempt for him. In the July 1935 issue of *Art Front* magazine, Davis wrote:

> We suggest that while the Commission was thinking along the line of "psychological unfitness," it might have done well to look to its own painter member. For, wherever particularly stupid and reactionary acts are committed in regard to art matters, one seldom has to look far to find the person of this back-slapping, hand-shaking, pot-boiling President of the National Academy of Design. . . .
>
> In using his position on the Art Commission to stop these murals, Jonas Lie has, I believe, satisfied a personal animosity, and at the same time has put himself forward in the press as the patriotic Boy Scout, always there to do his deed for home and country. Lie's charge of "anti-social content" is a lying charge, and he knows it, yet this man of mean ambitions is actually in a position to pass judgment on the work of artists.

Finally, Davis made a plea for Lie's dismissal and for a revamping of the entire commission:

By these and by other anti-social and anti-cultural words and behavior, Jonas Lie has proved himself unfit to hold a seat on the Municipal Art Commission, or to hold any public office, for that matter, outside that of a Fascist Censor. For these reasons the artists of New York are demanding his immediate removal from the Art Commission, as a menace to art, and as a person antagonistic to the civil rights of Americans."

The official response came from I. N. Phelps Stokes, president of the art commission. In the *American Magazine of Art* of October 1935, Stokes wrote that, in the opinion of the commission, the sketches were "lugubrious and unpleasant to look upon" and that the designs were disapproved "for one reason—and for one reason only—because every member of the Art Commission who was present when the submission was acted upon believed that, artistically, and in other respects, most of them were unsatisfactory and unsuitable for the location for which they were intended and submitted."

Shahn and Block were not quite ready to give up, however. With the help of Audrey McMahon, they sought to have the mural installed elsewhere in the state, outside New York City. In the early summer of 1935, at the suggestion of Corrections Commissioner Webster Thayer, they traveled to prisons in Elmira, Coxsackie, Woodbourne, and Wallkill, all of them possible sites for a mural. Early in July they reported to Thayer that the sketches meant for Rikers Island would not be completely satisfactory for any of these prisons, but they promised to work out, with the aid of the warden of the prison selected, the most appropriate solution to each problem.

When this didn't work, they proposed, as a last resort, a series of murals to decorate the various courtrooms at the Customs Appraisal Building on New York's Varick Street. Before nine elderly judges, who sat stolidly in a semicircle in front of them, Ben and Lou explained the need for these murals. The judges' answer arrived a few days later. After serious consideration, they had agreed that any money spent to decorate the building would best be used to repair and paint the judges' toilets.

CHAPTER SEVENTEEN

Washington, Bernarda Bryson, and a Trip to the South

BY THE SUMMER OF 1935, BEN WAS ONCE AGAIN OUT OF A JOB. He had no choice but to go back on relief, this time as part of the newly organized Federal Art Project (FAP) under the Works Progress Administration (WPA). Depressed at having to turn to the FAP because, in his words, "of the aura of poverty about it," Shahn was gratified to receive a letter from Fred L. Parker of the personnel department of the Resettlement Administration (RA), another New Deal Agency. Parker asked that Ben send a résumé of his educational and professional experience to the RA's headquarters in Washington. Shortly after sending the information, he was contacted by Rexford G. Tugwell, the agency's director.

Tugwell, an expert in agricultural matters and a distinguished professor of economics at Columbia University, had, in 1932, become a close adviser to FDR and a member of the president's famous Brain Trust. The next year he had come to Washington as an assistant secretary of agriculture. He played an important role in drafting legislation intended to ease the plight of American farmers, many of whom had been forced off their land as a result of the Depression. By the spring of 1935, however, both Roosevelt and Tugwell realized that the 1933 legislation, meant to help farmers by reducing the number of acres in production and developing conservation policies, was not accomplishing enough.

Upon Tugwell's recommendation, the president issued an executive order establishing the Resettlement Administration, whose main function was to help resettle small farmers and tenant farmers, many of them living on public relief, and to assist them in establishing rural cooperatives. Model subsistence housing and greenbelt towns were built, and seed, feed, and fertilizer were provided. In addition, the RA set up rehabilitation programs that offered financial aid, in the form of low-interest loans, to indigent workers and farmers.

It was a bold, radical approach to a complex problem, and it was vigorously opposed by conservatives in and out of Congress. In order to counteract their objections and to convince and educate the public as well as the legislators of the need for the program, Tugwell set up two divisions within the RA. The first was the Historical Section, the major function of which was to document photographically the economic and social conditions that had made the RA necessary. This division was to be headed by Roy Stryker, "an impressionable human being who could recognize and nurture talent, who could absorb and assimilate ideas from others, and disseminate them," according to John Vachon, who worked for him as a messenger and then a photographer. "A blend of old-style populist and New Deal Democrat," according to Vachon, Stryker had been a farmer, gold miner, social worker, Tugwell's student at Columbia, and finally an economics instructor there. Though not a photographer himself, Stryker understood that a contemporary visual record, provided free of charge to local and national publications, could arouse and disturb the public and the Congress even more than words could. Urban Americans, especially those in the East, had read of dust storms and soil erosion, just as they knew of the cruel plight of poverty-stricken farm families, but they had not *seen* or experienced them.

Ben was offered a job in the second division, the Special Skills Section. He had been recommended for the position by Ernestine Evans (she was not related to Walker), a brilliant editor, a close friend of Rivera's, and the first American to write seriously about the Mexican muralists. Special Skills had been created to produce posters, pamphlets, murals, and displays that would demonstrate the importance of the RA. Furthermore, the division would promote cultural activities and place works of art in the resettlement communities in order to build morale there.

Ben's official title was "Associate Art Expert, P-3" of the Fine Arts Division, which was headed by Adrian Dornbush. His appointment was effective September 19, 1935, and, his contract stipulated, would not extend beyond June 30, 1937. He was to be paid $3,200 a year—not only a decent income but, more important, a steady one.

Before Shahn began his work in Washington, Stryker insisted, he should take a two- or three-month trip through the South so that he might study at first hand the problems involved. Ben was elated. "I felt very strongly about the efforts that this Resettlement Administration was trying to accomplish resettling people, and so on," he told Richard Doud years later. "I don't think I ever felt that way before or since . . . totally involved." As for the charge made by critics of the RA that the agency's purpose was to disseminate propaganda, he scoffed at it. "I cannot separate art from life," he later told another interviewer, Forrest Selvig. "Propaganda is to me a noble word. It means you believe something very strongly and you want other people to believe it; you want to propagate your faith . . . art has always been used to propagate ideas and to persuade."

To prepare for his trip, Ben studied the areas of the country he was to visit—their histories, their social and economic problems, and the possible solutions to those problems. And he read the work of sociologists who had studied the South, among them Howard Washington Odum and Arthur Raper, as well as literary essays by Allen Tate and Robert Penn Warren.

Most important of all, however, he contacted Bernarda Bryson, then working as a lithographer in Woodstock, New York, and invited her to join him on this trip. In doing so, he formally if not legally put an end to his marriage with Tillie and began a life with another woman.

A headstrong, independent young woman, Bernarda Bryson was born in Athens, Ohio, on March 7, 1903. Her ancestors had arrived in New Hampshire in the early seventeenth century and had migrated to Ohio in 1797. Hers was a family of well-educated, emancipated women. Her mother, Lucy Wilkins Weethee, a graduate of Ohio University in Athens, was a professor of Latin. Her aunt, too, had graduated from college, as had her grandmother; her grandfather and his brother had founded their own coeducational college in Ohio.

The entire family was politically liberal. Bernarda's father, Charles H. Bryson, an enthusiastic supporter of Teddy Roosevelt's progressive politics, had been graduated from Ohio University; he owned and edited the *Athens Morning Journal*.

Bernarda was brought up in a world of books and ideas. She was introduced to Shakespeare by her father and read "The Rime of the Ancient Mariner" with her mother, who also encouraged her interest in art, buying paints and stretchers for canvases, which she taught her daughter to use.

Bernarda attended school until the age of nine, after which the family moved to the West. What she learned while there, she learned from her parents. She had, she remembers, more education than schooling at that time. When the family returned to Ohio, Bernarda was sent to the Columbus School for Girls, where she received the academic discipline she had missed.

Upon her graduation from high school, she attended Ohio University, where she majored in philosophy and studied art. During her senior year, she transferred to Ohio State University in Columbus, where she met and married Victor Parks, who was studying for his master's degree. The marriage lasted a year and a half. She remembers Parks as a "wonderful person" who was, unfortunately, an alcoholic. The experience persuaded her that she was not meant to be a wife.

Her first commercial job was at a department store, doing what she calls "institutional drawings." After that she made commercial drawings in Cleveland, where she also studied etching and lithography.

When the young woman returned to Columbus, where her parents lived, she began teaching at the museum's art school; she was also hired to write an art column for a local paper, the *Ohio State Journal*, which she enjoyed immensely. Once, she courageously denounced the director of the Columbus Museum for having spent a huge amount of money in order to bring *Arrangement in Gray and Black* ("Whistler's Mother") to the museum for an exhibition, when the money would have been better spent on poor, talented art students so that they might continue their studies. The museum director, furious, told her that if she couldn't write complimentary things about the museum, she should not teach there. Bernarda angrily replied that he was entitled to fire her only if her teaching was unsatisfactory. If she was to be fired for what she had written, she said, she would be forced to mention that in her newspaper column. Undeterred, the museum director called her editor to demand that she be relieved of her job, but her editor was delighted with her column and the controversial position she had taken, and he refused.

Bernarda had inherited her parents' progressive political views as well as their compassion for the underdog. Profoundly saddened by the terrible poverty that surrounded her during the first years of the Depression, she decided, when only twenty-five years old, to become actively involved in politics. Disheartened by the failure of the major political parties to remedy this tragedy, she concluded that she could be effective only if she joined either the Communist or Socialist party. She decided on the former, and told her mother of her intentions. When Mrs. Bryson expressed fears that such a move would only embarrass Bernarda's father, an organizer for the Republicans for FDR, Bernarda went directly to him to ask his advice. His reply was direct and unequivocal: she must, he told her, do whatever she really believed and pay no attention to the possible consequences.

Bernarda began to try to combine her interests in art and politics. She knew many works of social protest, but she had not yet found any that were of artistic merit. That soon changed. At a traveling exhibition shown at the Columbus Museum, she finally saw a painting by an artist who had something to say and was able to say it in his art. The painting showed Sacco and Vanzetti handcuffed to each other, and the artist was Ben Shahn.

Not long afterward, Bernarda was in New York, having convinced her editor that she should interview Diego Rivera concerning the scandal of the Rockefeller Center mural. Rivera, who was already working on the new mural at the New Workers' School, introduced her to one of his assistants: Ben Shahn. Excitedly, Bernarda told Ben of her great enthusiasm for his painting and also told him she had written a long article about it for her newspaper. Ben was gracious and asked her to send him a copy of the article as soon as she returned to Columbus, but she had to disappoint him by confessing that she never kept copies of anything she wrote.

A year later, Bernarda returned to New York, this time staying with an old friend, Lucy Temkin, and planning to explore the city. Her first night there, Lucy told her about a meeting of the Unemployed Artists Association in the nearby Church of All Nations. By the end of that meeting, Bernarda, though a newcomer, had been elected secretary of the organization, which, by vote, became the Artists Union. Through her political activities, she again met Ben. They worked together on the union's magazine, *Art Front.* In a very short time, disillusioned by what she considered its dishonesty, she left the Communist Party. She and Ben walked through the city together, their friendship increased, and when Ben told her that his marriage had come to an end, their relationship changed to such an extent that it was natural that he would ask her to join him in Washington.

Tillie was shocked and devastated by Ben's desertion of her and their two

Shahn and his son Ezra, in front of 333 West Eleventh Street, in a photo taken by Judy Shahn on her sixth birthday on July 14, 1935. The Kodak Brownie box camera she used was a birthday present from Ben.

children (their second child and first son, Ezra, had been born a year and a half earlier, in November 1933). She and Ben were, Tillie had believed, the perfect happy family: a loving husband and wife and two beautiful children. Others, who had observed Ben closely, were not nearly so surprised. For some time, he had been restless and irritable. He made no attempt to disguise his contempt for Tillie's family, whose values were too middle class and who were, he thought, hopelessly boring. He also resented what he considered their interference in his life. They had sent one of Tillie's sisters to be with her at the time of Judy's birth in Paris, for example.

In any case, Ben seems to have made no effort to keep his deepening relationship with Bernarda a secret from his friends.

Ben's separation from his wife and children, however, had broader implications than the breakup of the marriage. In leaving his family—abandoning them, really, for he gradually disappeared from their lives for a long time—he was also trying to distance himself from every aspect of his past: the traditions that had formed him, his religious and social origins, and almost all of the people associated with that past.

Ben's strongest tie had always been to his father, to whom he had been deeply attached, but Hessel had died in late 1933 or early 1934. His relationship with his mother had remained hostile. And now he had left Tillie, whom Gittel loved, and begun a serious relationship with Bernarda, a Christian from a completely different world; the hostility between mother and son only increased. It has been said that Gittel sat shiva—observed the seven days of mourning that Jews observe following the death of a loved one—after Ben left Tillie, but this seems unlikely. The Shahn family, though Jewish by tradition, was not strictly observant and would probably not have followed this custom. Nonetheless, as far as Gittel was concerned, her son Ben might have been dead. Though she asked about him and followed his career, she apparently never saw him again. Ben's relationship with his two sisters had never been close either; they rarely saw each other after his separation from Tillie. Only his tie to Phil remained. As for his few friends, they, too, faded out of Ben's life, and he saw them rarely following his separation from Tillie.

Many years later, Bernarda Bryson, who became Ben's second wife and remained with him until his death, told an interviewer that she believed she represented for Ben an escape from the ethnic pressures that had oppressed him. She believed that he wanted to erase completely that part of his consciousness. Bernarda and Tillie—both attractive, sensitive, extremely intelligent women—came from different worlds, and it was the world that Tillie inhabited that Ben wanted to leave behind. But Bernarda saw that this complete renunciation of his past embittered Ben more than he had anticipated. She believed that he might have "put a kind of moral scar tissue" over what he had done to himself, and she felt guilty for her part in that. When she first met him, he appeared sufficiently adult to know what he was doing and to understand the consequences of his actions. "After I knew him better, I realized that he didn't," she said. "He was a very impulsive person. He was thoughtful in some respects, and in other respects he wasn't. He was really torn with conflicts. When you first met Ben, you'd think he was sophisticated, widely read, much traveled, a funny, easy person. But he had come out of a background that was, to say the least, grim." According to Bernarda, because of his terrible temper, he could sometimes seem almost a "demonic character." At the same time, however, she recognized that "he was a very great person with a tremendous mind," and she believed that "the intensity of his work was probably the point of convergence between the conflicts."

When Ben left Tillie, he was already an angry, embittered man, capable at times of great, unreasonable cruelty. But in his work and in much of his life his anger and bitterness were aimed at injustice and bigotry, and it was for that justifiable rage that he will be remembered.

=====

In late September 1935, Ben—with Bernarda at his side and at the wheel of their small Model A Ford—set out to visit the South. This trip was to be a startling revelation to both of them: the Lithuanian-born, shtetl-bred New York artist, and the refined, intellectual Ohioan, who grew up in the world of academia. They had fought separately and together for the rights of artists impoverished by the Depression, and they had shared the struggle against injustice from the vantage point of New York. Now they were to see at first hand the poverty and desperation that characterized the lives of the millions of Americans who suffered in a world far from their own.

Ben's weapon against injustice this time was his small 35-millimeter camera. Except for the right-angle lens finder, it was without gadgets of any kind. He carried a separate light meter and had no interchangeable lens. Because of this, the camera was flat enough to carry unobtrusively in his back pocket. At first, the camera was to serve as a kind of mechanical sketch pad; the photos would be "notes" for the posters and pamphlets he had been hired to create for the Special Section. In a very short time, he realized that these images were valuable in themselves and not merely preparatory works. When Roy Stryker first saw them he was profoundly impressed. "I was taken by Ben's photos because they were so compassionate. . . . Ben's had the juices of human beings and their troubles and all those human things," he wrote. Believing that Shahn would be more valuable to the RA as a photographer than as an illustrator, he "borrowed" him from the Special Skills division, agreeing to furnish his film and pay for the development and printing of the photographs, which he kept in the files of the Historical Section. Ben retained the right to consult the photos whenever he felt they would be useful as resource material; Special Skills would continue to pay Ben's salary and travel costs.

Unlike the photographers who worked officially for Stryker and the Historical Section—among them Arthur Rothstein, Russell Lee, John Vachon, Walker Evans, and Dorothea Lange—Ben had no precise itinerary. He was free to go where he wanted and to choose what he wanted to photograph. Occasionally, at first, Ben would realize that he needed something he had failed to photograph; he and Bernarda would retrace their steps, sometimes five or six hundred miles. This could mean as many as three extra days' driving in their slow car. As time passed, however, he came to know instinctively what he was looking for and understand where he might find it.

In his interview with Richard Doud, Ben remembered the beginning of the first trip.

For instance, I remember the first place I went to on this trip where we were active, one of the resettlements that we built. I found that as far as I was concerned, it was impossible to photograph. Neat little rows of houses. This wasn't my idea of something to photograph at all. But I had the good luck to ask someone, "Where are you all from? Where did they bring you from?" And when they told me, I went on to a place called Scott's Run, and there it began. I realized then I must be on my own, find out, you know. I thought it would all be sort of given to me and from there I went all through Kentucky, West Virginia, down to Arkansas, Mississippi, and Louisiana—in other words, I covered the mine country and the cotton country. I was terribly excited about it, and did no painting at all in that time. This was it, I thought. I'm sort of single track, anyway. When I'm off on photography, photography is it, and I thought this would be the career for the rest of my life.

Unfortunately, neither Ben nor Bernarda kept a journal of their travels. Nor did they supply precise captions for most of the many photographs Ben took. However, file cards of negatives kept at the office of the RA, as well as the occasional anecdotes that Ben liked to tell, indicate the scope of his work and the subjects and places that attracted him.

Their trip began in coal-mining country. From the Scott's Run area, Morgantown, Purseglove, and Omar, West Virginia, they traveled to Jenkins, Kentucky, and then to Zinc, Arkansas. The suffering and poverty they saw astonished them. The few men who were employed, performing dangerous work in the mines, earned barely enough to cover their expenses. They were completely dependent on their employers, since most of them lived in company houses and bought at company stores. As an example, Ben related the case of one miner from Purseglove. His paycheck for two weeks was $25.77, from which $23.77 was deducted. His debits were: "Company store, $10.94; Company house, $4.50; Insurance, $1.00; Sick fund, forty-five cents; Lamp, seventy-five cents; check weighman, fifty-two cents; something else, sixty-one cents; and 'advance,' $5.00."

Ben's photos reflect his compassion for the plight of these workers and their families. "The photographs that Ben Shahn made in these coal mining communities cast a critical eye on the disparity between the 'haves' and the 'have nots,'" the art historian Susan H. Edwards has written. "The sociological slant of Shahn's photographs effectively brought to life the tribulations of Depression miners and mountaineers." Among his photos are overall views of mining towns and portraits of their citizens, a shot of a local post office and a theater, and detailed studies of an abandoned mine, as well as photos of lines of miners waiting for their relief checks, a scene of payday at the Purseglove mine, and posters for a showing of a movie, *Black Fury.* The latter was taken in Purseglove, where Ben also took a memorable photo of a black miner collecting his paycheck.

It didn't take Ben long to realize that all he knew about the South he had learned from a source of dubious value: political discussions on New York's Union Square. These completely misleading misconceptions in no way reflected the realities he now saw. He recounted one version (there were several) of how his romantic ideas concerning the relationship between the miners and their unions were shattered on a television program, A *Profile of Ben Shahn,* part of the series "The Open Mind," moderated by Eric Goldman:

> . . . I was in West Virginia during a little coal strike there and I went down to the mine pit and pickets were there. I thought the easiest way to open conversation with anybody was to offer them a cigarette, you know. And I carefully bought a pack of union-made cigarettes, Raleighs, and I offered them one and they said, "Nah, I don't smoke them," and I said, "Well, those are union cigarettes," and one said, "Look boy, I've been in the union for thirty years; here," and he offered me one of the more popular brands, you see.

There were other surprises. A bad word about John L. Lewis, the leader of the United Mine Workers of America, would be just cause for a lynching in the miners' view—but so would possession of a copy of the pro-union leftist magazine *The Nation.* "Those contradictions became gray all over," he noted; "they had been so beautifully black and white to me."

In Kentucky, Ben took photos of coal miners as they boarded a

Cotton pickers at 6:30 A.M., waiting for the workday to begin at the
Alexunder plantation.

Zinc, Arkansas, October 1935.

Street scene, Natchez, Mississippi, October 1935.

One of a series of photographs taken of a medicine man in a small town in Tennessee in October 1935.

bus on their way to the mines and loaded coal into freight cars, and he photographed the miners' shacks—all of these in Jenkins. He also documented street scenes, a post office, a bank building, and a horse and buggy in Middlesboro and Smithland.

In Tennessee, he traveled to the towns of Maynardville, Camden, Huntingdon, and Murfreesboro, and to the cities of Nashville and Memphis. He photographed a county courthouse, street musicians, the medicine show at Huntingdon, old riverboats docked at Memphis, deckhands in Murfreesboro, and a religious meeting on a Nashville street corner.

In Arkansas, an agricultural state whose farmers had suffered enormously from a drought in 1934, Ben and Bernarda were at first accompanied by Senator Joseph Robinson. The senator, known for his strong opposition to the striking farmworkers' union, was not only an embarrassment; he even attracted hostility, and soon Ben and Bernarda struck off on their own, traveling from the mountains to the delta country. Along the way, Ben took photos at a plantation in Pulaski County, tenant farmers in Boone County, a house with a roof ingeniously put together with auto license plates, and a blind street violinist in West Memphis. He also depicted life in front of a black church on a Sunday morning in Little Rock, and took a memorable shot of a child holding a ragged doll. The child, he commented, looked as horribly ragged as the doll.

In Arkansas Ben learned that not all RA employees had hearts of gold. When he presented his credentials to the RA regional director at Little Rock, the director snapped, "What the hell are you coming down here for, making more trouble for us?" He was, Ben learned, the owner of a large plantation. And, on one occasion, an RA employee asked, "You ain't seen any niggers around here, have ya?" Contempt for blacks was common; Ben and Bernarda were stunned by the stark disparity in racial attitudes between the North and the South. According to Nicholas Natanson in *The Black Image in the New Deal,* Ben's photos of blacks in the South had special value because they offered "subtle insights into the nature of race relations at the time."

Toward the end of this trip, Ben followed the Mississippi River south from Memphis to New Orleans and on to Plaquemines and Tangipahoa Parishes. He photographed mausoleums, cemetery workers, a rural church, and an abandoned paper mill. He showed deckhands, strawberry pickers, riverboats, merchants, tailors, Cajuns, and Creoles. He took a photo of a child seated inside a tenant farmer's darkened house in Louisiana and later explained why he refused to use a flash.

> I was really quite a purist about it, and when some of the people came in and began to use a flash I thought it was immoral. I'll give you a reason why. You know, you come into a sharecropper's cabin and it's dark. But a flash destroys that darkness. It is true that flash would actually illuminate the comic papers that they used to paste on their walls, but this wasn't the impact it had on me. It was the darkness, the glistening of the eyes, the glistening of a brass ornament on top of a big bed, a glass, a mirror that would catch light. I wanted very much to hold on to this, you see.

In Natchez, Mississippi, he captured the humor in the image of two women on their way to church; he later used these two figures in a well-known painting, *Myself Among the Churchgoers*. Toward the end of his travels along the Mississippi, Ben passed through the low country, land suitable for growing sugar cane and rice, fishing and trapping. It was yet another world and an equally foreign one to a man from New York. He took photos of the trappers, who lived on otter, muskrat, possum, wild boar, and alligator. These proud men wouldn't touch the soil lest they be mistaken for farmers. It was so beneath them to work the land that they would, Ben was told, stamp out anything green because their whole dignity rested on trapping, not on soil.

Though he took this first trip through the South on behalf of the Special Skills Section of the Resettlement Administration, in the end Ben succeeded in contributing to the files of the Historical Section some of the most sensitive photographs taken of the South during this tragic and troubled period. Given his background and education, he showed a surprising ability to understand and evoke the spirit of people whose world was so totally foreign to his own. As Susan H. Edwards has noted, "He cuts through the geographical center and fictionalized heart of the South. . . . What Shahn observed and fixed in the shadows of his photographs was the southern attachment to itself, its place, and its past."

A study of Shahn's remarkable photos reveals that his emphasis was on people rather than on landscapes or architectural sites. He showed a special gift for creating series of photos, resulting in a near-cinematic effect. Two of these immensely moving series deal with two destitute families, both living in Arkansas. Bernarda has written about each of them. Her words supplement but do not equal or replace the poignancy of Ben's images. Of the Mulhalls of Muskgrove, Arkansas, she wrote: "They were sweet and mild as dolls and were congenitally retarded. They had been resettled on submarginal land; it was almost solid rock. There were no windows in their home, a dirt floor and no water. What water they had was hauled from a great distance. Their cash crop of that year: $1.40."

The second family were the Twilligers, who lived in the Ozark Mountains. "Their cash crop for the year was $3.00," Bernarda wrote. "They had a very beautiful fifteen-year-old daughter. Ben asked her, 'Where do you go to school?' She replied that she never did. The school wasn't close enough."

Ben himself described the seventeen photographs he took of a traveling medicine show in Huntingdon, Tennessee: "I did a series of photographs of a Saturday afternoon in a small town in Tennessee of a medicine man selling bottles of cures. He had a little ventriloquist dummy and he had a Negro to help him. I don't think there were ten cars on the square. They were all mule-drawn carts that had come there. This was 1935. It was incredible to see." Once again, a verbal description seems flat compared to the force of the photographer's images.

One of the most successfully realized of Ben's series dealt with the cotton pickers of Pulaski County, Arkansas. Of all farm laborers, none suffered more from the Depression. Their plight stemmed from the 1933 decision by the Agricultural Adjustment Administration (AAA) to pay the planters not to grow cotton, an effort to offset the diminishing market. Though this clearly alleviated the problems of the powerful landowners, it had a disastrous effect on farmworkers, tenants, sharecroppers, and small farmers. These were forced to move elsewhere to seek work, for which they were inevitably paid little.

Shahn himself wrote of this series, a compassionate record of the daily activities of these desperately poor cotton workers during the fall harvest: "I came out to a plantation to take photographs. I knew I'd have to be there at 5:30 in the morning, when the crew got together and the sun was low, you know, just rising, and it was beautiful."

It was so cold that steam came from their mouths. They carried with them enormous cans of water, the kind farmers used for milk. By nine o'clock, it was hot; after about twelve hours of work, at five cents an hour, Ben and Bernarda drove the laborers back to the company store, where they would drink three Cokes, one after another—spending a quarter of their earnings. Shahn took superb pictures of the workers waiting near a plantation storehouse for a ride to the fields where they would begin their work. Some of these are so aesthetically correct and their composition so masterful that they seem almost staged (a charge leveled against many RA photographers, but never against Ben). He also took photos of the women at work in the fields, large sacks draped from their backs. Many of these photos are extraordinarily beautiful, theatrical, even lyrical. But Ben's intention was sociopolitical rather than aesthetic. Susan H. Edwards has commented: "He was not interested in the rhetorical valorization of the underprivileged or the dignification of labor. Just as in the mining country, he was looking for images that pointed to the concrete effects that a labor system, in this case, tenancy, had on real people."

CHAPTER EIGHTEEN

Washington: 1935–36

BEN AND BERNARDA RETURNED TO WASHINGTON ON NOVEM-
ber 8, 1935. The capital was then, as John Vachon described it, a
city where "large blue streetcars clanged along the tree-shaded
streets . . . and F.D.R. lived on Pennsylvania Avenue. Boy and girl
government clerks lived in rooming houses on K Street, and some
people were laughing at the antics of those two comic figures in
Europe, Hitler and Mussolini. It was a pleasant somnolent city.
Cattle were dying out on the drought-stricken plains of South
Dakota, and jobs were hard to find all over the U.S. of A."

Washington's temporary residents were, according to David
Brinkley, "social workers, farm economists, liberal lawyers, union
organizers, all of them political chiropractors eager to get their
thumbs on the national spine, to snap it and crack it until the
blood again flowed outward to all the extremities of American life,
returning it to health and prosperity."

Ben was proudly among these, more than willing and eager to do
his part. Upon his arrival, he delivered thirty-two rolls of 35-
millimeter film and nine rolls of 16-millimeter movie film to
Stryker, who realized that Ben's photos were special. Several years
later he tried to explain why. He told Margaret Weiss that he

believed Ben's rapport with his subjects was what made his photographs different:

> Something happens there in those pictures. Maybe it was in
> the wonderful tolerance, sympathy and feeling he had for peo-
> ple—for human beings. He [Ben] said, "I talk to them . . . I like
> them. I like people—and maybe they knew I liked them." Ben
> was a man of great experience—a man with a sense of life. He
> knew about lots of things . . . he knew about people. I believe
> that he did have the ability to reach out and reach into individu-
> als by his nature, his manner, his approach when he was taking
> pictures. In some way people opened up. They opened up and
> said, "Here we are." Looking at his pictures, one is sure that he
> related to those people and knew something about what was
> going on in their minds and troubled lives. His pictures project a
> sense of place, but not necessarily any particular locale. You
> know one scene is in a town, another is out in the country. All
> are part of a period which reflected an economic and social atti-
> tude born of hard times.

Stryker also expressed a devastating insight into Ben's motives,
however. In a 1964 interview with Richard A. Doud, he remarked
that Shahn "was after something that I couldn't have told him anything about. He was selfish, he was going out on a selfish project,
and sometimes selfish projects, selfish operations are the finest
things that ever happen because he was going out to get himself . . . a wonderful collection of pictures that would be useful in
making murals."

Stryker and Shahn, both strong-willed men, certainly had their
disagreements, but their collaboration—with Ben as the artist and,
in Bernarda's words, Stryker as "the enabler, the provider of any
needed piece of equipment, the unraveler of bureaucratic red
tape"—produced some of the finest photographs of the era.

Walker Evans, however, characterized their relationship as
essentially one-sided: "He could wrap Mr. Stryker around his finger; and he did," Walker told Paul Cummings in a 1971 interview.
"He could go over there and get a trip out of it. He could go up
with all expenses paid with his girl Bernarda. And they had a fine
time. Ben really worked Washington for all it was worth."

One of Ben's colleagues at the RA saw the artist's relationship with Bernarda as equally one-sided. According to Selden Rodman, this colleague said: "Ben and Bernarda, the quiet mouse, were always together. But what a patriarchal bastard he could be! When he wanted to hold the floor alone, he would think nothing of chasing her off peremptorily to wash the dishes." While praising Ben's qualities as a leader, this man continued: "He was that way with all women, and children, and still is, I guess. It was never 'Please, darling . . .' "

Nonetheless, Ben was sufficiently proud of and impressed by Bernarda's work to convince Dornbush that she, too, belonged in the group. Her experience, her knowledge of American history, and her skills as a printer, he argued, would make her an invaluable addition to the Special Skills Division. Dornbush agreed, and Bernarda was soon hired as a "junior art expert" to set up a lithographic shop.

As her first project, Bernarda proposed a series of thirty color lithographs devoted to the early history, absorption, and present condition of the American frontier. The lithographs would be bound into a book, with text on the facing pages. Once the project was approved by Tugwell, Bernarda set up the lithography shop for which she had been hired. She bought a press, the finest lithographic stones available, and the highest-quality paper. She stopped at nothing to establish her ideal print shop, even seeing to it that an entire interior wall was knocked down to provide ideal lighting. With characteristic energy and intelligence, she set to work at once on a series known as *The Vanishing American Frontier.* She and Ben were members of the same team. It was, as it would continue to be, a partnership, though an unequal one.

Bernarda's book was never finished, though she managed to complete nine black-and-white lithographs, one color poster, and several drawings and watercolor studies. In addition, during her time at Special Skills, she made drawings for a number of pamphlets, as well as what she called her *Underground Railroad* series, consisting of twelve watercolors of African-American heroes (among them Harriet Tubman, Nat Turner, and Sojourner Truth).

Ben was tireless. Special Skills, Roy Stryker remembered, "was full of screwballs, but into it by some act of providence came Ben

Shahn who not only gave it backbone but whose combination of toughness, vision, and *enormous competence* very soon affected the whole division." Ben was totally involved with his work at Special Skills. He had never before been able to commit himself so completely to any cause. He did every task with the same vigor and enthusiasm. "I attached the same importance to doing a line of lettering as I did to making a poster or the possible assignment of a mural," he told an interviewer, Harlan Phillips.

He was always busy. In early December, he was one of six artists working on a series of lithographic posters on such subjects as drought, ghost towns, cotton, and waste land.

The following year, 1936, which Ben spent in Washington, was especially active. Early in the year, he traveled to Baltimore, Philadelphia, and New York to investigate the methods of the two or three commercial lithographic shops still using stone lithography and producing prints that were works of art. Upon his return to headquarters, he presented Dornbush with a memorandum outlining what he had learned and what he recommended. The memorandum must have been impressive: Ben told Phillips that he was "offered a bigger job with a solid rug, some kind of crummy sofa, and a secretary." But he added: "I didn't want any secretary, and I would have loved the extra money. It was about $600 more, but I didn't want it, didn't take it." He much preferred active creation to overseeing and supervising assignments done by others.

Fervently dedicated to FDR's reelection in 1936, he created an exhibit for the Democratic convention in Philadelphia that June, traveling there to work with his staff on the mounting of the photographs and the lettering of the captions; he also checked the details of the construction, the color scheme, and lighting effects. The exhibition, intended to promote the activities of the RA as a New Deal success, was a triumph. Stryker told Richard Doud in 1965 that Ben's exhibit was "fantastic, cheap, easy to put together, and attracted no end of attention." It was, Stryker added, memorable because it was "so unique in design, so effectively selected, and so successful in the amount of people that stopped to see it."

Ben worked unofficially, too, for Roosevelt's reelection. After Tugwell introduced him to the UMWA's Lewis, he created posters for the newly formed Committee for Industrial Organizations, started by Lewis with the garment trade unionists David Dubinsky and Sidney Hillman. (This later became the Congress of Industrial Organizations [CIO].) In addition—under a pseudonym, because he didn't want to be criticized for doing too much outside work— Shahn created pamphlets for the CIO. He was confident that the work he did could make a difference in the lives of the many needy and downtrodden Americans.

He supervised the arrangement of a photographic display depicting conditions before and after homestead. He worked on poster sketches showing dust storms and soil erosion. His tremendously effective poster *Years of Dust* was published in June 1936. He joined other members of the artists' staff in arranging for a display of housing at the U.S. Chamber of Commerce Building. In addition, in early 1936 he designed a series of thirty traveling exhibits to be distributed to various clubs and schools, worked on a dummy layout of the RA exhibit for the San Diego fair (a photographic exhibit portraying RA programs, problems, and progress), went to New York to discuss methods of reproducing RA posters and to investigate the possibility of holding an exhibition of RA posters in the New York Public Library, and worked on a model for a display at an exposition in Dallas.

Later in the year, he helped prepare a four-color animated regional map that graphically presented a bird's-eye view of the Resettlement program and activities as developed in several regions. He was in charge of designing a photographic exhibition in Washington that would serve as a prototype for fifteen additional exhibitions, as well as a map of proposed landscape architecture for the Decatur Homesteads at the Decatur, Indiana, centennial.

His title was changed to "associate technical advisor" because of Civil Service Commission requirements, but everything else remained the same: he continued to work with the same boundless energy and enthusiasm. Almost obsessed with what he saw as a mission rather than a job, Shahn stopped reading for pleasure and gave up all his activities as a painter. He was always in a hurry, always had more work to do. He never took a trolley—they were too slow. Instead, he traveled by taxi. He was dismayed at 3:30 in the afternoon when he would find workers at government agencies already prepared to go home at 4:30. For him, there was no "closing time." He would work sixteen or eighteen hours at a stretch if he had a project to complete. At one point be became so ill from overwork that he had to be hospitalized and was warned to slow down.

In the fall of 1936, Ben further expanded his horizons when he began collaborating with Walker Evans on a two-reel, 35-millimeter sound film dealing with housing problems in the suburban town of Greenbelt, Maryland, a few miles outside Washington. Shahn and Evans were enthusiastic about the project at first, as was Stryker, who wrote to Dorothea Lange, one of the finest photographers on his staff, that the two men had been given permission to experiment with the project, and that he hoped they would "go to town" on the job. Apparently, however, the two friends quarreled, and by the time they were able to reach an agreement on the kind of film they wanted, the entire project was abandoned.

On October 6 of that year, too, Ben and Bernarda's family expanded, with the birth of their first child, Susanna. Ben was able to continue working with his usual vigor, but Bernarda, though she still worked as an illustrator, was forced to curtail her activities outside the home.

In the middle of December, word spread that the Resettlement Administration would lose its independent status and become a part of the Department of Agriculture. Inevitably, under this new system, the RA and its programs would be far more closely scrutinized. Cuts in spending as well as reductions in staff would be sure to follow.

Ben was understandably worried. His job, his way of life, and his mission were threatened. The RA was his only means of support, and he now had three children (though it seems he did not fully accept responsibility for the first two). Charles H. Bryson, Bernarda's father, was also concerned, but fortunately, as Ohio state chairman of the Republicans-for-Roosevelt League, he had a powerful contact in the administration: James A. Farley, the U.S. postmaster general, who directed Roosevelt's first and second presidential campaigns. On December 18, Bryson sent Farley a telegram urging that Shahn, "a man of extraordinary ability," be kept at his job: "To lose this man would be a definite loss to the public service." He asked Farley to pass the word on to the secretary of agriculture, Henry A. Wallace. Bryson followed this up with a letter emphasizing Ben's qualities. "Although an artist, Ben's character, experience, and temperament fit him for positions of large responsibility in the government. . . . Just a little help would save him."

Bryson's telegram and letter were effective. At the end of January 1937, Farley wrote back that he had checked with the Department of Agriculture and learned that no changes in Shahn's status were being contemplated.

Ben retained his job, but the mood in the capital had altered radically. In 1937, there were still 7.5 million unemployed, large numbers of homeless, and several hundred thousand dispossessed farmers, but Roosevelt's power had diminished and the impact of his social and economic programs reduced despite his landslide reelection in 1936. In *Washington Goes to War*, David Brinkley noted that after the election, "almost nothing had gone right for him."

> In 1937 he had sought to enlarge the Supreme Court and give it a liberal majority more likely to support his New Deal programs. The old Court had knocked those programs down, one after another. But his attempt to expand the Court was a fiasco. Congress and the public and the press saw the Supreme Court as one of the majestic pillars of American government, not to be tampered with, and they objected angrily to "Court-packing," as it came to be called, and defeated it. Further, in the fall of 1937 the economy, after making what had seemed to be modest progress from the depths of the Depression, fell backward into another severe recession. Unemployment, already high, rose again. The stock market crashed again. Production declined again. And then the 1938 elections brought a new group of conservatives to a Congress that was now even less willing to approve anything Roosevelt asked.

At the RA, now part of the Department of Agriculture, Tugwell, who had been the heart of the organization, was fired. At the same time, it was decided that the photographer who had produced the smallest number of negatives would be dismissed from the Historical Section. For this reason, Walker Evans, who had contributed very few because he was a perfectionist, was dropped. "It's what they call quantity control instead of quality control," Ben explained.

CHAPTER NINETEEN

Jersey Homesteads

IN SPITE OF THE CHANGES TAKING PLACE AT THE RA, NEITHER Bernarda's job nor Ben's seemed in danger. Whenever she could leave their infant daughter, Bernarda worked tirelessly at the congressional library, studying frontier history. Though she grew pale from spending so much time in the sunless room she'd been assigned, she remained enthusiastic.

Ben, too, continued to work hard, though his customary zeal was somewhat diminished by the new bureaucracy, which invaded his office, bringing with it ever-growing piles of paper that cluttered his desk. Most of the paperwork dealt more with administrative matters than with creative ideas and projects. Of these latter, one new project was of genuine interest to him, however; this was the possibility of executing a mural in the RA's new Jersey Homesteads project near Hightstown, New Jersey, only fifty miles from New York.

Jersey Homesteads was the dream of one Benjamin Brown, a Ukrainian who had immigrated to the United States at an early age, had worked his way through agricultural school in Pennsylvania, and had developed an almost obsessive interest in setting up cooperative settlements throughout the United States. With the passion of a visionary, this extraordinarily vital, intelligent man had already set up such cooperatives in Russia and in Utah. In the early 1930s, he decided to establish a homestead cooperative settlement in central New Jersey. The purpose of this community was to improve the lot of approximately two hundred unemployed Jewish needleworkers from New York and Philadelphia who had been forced to live in substandard urban housing, with little hope for work or for a decent future. Essentially, Brown wanted to create a kind of shtetl in the midst of New Jersey. It was to be a place where workers could peacefully ply their trade while enjoying the benefits of rural life away from the crowded, oppressive cities.

Central to Brown's ambitious project was the construction of a garment factory, where needleworkers would be employed for most of the year. During the summer months, traditionally slow ones in the garment industry, these same workers would be occupied with farming and gardening as well as with a proposed dairy and chicken enterprise. This would fulfill another of Brown's dreams: to find a way for Jewish settlers to make a living by working their own land, an occupation long denied them in the countries of their birth.

Under Brown's scheme, each family chosen to live in Jersey Homesteads would have to contribute $500 to a general fund that would finance the operation of the factory and farm building. Before that, however, it was necessary to find enough money to initiate the entire project. This was easier than Brown had ever imagined. A meeting with Secretary of the Interior Harold Ickes was arranged. Ickes needed little convincing to understand the value of the proposed settlement and readily agreed to finance it through his department.

The wheels were soon set in motion. Approximately 1,278 acres of land located in Monmouth County, roughly halfway between New York and Philadelphia, were purchased as a site for the new town. Construction of the two hundred homes and the factory as well as sewage and water works, poultry buildings, a firehouse, and later an elementary school/community center (the site of the proposed mural) began in mid-1935. At the same time, a 414-acre farm was set up.

After much wrangling and many bureaucratic delays, the

The artist in Washington, D.C., at work on the cartoon for the fresco mural for the community center at Jersey Homesteads.

dynamic young architect Alfred Kastner was put in charge of the design of the buildings and supervision of the project. Kastner had been appointed principal architect of the Construction Division of the Resettlement Administration, which had taken over the Jersey Homesteads project from the Interior Department in June 1935. He found the project in disastrous condition. Rampant corruption, endless red tape, and serious errors had led to long construction delays. Fortunately, Kastner had considerable experience dealing with intricate governmental bureaucracy. Born in Suhl, Germany, in 1900, and trained in Leipzig and Hamburg, he had come to the United States in 1924 and had since then made a name for himself designing community living quarters.

Working from a Washington office, he visited Jersey Homesteads weekly, firing most of the architects and engineers and reorganizing the entire staff. As part of this reorganization, he hired a young Russian-born American, Louis I. Kahn, as assistant principal architect for the new town. Kahn, then unknown, became, of course, one of the preeminent architects of the century (he has even been given credit, mistakenly, for the design of Jersey Homesteads).

Kastner was the Shahns' closest friend in Washington, and he had suggested the idea of a fresco mural to Ben. Tugwell approved on the condition that both Ben and Bernarda, as his assistants, would paint the mural on RA salaries.

Ben had conferred with the architect frequently, had visited the site of the proposed mural often, and, on his own, had conducted research for the project at the New York Public Library. In March 1936, Kastner wrote a memorandum to Adrian Dornbush, outlining the points that had been made during a meeting with Shahn. The general theme would, in Kastner's words, "center about contemporary life of the Jewish emigrant, touch on immigration and emigration, his assimilation into the country, industrialism and unionism, with contra-pointal adoption of pogroms elsewhere, and immigration to Palestine."

So far, all of Ben's attempts to complete a mural had come to nothing. Both the Prohibition mural and the Rikers Island project had been rejected. The Rivera mural, not his but one on which he had worked, had not been finished. In 1937, still another mural project was destined to fail. A competition was held by the Treasury Department's Section of Painting and Sculpture, the winner to receive a commission to execute a mural entitled *The Great State of Wisconsin,* for a new community near Milwaukee. Ben submitted a series of gouaches depicting the history of the Progressive movement in the state and praising the achievements of two prominent Progressives, Governor Robert La Follette and his son, Senator Robert La Follette, Jr. The proposal was rejected.

For the Jersey Homestead mural, no competition was involved. It was conceived under the best of circumstances. Ben and Bernarda spent hours with Kastner discussing plans for the mural as well as their dreams for the new settlement. Shahn and Kastner were ideal collaborators; it was a rare example of a mural painter and an architect working together on a mural.

Before Ben could begin his work, however, Kastner had to finish the school/community center. Obstacles were constantly being placed in the architect's way. He was often "furloughed," and his job was "terminated," and on at least one occasion, Charles Bryson came to his rescue as he had—several times—to Ben's, asking Farley to intervene so Kastner could be kept on the job until his work was completed.

Construction of the settlement, according to plans, was to be finished by the end of 1936; Kastner, determined to make the deadline, managed to keep a tight schedule. On May 1, the footing and footing walls of all the houses had been completed. On June 10, eight families were able to take possession of their homes; on August 2, Benjamin Brown officially opened the factory; on August 13, another twenty-seven houses were ready to be occupied.

With the homes and factory almost finished, Kastner turned his attention to the school/community center (financed with funds that the architect was able to save from the rest of the project) and to Ben's mural. By the fall of 1936, Kastner and Louis Kahn had worked out a design for the new building, but Kahn was furloughed in early 1937, leaving Kastner to come up with a final design.

In the fall of 1937, Alfred Kastner wrote a letter to Ben and Bernarda at Jersey Homesteads. He had stayed too long on the government job, he told them; and he was not at all satisfied with what had been done. "A blind man with his crutch can spot the construction faults of the Homesteads," he wrote. "In fact there is only one building which now emerges with architectural and structural merit—the sewage plant—which makes me a good sh.. architect."

As for Ben, he was still afraid of losing his job, especially once the Bankhead-Jones Farm Tenant Act, to assist tenant farmers, was signed into law. Under this law, Henry Wallace replaced the RA with the somewhat smaller Farm Security Administration. Ben's fears were justified. On July 15, he received word that, because of reduced funding, his services would be terminated as of September 30. Fortunately, Bernarda's father again intervened: he sent Farley a copy of the dismissal notice and a letter pleading, successfully, that Ben be retained until the completion of the mural.

Work on the mural, however, had not even begun, for during that summer, Ben had temporarily put aside his thoughts of Jersey

Homesteads and embarked on his second trip for the RA's Historical Section. This trip was quite different from the first one; as Susan H. Edwards has pointed out, "Shahn shifted his attention to focus on the positive effects of relief efforts. His photos from this series are more journalistic, less moving as social documents or art, but an appropriate closure to a narrative that began two years earlier."

This second trip was made difficult by the increased "sophistication" of the subjects Ben wanted to photograph. Since the first trip, the public had become far more aware of photography and its uses. The RA had placed its photos in a large number of newspapers and national magazines, including *Life,* which had been recently and very successfully launched as a picture magazine. Because of this, all too often when Ben took his camera out of his pocket, his subject or subjects realized that he was about to take their pictures, and so the photos were robbed of their spontaneity.

Nonetheless, the trip was a valuable one for the RA, emphasizing its accomplishments rather than the problems faced by the victims of the Depression. With Bernarda always at the wheel in their Ford, Ben toured Alabama, Tennessee, North Carolina, Pennsylvania, West Virginia, Maryland, and New Jersey. He showed America at work and at play, and almost always with a smile.

At Skyline, Alabama, he took pictures of square dances. At Crossville, Tennessee, he visited an RA project called Cumberland Homesteads, where he photographed the quarrying of native rock to be used for the houses' foundations, as well as construction and furniture building. There, too, he photographed women weaving and scenes of lively folk dancing. Music and musicians were the subjects of many of these photos of America at play. In Asheville, North Carolina, a little girl is seen singing while a boy plays the guitar. Another photograph shows a trio of Lovegood sisters singing; a banjo, violin, and guitar trio; and a number of smiling fiddlers. Musicians play the mouth organ, the guitar, and the violin at the Westmoreland County Fair in Pennsylvania, where Shahn also took photos of a painting class as well as a number of portraits of individual townspeople. In West Virginia, he visited a vacuum cleaner factory and a dairy barn, and in Acokeek, Maryland, he documented a modern version of a medieval jousting game.

By September, Ben and Bernarda arrived at Jersey Homesteads. Ben had been there often, on short visits, but now he, Bernarda, and Susie would stay there while he finally began work on the mural. Since no housing was available for them at the settlement itself, they were first put up at a cold farmhouse, and then with the family of a little man called Katzele whose home was even colder. Ben called it their "Siberian quarters."

For one month, Ben worked tirelessly on his sketches for the mural. Finding his office completely uncongenial, he got up at four in the morning and started work at five to avoid its noise and confusion. The peace and quiet he required lasted until nine o'clock, when the other employees arrived. Despite these distractions, the work on the cartoons for the mural went well. Dornbush did suggest a few changes he felt had to be made to satisfy the administration, however. The legend "Re-elect Roosevelt" was too political; it had to be changed to the simple "A Gallant Leader— Franklin D. Roosevelt." A graph showing the history of labor unions also had to be changed; the labor leader's head, eyebrows, and mane of hair modified so the picture wouldn't be interpreted as a likeness of John L. Lewis. These revisions presented no problems, technical or ideological, for Ben.

Assisted whenever possible by Bernarda, he began work on the mural itself in November 1937. Each day the school was filled with curious crowds watching Ben at work, just as crowds had filled the building in Rockefeller Center to observe Rivera. There was a major difference in the composition of the crowds: sophisticated New Yorkers, many of them artists, had come to see Rivera. Those watching Ben in Jersey Homesteads were needleworkers, most of whom thought a painter painted houses, not works of art. Nonetheless, Ben established an easy rapport with them. He was unfailingly affable, answering any and all questions put to him as well as he could. He enjoyed these spectators as they enjoyed him, and he used at least one of them, Irving Plungian, a carpenter, as a model for one part of the mural.

The mural was finished in May 1938. Set eight feet from the floor, it is forty-five feet long and twelve feet high. It dramatically depicts the flight of the Jews from Europe to the United States and their achievement of a happier life through trade unionism, government aid, and rural resettlement in a cooperative industry.

At the mural's far left, Albert Einstein (who, incidentally, lived in nearby Princeton, was active in the establishment of Jersey Homesteads, and later became a friend of Ben's) leads a group of immigrants down a gangplank, past the open coffins of two men sometimes mistakenly identified as Sacco and Vanzetti, to the Ellis Island reception area. (Einstein had not, however, arrived at Ellis Island.) In the upper left corner of the lefthand panel, a German soldier holds a sign in German: "Germans, don't buy from Jews."

In the central panel the immigrants find wretched working conditions and inadequate tenement housing in America. But then reforms begin; a crowd addressed by a labor leader (he still resembles John L. Lewis) gathers in front of the site of the notorious Triangle Shirtwaist Company fire. There 146 girls lost their lives; the scandal led to the first child labor laws and the first successes of the International Ladies' Garment Workers Union. Next to the

A section of the Jersey Homesteads mural of which Shahn wrote: "People really look at it. They know it by heart. To them it's like the building, a part of the community."

labor leader is a sign that proclaims, "One of the greater principles for which labor must stand in the future is the right of every man and woman to have a job, to earn a living if they are able to work." Farther to the right of the central panel, a new building is being constructed amid orchards, fields, and gardens; this building, along with a number of cooperative stores and a classroom in which a group of young men study the history of unionism, represents labor's victories.

Finally, in the last panel there is a ground plan of Jersey Homesteads. The leading members of its committee of directors are seated around a table beneath a poster of FDR, that bears the caption "A Gallant Leader—Franklin D. Roosevelt."

Ben had, at last, completed a fresco mural. He was not entirely pleased with it, however. He thought it was, like Rivera's work, crowded with too many details. He preferred the murals he would create later. Nonetheless, two esteemed critics who knew his work well disagreed. Francis V. O'Connor, an eminent art historian, noted the influence of Rivera in the mural's "high horizon lines, massively modeled figures, tiers of heads, shifting recessional space lines, and heavy reliance on architectural and industrial elements to serve as transitions." Yet he concluded that Shahn's work "expresses the ideology of the New Deal in its purest form and remains to this day one of the masterpieces of American social realism." Ben's friend James Thrall Soby praised it as well: "The mural remains," he wrote, "one of this country's eloquent visual projections of that immense and heartening social upheaval which was the Depression's one commendable product."

For Ben, whatever merit the mural had was due to its location within the community. People could see it every day, and it became a part of their lives. In that way he had achieved the success he had sought in creating his murals for public spaces.

CHAPTER TWENTY

Photographing Ohio and a New Approach to Art

On May 14, 1938, Ben's position with Special Skills was finally terminated, and he was returned to the RA's Historical Section. His title was "Principal Photographer," and his salary was $2,300 a year. This was half what he had been getting, but there was some compensation in finally joining, officially, the company of Dorothea Lange, Arthur Rothstein, Walker Evans, Russell Lee, and the other great photographers who worked under Stryker and who collectively became known as the FSA photographers.

Sometime in June, before Ben was given his first assignment, he, Bernarda, and Susie moved to the Bryson house in Worthington, a suburb of Columbus, Ohio. It was to be a summer dominated by domesticity; on June 17, Jonathan, their first son, was born, and during the summer Susie learned to walk. Also living in the house were the three children of Bernarda's late sister Phyllis. Following the death of their mother, the two boys and one girl had been adopted by their grandfather Charles Bryson. In spite of the presence of all these children, Ben and Bernarda were relatively free to do what they wanted. Bernarda's mother having died recently, Charles had hired a young naval officer and a woman Bernarda remembers as his "ruthless wife named Ruth" to share the house and take care of the children.

Before they could settle in completely, Ben was given his first assignment by the Historical Section: to cover what Stryker called "the harvest" in Ohio. Though it meant that he and Bernarda could be on call whenever needed by their children, Ben hesitated before taking on the assignment. He explained his reluctance to Richard Doud in 1964:

> It was so completely different from the South and from the mine country. It was neat and clean and orderly, and I didn't think it had any photographic qualities for me. At first I said, "Well, I can't do anything about it." Then one day it sort of came to me. I felt it after about two weeks, so I called Roy and I said, "I'll take the job." I stayed about six weeks with this, and worked just day and night on the scene. It was an entirely different thing. In the South and in the mine country, wherever you point the camera, there is a picture. But here you had to make some choices, you see.

Those choices were, as always, to be his own, but it does seem that some kind of script had been prepared. According to Carolyn Kinder Carr, in September 1936 Roy Stryker had met with the prominent sociologist Robert Lynd, who with his wife, Helen, wrote *Middletown*. During this meeting, they listed more than two hundred items detailing every aspect of life in a small town. When, two years later, Lynd learned that Ben was to travel through Ohio for the FSA, he asked Stryker to have him study the impact of women's clubs in the towns he visited. Ben wrote in reply: "If you will send me psychological lenses and philosophical film, I'll do this job for you." Although Ansel Adams once told Stryker, "What you've got are not photographers. They're a bunch of sociologists with cameras," Ben made it clear that he was not a sociologist. He would approach his Ohio assignment as an artist-photographer would.

The trip was far different from Ben's previous travels, in many ways. For one thing, unemployment was not nearly as widespread in Ohio as it had been in the South. (A 1937 survey found that the state's overall unemployment rate was 15.3 percent.) Farms and industry were both hard hit by the Depression, of course, but poverty was not as severe. Furthermore, Ohio was familiar territory to Ben—and especially to Bernarda, who was a native Ohioan—so the exotic, surprising element was missing. Nonetheless, Shahn's Ohio photographs are among his most admired and treasured.

Ben limited himself to a fifty-mile radius around Columbus, taking pictures there as well as in the small towns of Ashville, Buckeye Lake, Circleville, New Carlisle, Lancaster, Linworth, London, Marysville, Mechanicsburg, Plain City, Somerset, Springfield, Urbana, Washington Court House, and Worthington. He told Stryker he wanted to photograph the average American, and Stryker agreed enthusiastically. "I was tickled with Shahn because he was so trustworthy, so valuable that I was delighted to have him go out there," he told Robert W. Wagner in a 1968 interview.

Ben had had enough of photographing the tragic, despairing faces of the Depression. He took pictures of everyday life in central Ohio: main streets, baseball games, lunchrooms, a street carnival; a post office in Plain City and a church in Linworth. He also took pictures of men and women at work, cutting corn, threshing wheat, and baling hay. Informal anecdotal captions accompany a number of the photographs. Typical of these captions are the following:

> Hard-pressed farmer came to banker for loan. Farmer not a "good risk." Banker refused coldly. Farmer pleaded Banker, moved by the plea, makes a sporting offer- "one of my eyes is glass. It is considered a perfect match for the other. Guess which eye is glass, and I'll let you have the loan." Farmer gazed intently at both eyes. Finally pointed at left eye, saying, "This is the glass one." Banker, amazed: "How did you guess?" Farmer: "It looked kinder."
>
> *Circleville's "Hooverville."* Begins to talk: "No man in the United States had the trouble I had since 1931. No man. Don't talk to me. I'm deaf. I lost my farm in 1931. I went into town to work with a painter. I fell off a scaffold and broke my leg. I went to work in an acid factory. I got acid spilt on me. Burnt my nose, made me blind. Then I get those awful headaches. I've been to lots of doctors, but that doesn't help me. They come on at sundown. No man in the United States had the trouble I had since 1931." (This last repeated many times throughout his talking.) "No man. It must be getting on to 6 o'clock now. My head's beginning to pain."

Buckeye Lake is the week-end/resort for all of Central Ohio. Its patrons are clerks, Columbus politicians, laborers, business men, droves of high school and college students. The rich occupy one side of the lake, the rest rent cottages on the other side. It has an evil reputation and an evil smell. It has furnished Columbus and the neighboring small towns and cities with dancing, cottaging, swimming, etc., for several generations. This is the most unsavory place the photographer ran across in Ohio.

Circleville, County Seat of Pickaway County. Average small Ohio City, depending upon surrounding rich farm lands for its livelihood. Because of its non-industrial surroundings, retains much of old-time flavor. Outstanding industries—*Eshelman's Feed Mill.* Employs 150–200 men the year 'round. Pay averages about 85 cents an hour. *Container Corporation of America* makes paper out of straw; can absorb by-product of all neighboring farms. In addition, a number of canneries and feed mills. During depression many farms of the district were foreclosed. People who lost homes naturally gravitated toward the town. A town of its character is unable to house new influx of population. Consequently, there spring up around it an extensive Hooverville. Circleville got its name through having been built in a circle as a better protection against the Indians. (For any further information Chamber of Commerce, Circleville.) (Circleville is the home of Ted Lewis.)

His photos of Ohio, approximately three thousand of them, lack the passion and drama of the photos taken through the South, but they are honest, and therefore successful evocations of small-town life in the American Midwest. A number of them were included in the 1940 book *The Ohio Guide,* compiled by workers of the Writers' Project of the WPA, and in *Home Town,* a collection of essays by Sherwood Anderson.

At the end of the summer, Ben resigned his position with the Historical Section, although it was effective through the end of the following June: he had a contract to execute an important mural in New York. Roy Stryker, who knew of Ben's commitment to work in New York, was not surprised, but many of Ben's colleagues were stunned. Work for photographers was almost impossible to find,

The photographs Shahn took in Ohio during the summer of 1938
were in sharp contrast to those taken a few years earlier in the South.
The reflection of the photographer is seen in the window behind
the two seated men.

and it seemed unthinkable that anyone would give up a job guaranteed to last for several more months. What they didn't know, according to Bernarda, was that Ben was beginning to feel trapped by the camera. Even if he had not already agreed to execute the mural, he would have left the FSA. "Photography ceased to interest me suddenly," he told Richard Doud. "Suddenly, just like that. I felt I would only be repeating myself and stopped dead."

After the summer of 1938, Ben did occasionally pick up his camera, but only to make snapshots, not to take photos for publication. His renunciation of the camera represented a real loss to the world of American photography. Fortunately, several thousand photographs remain. They attest to his unique skill as a photographer. These photos show some of the same qualities that distinguish his drawing and painting: a fascination with the alphabet; the use of letters and words to enhance the image; a wry humor; and, above all, genuine compassion. His photos of the 1930s bear visual witness to the special way he felt about the past. "The difference now," he told Doud thirty years later, "is that if we feel anything, it's a sympathy, where in the 30s it was an empathy." Susan H. Edwards noted this, too. "Shahn's photographs," she wrote, "stand apart from the others made by the RA/FSA photographers because of his primary commitment to the social basis of art. As a champion of the disenfranchised, he transferred an empathy for the victims of intolerance and discrimination to insightful advantage. Shahn's concept of a successful photograph was grounded not only in visual aesthetics but also in an image's potential for conveying a message."

Vicki Goldberg, writing in *The New York Times* of April 9, 1995, also remarked on Ben's empathy: "Shahn considered himself a worker like his subjects and identified with them; his photographs have a quiet humility of observation and a basic trust in the worth of ordinary people." Yet he was not sentimental. According to Bernarda, "he could not tolerate the idealized figure of 'the worker' or the 'downtrodden' that in the early 1930s were becoming a distinct theme in the art world. 'It's all right,' he said, 'to have a soft heart so long as you have a hard eye.' "

Ben was impressed by the FSA photographers' work and he was proud to be one of them. He summarized his feelings in the 1944 interview with John D. Morse. "We tried to present the ordinary in an extraordinary manner. But that's a paradox, because the only thing extraordinary about us was that it was so ordinary. Nobody had ever done it before, deliberately. Now it's called documentary, which I suppose is all right. . . . We just took pictures that cried out to be taken."

=====

Ben's decision to abandon photography coincided with a major change in his approach to painting. His contact with and subsequent understanding of the people he encountered during his travels for the RA/FSA enhanced his perceptions as a painter and led to a change in the direction of his art. In *The Shape of Content*, he explained:

> Theories had melted before such experience. My own painting then had turned from what is called "social realism" into a sort of personal realism. I found the qualities of people a constant pleasure; there was the coal miner, a cellist, who organized a quartet for me—the quartet having three musicians. There was the muralist who painted the entire end of his barn with scenes of war and then of plenty, the whole painting entitled, "Uncle Sam Did It All." There were the five Musgrove brothers who played five harmonicas—the wonderful names of people, Plato Jordan and Jasper Lancaster, and of towns, Pity Me, and Tail Holt, and Bird-in-Hand. There were the poor who were rich in spirit, and the rich who were also sometimes rich in spirit. There was the South and its story-telling art, stories of snakes and storms and haunted houses, enchanting; and yet such talent thriving in the same human shell with hopeless prejudices, bigotry, and ignorance.

However, much as he valued this experience, he foresaw an even greater change in his goals as an artist. "Personal realism, personal observation of the ways of people, the mood of life and places," he concluded, "all that is a great pleasure, but I felt some larger potentiality in art."

CHAPTER TWENTY-ONE

The Bronx Mural and a Fight over Walt Whitman

IN THE FALL OF 1938, BEN AND BERNARDA RETURNED TO NEW York, very happy to be back. Bernarda remembers that both she and Ben had been "New York hungry."

It was a tense period. Germany mobilized and France called up its reserves. War seemed inevitable. That fall Neville Chamberlain, the British prime minister, met with Adolf Hitler at Berchtesgaden and at Godesberg, and, after the notorious Munich conference in late September, attended by Chamberlain, Hitler, Mussolini, and the French premier, Edouard Daladier, it was clear that Germany intended to be the dominant power in Europe as well as throughout the world.

The couple moved into a fifth-floor walkup at 300 East Eighty-ninth Street, near Second Avenue, and Ben had also rented a room, once a bar, on the ground floor to serve as a studio. The area, Yorkville, was the heart of New York's "Little Germany," inhabited largely by German Americans, many of whom spoke German rather than English. Many of them, too, saluted each other in military fashion and greeted each other with "Heil Hitler" as they went into their butcher shops and beer halls and pastry shops. Yorkville was also the home of the German-American Bund, whose members were openly pro-Nazi. Consequently, life there was often uncomfortable and even frightening for a Russian-American-Jewish artist. Ben's friends urged him to move back to Greenwich Village, but to live there, he believed, would give him "a false sense of security." Yorkville reminded him of the realities of a deeply troubled world.

Yorkville also had one other advantage over the Village. It was closer to the Bronx Central Post Office, between 149th and 150th Street on the Grand Concourse, near Yankee Stadium, where Ben and Bernarda had been commissioned to execute the mural. This time the assignment was not part of a job, as the Jersey Homesteads mural had been. Instead, he and Bernarda had won a competition organized by the Section of Painting and Sculpture, a New Deal program established to commission art for new federal buildings, primarily post offices.

The competition had been formally announced in January 1938. It was open to artists from New York, New Jersey, Pennsylvania, and Connecticut; the winner would be paid $7,000 to produce a mural on the theme "Resources of America."

The section of Painting and Sculpture was headed by Edward Bruce, a distinguished banker, lawyer, art collector, and painter, who devoted much of his life to the cause of government art patronage. His assistants were Edward Rowan and Forbes Watson.

The chairman of the advisory jury was Henry Varnum Poor, a painter, ceramist, and muralist. The other members of the jury were Thomas Harlan Ellett, the architect who built the Bronx post office, and George Harding, a muralist from Philadelphia.

Each artist was to submit his or her designs by May 14. (Ben and Bernarda must have worked on their designs before going to Ohio.) Entries were to be unsigned; the name and address of the artist were to appear only in a plain sealed envelope accompanying the design. The envelopes and the designs were numbered when they arrived at the Section, and the envelopes would be opened only after a winner had been chosen.

One hundred and ninety-eight entries were submitted, but the judges made up their minds quickly. Surprisingly, they chose two designs: numbers 95 and 96, those of Ben Shahn and Bernarda Bryson. The jury's decision and the speed with which it was made raised some questions. Did Henry Varnum Poor, a good friend of Ben and Bernarda's, recognize the winning submissions as those of his friends? He was, after all, familiar with their work. And why was it that two different entries won? According to Bernarda, her design and Ben's were indeed different (she deferred to Ben's design and immediately and instinctively assumed the role of his assistant). She too wondered just what had happened, and how there could possibly have been two winners.

Warm, enthusiastic letters of congratulations arrived from Edward Rowan and Edward Bruce, and in the middle of June a contract arrived, made between the United States of America and Ben Shahn. Everything had been done correctly. Not only had Stryker been told of Ben's desire to do the mural before the artist went to Ohio, but Ben had obviously asked Bruce's permission to work for the FSA for a limited period of time before starting work on it.

Ben and Bernarda began work on the cartoons as soon as they were settled in New York. The first panel, which was to be placed above the "Postal Savings" window on the north wall, showed Walt Whitman pointing to a quotation from one of his poems, which he had written on a blackboard. It set the tone for the entire mural:

Brain of the New World, what a task is thine,
To formulate the modern out of the peerless grandeur of the
*   modern;*
Out of thyself, comprising science to recast poems, churches, art,
(Recast, maybe discard them, end them—maybe their work is
*   done, who knows?)*
By vision, hand, conception, on the background of the mighty
*   past, the dead,*
To limn with absolute faith the mighty living present.

Details of the finished work were still subject to revision, and Rowan had asked for some changes in the first sketch of this panel (as Bruce's assistant he had the right to do so). Ben sent the new sketch to Rowan for his approval in the middle of November. In his accompanying letter he expressed his eagerness for all the cartoons to be approved before he went ahead, and offered to put them up in place at the post office.

Rowan replied a few days later. He wrote that he felt the changes made in the "Whitman panel" very much improved it, and he gave Ben the go-ahead to proceed with the full-size cartoons. He also suggested that Ben arrange to hang them at the post office before the Christmas rush, which began on December 10, so that they might be more easily judged.

Reaction to the cartoons, specifically the Whitman panel, was not as unanimously favorable as Ben and Rowan anticipated. In early December, Ben wrote to warn Rowan of a potentially serious problem:

> There has been some milling about of persons connected with several Catholic organizations. Whitman, it seems, is on the Catholic Index. These people have objected to the quotation which I selected to touch off the "Resources of America" idea.

Though he vigorously protested the interference of a number of religious groups, Shahn was willing to change the Walt Whitman quotation used in the Bronx Central Post Office mural.

It can be easily changed. There are other Whitman quotations which strike much the same note and which might perhaps not be found objectionable.

I want to convince you of one thing definitely—We want to get to work on this mural with just as little complication as possible. We also want nothing to appear there which hasn't been openly viewed and discussed beforehand. In other words, anything approaching a controversy would be distasteful and a nuisance to both of us.

On the other hand one must protest that Whitman is one of our most loved and honored American poets. He is a part of our cultural tradition. A clerk in the Post Office told me that he was required as a part of his high school commencement exercises to know this particular poem by heart.

I question whether it is the right thing for a limited group of people to try to impose their particular Index on the general public. With Democracy rather on its mettle these days anyway it gives one something of a shock to hear "Verboten!" directed against a traditionally celebrated American poet.

In putting up the sketches I might have left the blackboard beside Whitman blank. But this seemed to me an inspiring set of lines and, quite honestly, I anticipated no protest whatsoever.

I don't know how much authority these people may have in what goes in or out of the building. That is for you to decide. As for me I believe that the idea incorporated in these is truly fine. I believe that most people do.

"Anything approaching a controversy would be distasteful and a nuisance to both of us"—these are curious words from a man of principle who fought with courage for justice and who never avoided controversy in doing so. However, Ben had learned a bitter lesson from his experience with the Rivera mural, and he was anxious about the possible destruction of his own work. In addition, he realized that the entire federal arts program, already criticized by conservatives in the government, might be endangered if a controversy over the Bronx Post Office mural became a major issue. Further justifying his willingness to give in, he noted that though the Whitman quotation had initially been approved by the jurors, by members of the Section, and by Edward Rowan, he had, after all, agreed in writing to make any changes in the designs that Christian J. Peoples, the director of procurement, might request, and that Peoples believed that the Whitman was "contrary to the spirit of our own Constitution"—had, in fact, written to Bruce demanding that Shahn select something more appropriate.

In spite of Ben's willingness to compromise, there was no way of avoiding a battle at this point. On December 9, Arthur J. McBride, a New York attorney, had written to Postmaster General James Farley, enclosing a copy of the Whitman inscription.

> A single reading of the enclosed inscription [McBride wrote] will I am sure satisfy you that the wish is the father to the thought contained therein and is utterly distasteful to a great multitude of American citizens who still cherish the institutions which have contributed so much to the progress of our nation. As a member of the Democratic Party and an American citizen and as a Roman Catholic, may I respectfully request that you take the necessary steps to prevent the painting of this objectionable matter on the walls of the said Post Office.

On Sunday, December 11, the Reverend Ignatius W. Cox, a professor of ethics at Fordham University, launched a major attack on the mural before a crowd of three thousand parishioners at the Church of Our Lady of Angels in Brooklyn. Denouncing the inscription as "government propaganda for irreligion . . . and an insult to all religious-minded men and to Christians," he urged his listeners to join in an appeal to Albert Goldman, postmaster of New York, to change the words written on the mural. The press gave front-page coverage to Cox's speech, but Ben's offer to substitute another Whitman quotation for the offending one was only briefly noted. The next day, Donald O'Toole, a member of the Post Office and Post Roads Committee of the U.S. House of Representatives, joined the battle by sending a telegram to Postmaster General Farley protesting the use of the quotation because "it is repulsive to a majority of our people and promotes irreligion." He went on to suggest that "in these godless days some mention might be made of the recognition of the existence of God by the American people."

The same day, the very influential Chancellor J. Francis A.

McIntyre of the Archbishopric of New York also wrote to Farley, complaining that the sentiments expressed by Whitman are "far distant from American ideals" and "suggestive of Asiatic philosophy." Still other superfluous letters of protest were sent—superfluous because the goal of the protest, the elimination of the offending quotation, had already been achieved. One writer claimed the inscription expressed a "strictly pagan philosophy"; another felt it was "an insult to all religious-minded men and to all established forms of religion, inasmuch as it propagates atheism and irreligion."

Even as these letters were being sent, Ben, with the help of Rowan, was seeking alternative quotations. It was a diligent search, for not until three months later was he able to inform Rowan that five lines from Whitman's "As I Walk These Broad Majestic Days" had finally been chosen:

> We support all, fuse all
> After the rest is done and gone, we remain;
> There is no final reliance but upon us;
> Democracy rests finally upon us (I, my brethren,
>   begin it)
> And our visions sweep through eternity.

In the meantime, Ben and Bernarda had continued work on other panels of the mural, which was being executed in egg tempera, a medium almost as classic as fresco. "People seem to like the mural very much," he wrote Rowan, "and, needless to say, this sort of daily approval is about the most pleasing experience one can have."

By the end of June 1939, eleven of the thirteen panels were completed, but Ben sensed that Rowan was not completely satisfied with the substitute Whitman quotation. He proposed a meeting in Washington, but it turned out that Rowan only wanted to be assured that no reference be made on the mural to the quotation first selected. In August, the mural, signed by Ben Shahn and Bernarda Bryson, was completed and installed.

Ben enjoyed the months spent in New York. Having hired a young woman to take care of their two children, he and Bernarda were free to live at a leisurely pace when not working. They wandered all over the city and frequently walked all the way from their apartment to the Bronx Post Office, a distance of more than three miles.

The work, however, was exhausting. Ben had found great satisfaction in conceiving and designing the mural, but he did not enjoy facing what seemed an endless space of wall each morning. He had only one assistant, Bernarda. Her job was essential. She collaborated in the execution, in painting details, and in "mulling colors." The latter involved taking finely ground colors and grinding them still finer, before mixing them with egg yolk and distilled water. The eggs were delivered fresh each morning, and Bernarda remembers making a great many angel food cakes during that period. Bernarda also helped apply a thin coat of gesso to even up the plaster in order to make the surface suitable for the application of the tempera. This last procedure was necessary because the plaster wall had been previously covered with canvas, which upon removal had revealed a somewhat mildewed surface.

Ben enjoyed talking to the onlookers, many of whom had nothing better to do than watch him work on the mural. One observer wanted to know why a woman in the mural was making snowballs. Ben answered patiently that the woman was picking cotton and not making snowballs. "Oh," the questioner retorted, "I thought that stuff was something that growed on trees."

A superpatriot expressed dismay each time she passed in front of the mural: there were too many paintings of all these Communist workers on the wall. Once, when she informed Ben that her ancestors fought in the Revolution, he got so angry he kicked over a pot of paint. His ancestors had fought in the battle of Jericho, he told her, but he didn't go around bragging about it. She stubbornly pursued him, even following him to the men's room where he had fled to escape her.

The eagerly awaited last day in the post office was disastrous. Ben was on his movable scaffold. He himself had made it, with large wheels so that it could be pushed easily, as well as brakes to allow him to stop. Rolling along to put a final touch on one of the panels, he collided with a huge chandelier and shattered one of its globes. (Replacing it cost him $60.) Later, at the end of that seemingly endless day, he and Bernarda were so hot and so tired of their work that they agreed to throw their last two eggs at the next person who came into the post office. They raised their arms, waiting for the innocent victim of their fatigue, then quickly lowered them as two nuns stepped through the door.

Reactions to the finished project were completely favorable. Both Bruce and Rowan were enthusiastic; the art critic Forbes Watson wrote to Rowan praising Ben for doing "a remarkably fine job" and calling it a work of "great dignity." Later judgments concurred. In his book about Ben's paintings, James Thrall Soby wrote that Ben and Bernarda "succeeded in their exalted aim":

> The contrasts between deep perspective and close-up figures are managed with extreme dexterity, and there is, throughout, an uncanny sensitivity to lighting effects, whether natural in source, as in the agricultural scenes, or artificial, as when the flames of a blast furnace illuminate steel girders and the face of a worker. On a very large scale the murals typify what has been a constant of Shahn's aesthetic—a love of evocative juxtaposition. "Most important," he once said, "is always to have a play back and forth, back and forth. Between the big and the little, the light and the dark, the smiling and the sad. . . . I like to have three vanishing points in one plane, or a half dozen in three planes." To which might be added that Shahn has always loved oppositions between inanimate rigidity and human warmth. In the Bronx panel called "Textile Mills," for example, the definition of the bobbins, the architecture, and the metal sign is extremely precise, whereas the figure of the worker is softly rounded in contour. The Bronx murals as a whole abound in such subtle shifts of technique and mood, yet they arrive at a cohesive monumentality far more pronounced and impressive than that of his earlier mural in Roosevelt.

In her study of Ben and his art, written many years later, Bernarda observed:

> His colors were becoming continually higher in key, more luminous; the black underpainting he had inherited from Rivera had now given way, first to ochers and siennas, then to an increasing range of colors. Ideologically Ben was at that time more under

the influence of Walt Whitman than of Rivera, an orientation strongly supported by his travels in America and by his Leica observation.

Ben himself articulated his feelings about the mural in the 1944 interview with John D. Morse.

> My idea was to show the people of the Bronx something about America outside New York. So I painted a cotton picker, along with another panel showing a woman tending spindles in a city mill. I painted wheat fields, and power dams as well as steel workers and riveters. I stuck to big, simple shapes and solid warm colors. I think I handled them better than I did the one panel at Jersey Homesteads, but I'll bet not as many people really look at them. They were not planned as part of the building or community. They were an architect's afterthought. I went back to look at them one day and the service crew foreman saw me. "You the guy who did these pictures?" I said yes and asked him how he liked them. "Not particularly, but I'm sure glad you put all these guys in overalls up on the walls. It helped me organize the building crew. Made 'em think they were important."

Even before finishing the Bronx mural, Ben had started work on the sketches for another competition. This mural was to be a large one, covering a total of three thousand square feet of wall space in the main post office in St. Louis, Missouri; the prize was an exceedingly generous one of $29,000, then the largest commission ever awarded by the federal government.

The mural's themes were to be "The Four Freedoms," "History of the Frontier and River Life," "State History," and "Immigration." Ben created a series of nine designs: Freedom of Religion, Freedom of Speech, Freedom of the Press, River Traffic, the Missouri State Seal, Vox Pop, Opening of the Frontier, and two sketches on the theme of immigration. Pleased with his work—and eager for the large prize—Ben was particularly disappointed to learn that the jury had rejected his sketches as too political. Instead, the commission was given to two Chicago-based artists, both of whom had been strongly influenced by the Mexican muralists. Surprisingly, both were as intensely political as Shahn was, and both had been harshly criticized on that basis. One was Mitchell Siporin, whose work had been criticized by the *Chicago Tribune* as "un-American" and "showing Communist influence." The other winner was Edward Millman, whose mural for a Chicago school had been plastered over because of its political content.

Ben diplomatically wrote a letter to Edward Rowan saying he was very pleased that Siporin, whose work he knew well, had won, and congratulating both artists on their victory and the Section on its choices. He also authorized the use of his losing sketches for an exhibition in St. Louis.

His diplomacy apparently paid off. To make up for his disappointment and perhaps reward his generosity, he was commissioned to execute a small panel, eight and a half feet by sixteen feet, on the theme of the First Amendment. The panel would be placed over the door of the Woodhaven Branch Station Post Office in Jamaica (Long Island), New York. For this noncompetitive assignment, Ben would be paid $1,750. He decided to letter the words of that amendment, so close to his own ideals, at the bottom of the panel.

By the end of February, Ben was working on the preliminary sketches; his black-and-white proposal was approved in mid-March. Rowan asked for a photo of the full-size cartoon when it was ready, so that it could be reviewed by the office of the Section of Painting and Sculpture.

In early June, Rowan showed the photo of the cartoon to members of the Section. As usual, they were not about to let Ben go ahead without suggesting a number of changes. The material was too crowded, the scale of the men portrayed on the canvas was not consistent, and the raised arms of one man seemed forced, they believed. More important, they found the inscription at the bottom unnecessary. Ben agreed to most of the changes, but the problem, he felt, was that the small photograph he had submitted was necessarily misleading. He insisted, moreover, that the inscription was essential. Citing the example of mural painters from Giotto to George Biddle who had used words on their murals, he wrote: "I designed the mural, using the inscription as an integral part. I think the panel would lose by its removal. . . . It will enhance the

CHAPTER TWENTY-TWO

Moving to Jersey Homesteads, Tillie Alone, and a One-Man Show

LATE IN 1939, AS THEIR WORK ON THE BRONX MURAL WAS coming to an end, it was reported in the press that the experiment at Jersey Homesteads had failed. The settlers from New York didn't know how to run a farm or a dairy and were unable to learn. Nor could they manage a factory profitably. The community was torn apart by disagreements, suspicion, hostilities, and confusion. Word of the town's problems spread, making matters even worse, since it became increasingly difficult to raise the obligatory $500 for a venture that seemed likely to fail. Even people who had signed up backed out. For a long time more than one hundred houses remained empty, until in desperation it was decided to open the town to outsiders, those who were not a part of the cooperative. The empty houses would be rented and, it was hoped, soon sold.

This was good news for Ben and Bernarda, who were ready for a change. Rent for a comfortable house in New Jersey would be only $16 a month, far less than the $100 they were paying in New York for a crowded apartment. In addition, it would doubtless be easier to raise their children in the country than in New York. Even better, they soon learned that a particular house they had both liked would be among those up for rent.

public value of the mural as well as its expressive value to me." He felt so strongly about the matter that he himself brought the cartoon to Washington in August. There, after a discussion with Rowan and other members of the Section, it was agreed that the quotation would remain.

Still, Ben was hesitant. He hated planned communities and loved city life. Jersey Homesteads could have reminded him of the shtetl of his childhood. Bernarda, on the other hand, had lived much of her life in the country, enjoyed the outdoors, and looked forward to living in a home from which they would walk directly into a garden. A compromise was reached: they would rent the house, but they pledged to remain in Jersey Homesteads for no more than one year, after which they hoped their income might permit them to live elsewhere. They also agreed that they would in no way involve themselves in the affairs of the small community. They kept neither promise. Jersey Homesteads would remain their home for the rest of their lives; and, for at least the first years there, they would become an integral and vital part of the community.

═══

In dictating his "autobiography" to an unidentified writer several years later, Shahn spoke of this move from New York to Jersey Homesteads; he mentioned only in passing his older children and his first wife, "who died." Ben's vagueness about his two older children was understandable. He had paid little attention to them, and they played only a small, if any, part in his life at this time. As for Tillie, she was not at all dead but doing her best to bring up those two children who had temporarily lost their father.

Ironically, in the fall of 1935 Tillie had found a Resettlement Administration job, to do with the construction of Jersey Homesteads. For a short time, she worked in Hightstown and lived there with the children. Ben visited them there on occasion.

Then, in the winter of 1936, Ben began visiting his older children each Thursday. They had returned to New York and were living on the top floor of an apartment house at 347 Bleecker Street, on the corner of West Tenth Street. Ben would spend one Thursday with Ezra, then barely three years old, the following Thursday with six-year-old Judy, and the third with both children. During that time he built for each child what he or she wanted the most. Ezra wanted a rowboat; Ben made him a miniature green one. Judy wanted a puppet theater, and Ben built one of Masonite. "It folded so it could be stored away when not in use and had red corduroy theater curtains," Judy remembers. These visits ended after little more than a year, however; the children did not see or hear from their father again for eight or nine years, although Judy once had a glimpse of him. It came about as follows.

In the spring of 1938, Doris and Herbert Mayer, who had been friends of both Tillie and Ben, gave a farewell party for themselves. Herb, a chemist with a great interest in art, had suddenly been offered a job in Washington that began almost at once. This meant that they had very little time to close their New York apartment, move their things to Washington, and also organize a party. Since few of their friends had telephones, the Mayers decided that they would each inform as many as possible, in whatever way possible.

Neither thought of inviting Ben or Tillie. But during her lunch hour one day, Doris ran into Tillie and asked her to the party. Tillie said she would be happy to come if she could bring the children, which, of course, was all right with Doris. At the same time, by coincidence, Herb had encountered Ben and invited him. Both Herb and Doris were, of course, uneasy over the possibility of the parties' meeting, but they could do nothing about it. They consoled themselves with the thought that probably neither Tillie nor Ben would come.

Shortly before the party was to begin, Doris went out to buy more food. As she was walking home, she saw Tillie and the children on the sidewalk. At the same time, a car drove up to the entrance of the Mayers' apartment house. Doris couldn't tell who was in the car, but Judy recognized it right away and ran toward it, shouting, "Daddy, Daddy!" The car—with Ben and a woman in it— drove away immediately.

In New York, Tillie began working for the Index of American Design, a New Deal organization established to record and index the main types of American decorative art from colonial times onward. She held a good administrative position and was reasonably well paid. Both facts were important: Ben was not usually prompt in sending her the $100 a month in child support that he had agreed to pay. In late 1940 or early 1941, however, Tillie came under suspicion of "red" activities; the FBI interrogated her, and FBI agents began snooping around the neighborhood, questioning neighbors and local merchants about her activities. In the spring of 1941, she was fired, in spite of the fact that, though politically on the left, she hardly had the time—as a single mother of two working full-time to support her family—to engage in any subversive political activity.

It was later learned that the probable reason for the FBI harassment was that one of Ben's paintings, *Demonstration*, hung in Tillie's living room. From the Tom Mooney series, it shows a group of angry people with raised, clenched fists. Some visitor to the apartment had apparently described it to someone as a "red" painting.

Tillie had a hard time finding another job. As a result, she had to give up her comfortable $35-a-month apartment. Ezra and Judy were sent to summer camp on a full scholarship, while their mother tried to make future arrangements for them. Val, a woman who had cared for the children while Tillie was at work, was let go, and Tillie moved in with some friends who had a small guest room in their apartment at 425 West Broadway, then a bleak industrial street. In the fall, Ezra was sent away to boarding school on a full scholarship, and Judy moved in with her mother. "My whole childhood life fell apart at that point," Judy remembers.

It took Ben and Bernarda some time to adjust to life in Jersey Homesteads. At first, Ben missed the pace and energy and sounds of the city. Rural landscapes meant little to him. He found little pleasure in them as a man, and as an artist he was rarely inspired by them. He had never before owned a lawnmower and wasn't interested in discovering what to do with it. As for Bernarda, although she was considerably more at home in a small town and in a country setting, she too felt isolated at first. There were only two telephones in Jersey Homesteads, which intensified her feeling of isolation, and she and Ben were among the few English-speaking families in the Yiddish-speaking community, which limited the possibility of social contact. She was unfamiliar with the wry yet warm Jewish humor, even ill at ease with it. She was the "shiksa" in town—there were few—she felt very much a foreigner so everyone wanted to teach her Yiddish. She was also one of the youngest of the adult residents, so everyone wanted to mother her. In the beginning she felt extremely uncomfortable in this American Vilkomir.

Ben's work benefited greatly from the move, however. Though

he had never abandoned easel painting, this was his first chance in a number of years to devote time exclusively to it. He began to take advantage of the relative peace and quiet of the country, with its few distractions to interfere with his work. Although his paintings were not selling, he was not discouraged: no works of art were selling. His name was kept before the public, moreover, both through press coverage of the murals he worked on and through his representation in a number of important group exhibitions. One of these collected work done by artists in the Federal Arts Program, held at the Corcoran Gallery in Washington; another was the Second Annual Membership Exhibition of the American Artists Congress, held at the John Wanamaker Gallery in New York. In 1939, Ben's painting *Scotts Run, West Virginia* was shown at the Whitney Museum as part of "Twentieth Century Artists: A Selection of Paintings, Sculpture, and the Graphic Arts from the Museum's Permanent Collection." (The museum bought it for $200 once the show closed.) The most important of all these exhibitions was organized by New York's Museum of Modern Art and held in Europe. This major event, the first extensive exhibition of works by American artists ever held on the Continent, encompassed three centuries of American art—film, photography, sculpture, and graphic arts, as well as paintings.

To represent twentieth-century painting, forty artists were invited by the museum to submit their works. Thirty-six of the forty sent paintings, but museum officials accepted only six or seven of these. The rest of the paintings sent to Europe were selected by the museum's president, A. Conger Goodyear. Goodyear included works by America's most illustrious artists: painters of the Ashcan school, as well as John Marin, Charles Demuth, Arthur Dove, Joseph Stella, Georgia O'Keeffe, Edward Hopper, Charles Burchfield, Thomas Hart Benton, and Ben Shahn, who was represented by *Six Witnesses Who Bought Eels from Vanzetti.* Inclusion in this prestigious show was a strong indication that Ben was gaining official as well as public recognition.

Although Ben was receiving substantial publicity, he had not had a one-man show for seven years, since he last exhibited his work at Edith Halpert's gallery. It's uncertain why; either Halpert was not interested in showing his work in the late 1930s, or Ben was not willing to have it exhibited in her gallery, or both. Each was stubborn and quarrelsome; most likely, they had argued. In any case, Ben needed a dealer.

He found one in Julien Levy. Levy was the owner of a small but lively gallery that had earned a reputation as one of the most forward-looking in the city. A slender, dark-haired man with aristocratic features, he was responsible for introducing Surrealism to the American public, and he had shown the works of Alexander Calder, Salvador Dali, Max Ernst, René Magritte, Albert Giacometti, and Joseph Cornell (whose first solo show was held at Levy's). He was also the only dealer to hold regular exhibitions by photographers, such as Henri Cartier-Bresson (whose photographs Ben admired immensely) and Walker Evans (who was probably the one to introduce Ben, or his paintings, to Levy). Successful in promoting his artists, he was nonetheless bored by business, willing at any time to give up a remunerative transaction in order to play chess with Marcel Duchamp, one of his favorite artists.

Sometime in late 1939 or early 1940 (he rarely dated his letters) Levy wrote to the artist, saying he had heard that Ben was no longer connected with Edith Halpert and suggesting that they meet to discuss the possibility of a show to be held in the spring of 1940. Ben assumed that Levy wanted to exhibit his photography. This was not the case, however. Levy assured Ben he wanted his paintings, specifically some "class-conscious paintings."

The exhibition was to open on May 7, 1940, in Levy's second-floor gallery at 602 Madison Avenue. The gallery was the first to have curved walls—these, Levy believed, would allow the viewer to attend more easily to one painting at a time. Ben and Levy chose some twenty works, the finest part of his output since his last one-man exhibition.

The show—it was called "Sunday Paintings"—focused on Americans at leisure. Not only was there no catalogue; the works exhibited were not even given titles. Ben named them later, having come to the conclusion that "the absence of them [titles] left one . . . with a certain sense of vagueness or lack of orientation." In her book on Ben, Bernarda characterized the paintings of this period as "the very essence of the America that he was just coming to know, but to know well." She saw in them "a sense of identity, of friendship, even a sort of glee that these people are so real and are so ordinary, and that each one, in his ordinariness, is so markedly unique."

Willis Avenue Bridge, whose composition was inspired by a photograph Shahn took while living in New York, shows two women seated on a bench on the bridge. One holds crutches; the other wears a shining pearl necklace. The cross supports of the bridge are painted red; Shahn preempted all scholarly interpretations of these latter by explaining that no complicated symbolism was meant. He had walked over this bridge many times on his way from the Eighty-ninth Street apartment to the Bronx Post Office; it was spring, and the bridge was getting a coating of red paint.

Myself Among the Churchgoers takes a humorous look at the controversy surrounding the Whitman quotation in the Bronx

The artist/photographer himself is seen using his right-angle viewfinder in Myself Among the Churchgoers *(1939), which takes a wry look at the controversy surrounding the Bronx mural.*

mural. Two serious-looking, undoubtedly pious, black-clad women pass in front of a clapboard church. On the announcement board appears the title of that week's sermon: "Is the Government Fostering Irreligion in Art?"—the sermon given by the Reverend Cox at the time of the Whitman controversy. Ben himself, tweedy and urban, is depicted off to one corner, photographing the scene, unbeknownst to his subjects, through his right-angle viewfinder. The image of these women is based on the photo Ben had taken of two small-town ladies walking down a Mississippi street.

Seurat's Lunch is another example of Ben's humor. A serious-looking man, hands folded and knees crossed, sits in front of a restaurant window. Signs in the window offer roast beef and special whiskeys (at ten cents); once again Ben uses lettering as an important element in a painting. The façade of the restaurant is dotted, a witty reference to the French master of pointillism.

Pretty Girl Milking a Cow is more melancholy in mood. A solitary man, wearing a pinkish shirt, sits on a hillside, which is strewn with reddish-brown autumn leaves. He is playing a tune on his harmonica. It is futile to look for a connection between the painting and its title: the title, later suggested by Bernarda, is the name of the song the man is playing.

Two of the small paintings shown at this exhibition are among Ben's most enduring works. Again, both are based on photos he took in New York. *Vacant Lot* was first called *Man Doth Not Live by Bread Alone.* It shows the small figure of a lonely boy, hitting a baseball against a huge red brick wall. The artist himself once explained this small masterpiece to C. C. Cunningham of the Wadsworth Atheneum in Hartford:

> The lot in the picture is (was) the corner lot at Greenwich and Bethune Streets, in New York. I had a studio in the adjoining building at a time when an old place was torn down. The new space had a curious sort of allure, a strange kind of unreal emptiness, an unfamiliar kind of light. It drew the usual contingent of youngsters, but the picture is no actual happening, no real boy. It's simply a sort of response to the attraction and the sense of loneliness that such a place has. It's an emptiness full of something that was there before.

The reviews of the exhibition were mixed; there were complaints that Shahn's new paintings were gloomy and depressing. Other critics praised the artist for his sincerity and honesty as well as the haunting quality of some of his work. Only Robert Coates of *The New Yorker* expressed unqualified admiration for an artist who possessed "about as keen and intelligent an eye as we have around today."

Commercially, the show was a failure. Only two works were sold—*Willis Avenue Bridge* to Lincoln Kirstein, who later presented it to the Museum of Modern Art; and *Vacant Lot* to James Thrall Soby, who purchased it on behalf of the Wadsworth Atheneum. Soby bought the painting even before the exhibition opened. He paid $200. Levy knew this was too little but, he explained to Ben, the sale carried with it a great prestige which would help the artist launch future exhibitions.

There were no further Shahn exhibitions at Levy's gallery, however. The two men parted ways over a matter of policy and, perhaps, generosity or courtesy. As compensation for his expenses— advertising, announcements, shipping, and often, though not in Shahn's case, a catalogue—Levy asked all his artists to give the gallery one work from each exhibit. Ben had agreed to this condition before his show opened, but once it closed he changed his mind—because, he told Levy, he hadn't sold much. Furthermore, he thought the practice was an exploitation of the artist. "I said," Levy wrote in his memoirs, " 'all right, take your picture, I won't hold you to it.' So I have no Shahn, nor were we ever very friendly again."

CHAPTER TWENTY-THREE

The Washington Mural

BY EARLY 1940, BEN HAD SPENT EVERYTHING THAT HE AND Bernarda had earned for the Bronx mural, and he was heavily in debt. Though he looked forward to the exhibition at Julien Levy's gallery, he realized that few if any of his paintings would be sold there, and that his earnings from it would never come close to solving his financial problems. In addition, the family was growing, for Bernarda was pregnant with their third child.

In March, there was a glimmer of hope: an announcement of another anonymous mural competition, this time for the decoration of the main corridor of the new Social Security Building in Washington. Once again, the competition was under the auspices of the Section of Fine Arts, which had sponsored the Bronx mural competition.

Ben set about preparing the preliminary designs with enthusiasm. He had every reason to be optimistic. He had already proven his skill as a muralist, and the same people who had judged his work on the previous mural would be judging this one. However, the winner would not be announced until the fall; the wait, because of his eagerness to win, seemed interminable. Meanwhile, as he had foreseen, the exhibition at Julien Levy's brought him added fame but little money, and there were further debts, at least one to Bernarda's father.

The anxiously awaited news arrived in late October. Ben was visiting friends when Bernarda called and breathlessly announced that a telegram had arrived, bringing the news that he had won the competition. He was incredulous, certain that it was a cruel joke. People sometimes called friends to announce that they had won one of the popular radio contests . . . this had to be a similar prank. A phone call to Washington, however, confirmed that it was true. He was indeed the winner. And with the commission went a fee of close to $20,000. It seemed a miracle: one moment he had been desperately broke, and in the next he was walking on a cloud.

"The Meaning of Social Security"—Unemployment, a section of the mural.

U.S. GENERAL SERVICES ADMINISTRATION, PUBLIC BUILDINGS SERVICE.
PHOTOGRAPH BY DAY WALTERS

Word spread quickly through Jersey Homesteads: the following morning, when Ben went out to wash his car, his next-door neighbor called out to him, "You're not going to wash the car anymore yourself, are you?"

The jury had reviewed the work of 375 painters, and its decision had been unanimous. The official announcement read, in part:

> The jury praised Mr. Shahn's work on account of "the indications that the artist drew from life, not relying entirely on his supreme knowledge of design." The jury further reported that "there is a variety in the tempo and texture. The pattern advances and recedes, changing its beat, the crowded parts always finding relief. The color is somber, but good, and in keep-

ing with the meaning of the subject theme. It is well integrated in the design. There is continuity, and the mural as a whole is well bound together. The enlarged detail promises a proper execution of this work and we feel well satisfied and confident in our unanimous choice."

The theme of Mr. Shahn's mural is, in general, "The Meaning of Social Security." He relates it to building, agriculture, the poor, child labor, the invalided, recreation, unemployment and other conditions to which the principles of social security apply. His sketches suggest the power and imagination which have made Ben Shahn a leader in the field of mural painting.

Never before had Ben been so wholeheartedly enthusiastic about a commission. This one gave him a unique opportunity to express his deepest convictions through his art—and, thanks to its location, it would be seen every day by thousands of people. Shahn wrote to Edward Bruce: "To me, it is the most important job that I could want. The building itself is a symbol of perhaps the most advanced piece of legislation enacted by the New Deal, and I am proud to be given the job of interpreting it, or putting a face on it." The presidential elections had just taken place, and Ben reported in a handwritten postscript, "Jersey Homesteads went 93% for Roosevelt!" The next day he sent Bruce another letter: "It seems to me that in all my work for the past ten years I have been probing into the material which is the background and substance of Social Security . . . all of it having to do with the problems of human insecurity."

At the same time, he sent Edward Rowan a detailed description of the sketches, with titles for the separate panels. His mural on the west wall would be concerned with positive values:

I have used the long unobstructed wall on the west side of the building to interpret the meaning of social security, and to show something of its accomplishments. On this wall I have developed the following themes:
"Work"   "The Family"   "Social Security"
As a plastic means of emphasizing these themes I have placed

ing to Ormai, Ben was aggressive and fastidious, "worrying" paint into the plaster.

There were a few small problems. On one occasion, an influential member of the Social Security Board complained that Ben's boy in crutches was "deformed." In spite of Rowan's plea that Ben give in, the artist refused. On another occasion, a secretary of a structural steel firm corrected Ben's engineering in the "public works" panel, informing him that the presence of two rivets in the center line of a member would prevent the installation of a girder. Ben balked once again: he preferred art to reality. He did make one change, however. Giving in to Rowan's request, he removed an eye patch from a Social Security applicant.

These were minor issues. A far more serious problem arose in July 1941, when Ormai was ordered by his New York draft board to report immediately for induction into the army. Ben was desperate. He contacted Edward Bruce, asking that he find a way to have Ormai's induction deferred. Ormai was "an almost indispensable assistant," he wrote, and "an expert fresco plasterer (a rarity, you may know)." Since he was planning to execute the mural in *buon fresco*, Ormai's participation was absolutely essential.

Ben's words, in this case, had no effect. On July 18, Rowan replied that Bruce had tried before to obtain deferments for artists and had always failed, as he was sure to do this time. As it happened, however, Ormai—who in any case was a conscientious objector—failed his physical: he had had tuberculosis, and suffered from anemia and a circulatory problem.

Relieved, Ormai returned to the Social Security project, where he and Shahn discovered that to work in *buon fresco* would be impossible. Upon examination, they found that government assistants had given the wall only two layers of plaster, both of them relatively arid, instead of the six that were necessary. Because the surfaces were excessively porous, the paints and glazes tended to dry unevenly and consequently to crack. Ormai was upset. "It shouldn't be like a placard that is whitewashed," he said. "What we had was kind of cheesy." Ben agreed. "The walls," he said, "were dead cinder."

There was no choice but to change the medium to egg tempera, applied on dry plaster (*fresco secco*). Yolks bind paint better than

Early in the preparation of the mural, Ben worked with John Ormai, a twenty-one-year-old student at the Art Students League, whom he had hired to be his assistant. The dazzlingly brilliant Ormai, who had only recently decided to trade a career as a sculptor for one as a fresco muralist, was one of the artists who had lost the Social Security contract to Shahn. His job was to mix the plaster and to mix pigments with distilled water and slaked lime. Precision and speed were essential, since one mistake, even a small one, could ruin a day's work.

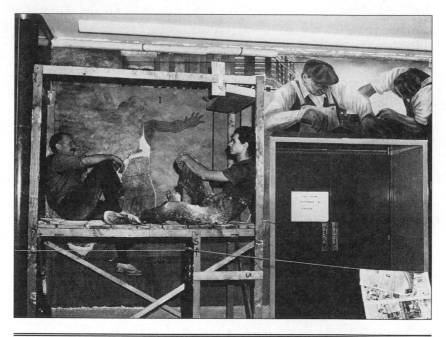

Shahn and John Ormai at work on the Washington, D.C., mural, 1940.

After preliminary work in New Jersey—where the deeply religious, idealistic Ormai stretched Bernarda's considerable skill as a cook by asking that she prepare meatless dishes since he was a vegetarian—Ben and the young man moved to Washington to begin work on the site itself. Ormai, a perfectionist, proved to be of great help. Arriving at work at four o'clock each morning, he would spend five hours wetting, plastering, and mixing, after which Ben would arrive at the Social Security building, ready to work. Accord-

lime water does, and gesso is a less absorbent surface than lime plaster. Because *fresco secco* did not call for the speed and accuracy required by *buon fresco,* Ormai was released.

Dismayed at having lost his job and unable to find another in Washington, Ormai returned home to Bethlehem, Pennsylvania. From there he wrote Ben: "I know your job will come through with flying colors. I wish I were in Washington to see it progressing." But Ben had not yet been able to return to his work either. The replastering of the wall would take several months.

Meanwhile, Ben remained in Jersey Homesteads, though he often visited Washington. In late September, he received word that the commission had fully approved the full-line drawings and detail studies and that he was officially authorized to go forward with the mural. He learned, too, that the wall would soon be ready, and he made preparations for the move to a more permanent home in Washington.

Ben, Bernarda, and the three children—a daughter, Abby, had been born on July 31, 1940—drove to Washington on December 8, 1941, the day after Pearl Harbor. On their way down to the capital they saw thousands of trucks, filled with soldiers, going in all directions. An enemy attack at any time and any place seemed a possibility.

It was sundown when Ben and his family arrived at their rented apartment in Arlington, on the Virginia side of the Potomac. Their furniture had preceded them and was spread haphazardly throughout the rooms. Ben was unconcerned. What moved him were the splendid lights on the dome of the Capitol, which could be seen from their apartment. He called the children over to enjoy the marvelous view, but by the time they arrived it was too late. The lights that illuminated the Capitol had been put out for the duration of the war.

The mood in Washington had changed dramatically since Ben and Bernarda had last lived there. "As the forties began," David Brinkley wrote,

Washington was mainly a middle-class town, grown up around a middle-class government. . . . The war transformed not just the government. It transformed Washington itself. A languid Southern town with a pace so slow that much of it simply closed down for the summer grew almost overnight into a crowded, harried, almost frantic metropolis struggling desperately to assume the mantle of global power, moving haltingly and haphazardly and only partially successfully to change itself into the capital of the free world.

In the months before Pearl Harbor, the capital's population was growing by more than 50,000 a year. From 621,000 in 1930, the number rose to well over a million by the end of 1941. Seventy thousand new people came in the first year after Pearl Harbor. "People arrived from all over the country and wandered bewildered out of the crowded waiting room of Union Station into strange, crowded streets, looking for jobs and—in this labor-starved town—usually finding them," Brinkley wrote.

Between 1941 and 1942, the themes of American popular songs changed abruptly. The hits of 1941 included "Chattanooga Choo-choo," "Bewitched, Bothered, and Bewildered," and "Deep in the Heart of Texas." The popular songs of 1942 spoke of loneliness, nostalgia, patriotism, and war: "I Left My Heart at the Stage Door Canteen," "The White Cliffs of Dover," and "Praise the Lord and Pass the Ammunition." The books America read, too, reflected the changing times. Among the best-sellers of 1941 were William L. Shirer's *Berlin Diary,* Joseph Davies's *Mission to Moscow,* and Winston Churchill's *Blood, Sweat, and Tears,* all of which depicted the prelude to World War II. The next year's successes dealt with war and the German occupation: Steinbeck's *The Moon Is Down,* the story of the Nazi invasion of a Norwegian village, and W. L. White's drama of the PT in the Pacific war, *They Were Expendable.*

Priorities had changed in Washington and elsewhere. The scaffolding was up and the walls had been properly prepared, but Ben was troubled by the idea of beginning work on the mural so soon after Pearl Harbor. The mural itself and his work on it seemed trivial beside the overwhelming drama of the war. Nonetheless, he was advised to begin at once.

His working conditions were complicated by the fact that what was to be the Social Security Building was converted into the War Production Board Building. Literally thousands of busy people now passed through this corridor every day. Many of them stopped to look, and—as had been the case with his earlier murals—some of them commented on what they saw. An Englishman noticed Ben's image of two youngsters jumping for a ball in the course of a basketball game, and thought he saw one of them hitting the other in the face. "American sportsmanship," he complained. On another occasion, a general walked by with members of his staff and remarked to his companions disdainfully that the artist had been at his work for a very long time. Ben, annoyed, told the general that the army, too, was rather slow, having bragged that it would end the war in two weeks. Another time, Ben heard someone call out, "You're a traitor." It was the great photographer Edward Steichen, in naval uniform, humorously referring to Ben's abandonment of photography.

One incident particularly pleased Ben. Coming off the scaffold, covered with dust, he was on his way to the cafeteria for lunch one day when he was approached by a very attractive black woman who asked how many blacks would be represented in his mural. Ben bristled—he didn't like to be challenged or pressured—and replied that it was none of her business; he would put in as many or as few as he needed. This was the beginning of a conversation which led to Ben inviting the young woman to join him for lunch. As soon as they were seated, all the tables around them emptied. Though Ben hadn't been aware of it, this was the first time a black person had come to eat in the cafeteria. He and his new friend lunched together every day for one week and during that time, out of necessity because of crowded conditions, the tables around them started filling up. Without plan or fanfare, the cafeteria had been peacefully integrated.

Most of the comments made in front of the murals were gratifying to the artist. "I know the details are right," he told John D. Morse,

> because all sorts of people stopped to talk to me while I was working. One day when I was finishing the steel construction panel a rigger who had worked on the building pounded me on the back and said, "Good job, bud, good job. That stone carving out in front of the building ain't got nothing to do with anybody."
>
> Then there was the guard in the corridor who had been standing there for weeks without taking any notice of the mural at all. Suddenly there he was beside me. I was painting the man letting

wheat pour through his fingers, and the guard said, "Say, that's the first wheat I've seen since I left the state of Washington." I also liked the man from Iowa who stopped by when I was finishing the overalls on one of the carpenters. "Why," he said, "that's the spit'n'image of my friend Ed Talbot."

But I liked best the Army colonel who came up one day when I was eating lunch in the building cafeteria. "I finally got the courage to come up and talk to you," he said. "I've been wanting to tell you that what you're painting up there on the wall is important to keep in front of all of us while we're fighting this war."

Ben, too, had come to believe that his murals held a special place in the body of his work. He said:

Handball (1939), *one of the artist's best-known paintings, is based on a photo taken in New York in 1930–31.*

I'm not sure what I think about Tolstoy's definition of great art as the kind that pleases the most people. I suspect it's one of those half truths. I don't know. But I do know I get a kick out of being able to paint in the same picture the spit'n'image of Ed Talbot and the war aims of an Army colonel, while all the time other pictures of mine are hanging in the Museum of Modern Art. Back and forth, you know, between the big and the little shapes, between light and dark, serious and comic. Three vanishing points in one plane.

On June 22, 1942, Ben completed his job. He was more than pleased with the results: "I think the Social Security mural is the best work I've done. Anyway, it was the most satisfying. I felt I had everything under control—or almost under control—the big masses of color to make it decorative and the little details to make it interesting."

Present in the mural are elements from *Handball* (a painting inspired by an earlier photograph taken in New York) and from *Vacant Lot*. There are unemployed miners at Scotts Run, workmen, brick walls, the tragic figure of a woman with a crutch from *Willis Avenue Bridge*, welders, a crippled boy, and a homeless father and son. More than fifty years later, at the rededication of Shahn's mural following its badly needed restoration in what is now the headquarters of the Voice of America, Bernarda reflected on the impact and importance of the mural:

> In these mural panels, we see the optimism of people at work, the pessimism and tragedy of the unemployed, a black woman with crutches, a man beside a ruined wall, children lying on the ground, peering out of windows, curiously lonely in most instances. Shahn was acutely aware of continuing hardships, the situations with which Social Security had coped and still must cope. We see the unemployed sitting on curbstones, leaning against brick walls, waiting, talking. We see a rural area of apple-picking, the vignette of a family, people at play, people—all sorts of people, building—then, the long side-wall of a factory—actually the factory built by Resettlement for the village of Jersey Homesteads.

All this is framed, emphasized, pushed back, brought forward, shaped in a series of interrelated forms, industrial forms, architectural forms, essentially American, familiar to us all, and at the same time serving to move the eye along from wall to wall, uniting the recessed panels into a continuous movement, interrelating the opposing walls. As Shahn hoped and planned it does encompass his view of America as it was, as it had been, and as, he felt, it could be. Above all, it expresses his remarkable experience as an active participant in one of the most courageous, inventive and caring experiments ever undertaken by government—Social Security.

CHAPTER TWENTY-FOUR

The OWI
and the War
that Refreshes

BEN'S REPUTATION AS AN ARTIST GREW WITH THE UNQUALIFIED success of the Social Security mural. He became a significant part of an illustrious circle of writers and artists who had come to Washington during the early forties to join the war effort. Shahn was charming and witty, with a strong personality and an imposing physical presence—burly, avuncular, with a small mustache and smiling blue eyes—that made him stand out in a crowd. A relentless storyteller—and usually the often-repeated stories were good ones—he demanded the attention of those around him, much as he had as a young man. He not only knew how to take charge; he insisted upon doing so. He could not be interrupted or challenged. According to a friend, he far preferred a monologue to a dialogue. Many years later, another friend and admirer, the artist Leo Lionni, noted that he always wanted to be in a circular room with Ben, to keep from being cornered by him. Shahn, it was said, did not enjoy attending concerts, because he was unable to talk while the music was being played.

Even before he had completed the mural, Ben was offered a job at a wartime agency, the Office of Facts and Figures (OFF), that would keep him in Washington for another few months. The offer

came from one of two people: the director of the OFF, Archibald
MacLeish, the distinguished poet (on leave from his post as
Librarian of Congress), who had used some of Ben's photos for his
illustrated poem *Land of the Free;* or Thomas Mabry, acting chief
of the Graphics Division of the OFF, for whom Ben had already
worked on some war posters. By the time Ben took up his new
position in August, the OFF had become the Office of War Information (OWI). Ben's official title was "Senior Liaison Officer,
OWI, Design and Services Section, Graphics Division, Bureau of
Publications and Graphics." His salary was $4,600 a year.

Roosevelt had established the OWI's predecessor, the OFF, in
the fall of 1941. The OFF's stated purpose was to further an
understanding of the "status and progress of the war effort and of
the war policies, activities, and aims of the government." This was
before Archibald MacLeish wrote Roosevelt a letter saying that "a
full knowledge of what we are fighting for would be a positive
weapon in winning the war."

MacLeish meant to achieve his goal by means of posters and
pamphlets. He began an extensive search for writers, artists,
designers, illustrators, cartoonists, and photographers to portray,
in his own words, "in the simplest possible terms that can be
understood by the mass mind the extreme gravity of the situation
now confronting us, and the extraordinary measures which must
be taken to achieve victory." In other words, it would be necessary
to shock and awaken the consciousness of all those people who
had not yet fully realized the gravity of the peril that had engulfed
half the world.

Some of the country's best scholars, writers, and artists
responded enthusiastically to MacLeish's recruitment drive. As the
agency grew, however, he realized that he and his people were all
too frequently duplicating the work of other government agencies.
To solve this problem, MacLeish suggested to President Roosevelt
the creation of one strong agency, the Office of War Information,
which would consolidate the jobs previously done by several different agencies. Roosevelt responded favorably and on June 13,
1942, the OWI was established. Shortly thereafter, Elmer Davis, a
highly respected news analyst and radio commentator, known for
his integrity and objectivity, was appointed to head the newly created agency. (MacLeish remained as assistant director for a short

time.) Like his predecessor, Davis believed that posters and pamphlets were a most effective means of educating the public; he soon announced the establishment of the OWI Bureau of Publications and Graphics. At the same time, he appointed Francis (Hank) Brennan, the art director of *Fortune,* chief of both the Writers and Graphics Sections.

One of Brennan's first and most important tasks was to recruit gifted, established artists for the organization. He also planned to look for less well known men and women. "It was a time," he said, "to find out if another Goya is fuming in Iowa and another Daumier sketches acidly in Vermont."

In many ways, Ben's new job would be similar to his job at the RA, where his goal was to use photographs to explain the tragic effects of the Depression and to urge the American people to accept appropriate social reforms. In his new job at the OWI he would seek to explain the reasons for World War II to the American people who would, as a result, accept the restrictions imposed by the war.

Ben's enthusiasm for his new job, unfortunately, soon disappeared. His posters and campaign ideas were too realistic, too strong, and too brutal for both the men who ran the organization and the psychologists they consulted in their mission to educate the public. Most of the OWI's administrators were businessmen or advertising executives who discouraged Ben and his colleagues from emphasizing the ugly side of war and the nature of Nazi crimes. Even the word "Nazi" was not permitted, because they believed that much of the public had never heard the word and did not know who the Nazis were. The word "enemy" was acceptable as a substitute.

What the OWI heads preferred were more positive posters and pamphlets that explained the need for food rationing, increased production of war matériel, and, perhaps their favorite theme, the necessity for total secrecy on the part of workers in war plants and citizens who, because of their contacts with members of the military, might inadvertently reveal troop movements. As far as Ben was concerned there were far too many series with the theme "Don't talk"—a hand coming out of the waves, figures sinking, and a ship's captain saying, "Someone talked."

Ben's dissatisfaction and frustration are easy to understand.

Some of his ideas were imaginative and brilliant, at times strikingly innovative. They would certainly have been effective, but most of them were rejected. His proposal for a magazine to be circulated in war plants as part of a comprehensive educational program was rejected, as was his idea for a thirty-two-page booklet, to be called "Dear Adolf," including photos of farmers and food production all over America, with quotations and other documents indicating the power and fighting spirit of the United States. The text was to be written by Stephen Vincent Benét.

Among Shahn's rejected posters were two series, "Nature of the Enemy" and "Method of the Enemy"; the latter included *Farmers—Victory Is in Your Hands,* and *Unfair Labor Practices.* Among the rejected single posters were *Stalingrad Story* and *The Enemy Won't Know Its Bow from Its Stern* (this quoted an FDR speech following his trip to Africa), both of which were all-type posters; *Unconditional Surrender; Ask the Women and Children; German Americans: What Nazis Think of German-Americans,* an idea that grew out of a discussion held at a staff meeting; *May Pole Dance,* showing Axis partners wound up by ribbons on a maypole; *Slavery,* a figure standing behind barbed wire; and *Murder,* depicting a woman lying dead.

Because of the unreasonable limitations and restrictions imposed upon the artists, the OWI actually published and distributed only two of Shahn's posters. Although it is impossible to understand why these were chosen while so many others were rejected, they are undeniably most effective. One of them announced the annihilation of the small Czech village of Lidice and the murder or deportation of most of its inhabitants by Nazi soldiers. (This atrocity was committed in revenge for the killing by anti-Nazi Czechs of Reinhard Heydrich, chief of the Nazi security police and "Protector" of Bohemia and Moravia.)

In its stark simplicity, Shahn's poster was enormously powerful. The news of the destruction of the village and its people appears on printed ticker tape, above which are the words "This is Nazi brutality." The large figure of a hooded and handcuffed prisoner stands behind these words. Behind him are bare brick walls and a threatening blue sky.

Though the OWI did print this poster, Ben learned that it was too harsh for some of its intended audience. Forty thousand copies which were to be distributed by a Czechoslovakian-American organization were withdrawn on the grounds that, according to a civilian psychologist, the message was "too violent."

The other poster judged suitable for distribution by the OWI depicted a group of Frenchmen, hands held high in surrender before a bright red notice proclaiming that all French citizens between the ages of eighteen and fifty are obliged to work at whatever job was deemed necessary to the well-being of the Nazi-controlled Vichy government. Simple, large letters at the top of the poster read: "We French workers warn you . . . defeat means slavery, starvation, death."

The creation of this dramatic poster marked Ben's first collaboration with a brilliant young graphic artist, William Golden, art director for the Columbia Broadcasting System, who had taken a leave of absence from his job to work for the OWI. Ben wrote of this experience:

> We sat together through a session or two and discussed what a war poster ought to be. . . . We then began to suggest, discard, work toward specific image ideas. We agreed upon such an image idea and I undertook it at home over a weekend. I felt its urgency and did not want to undertake it in the unresolved atmosphere of the OWI studio.
>
> Once I had begun to put our poster idea into image form, I became acutely aware of fallacies in it that would never have emerged in a simple conversation. I played around a little with the idea, then came up with a new one, totally different, that was visual and not verbal. It was ultimately known as the *French Workers* poster.
>
> Bill's reaction to what I had created was apoplectic. It wasn't what we had talked about or what we had agreed upon. If (I said to myself) he expected me to labor and belabor an idea that was neither visual nor valid, he was working with the wrong artist.
>
> I think that both Bill and I solidified our graphic futures more through that impasse than through any subsequent single experience. What I learned was a hardened determination to put the integrity of an image first and above all other considerations;

one must be prepared to retire from any job whatever and to let someone else make either a mess or a success of it, rather than abandon the clear vision that he may have. I took this position.

In spite of this beginning, Shahn and Golden became close friends and collaborators. In all the years of their friendship, the subject of the *French Workers* poster was never again raised.

In November 1942, after Ben had been with the OWI for only a few months, the Design and Services Section was moved to the penthouse of the Fisk Building at 250 West Fifty-seventh Street in New York City. The reason for the move was the need to be closer to the offices of the magazines and newspapers, most of them in New York, that used OWI graphics.

Many members of the Washington staff moved to New York; Ben, Bernarda, and the children returned to Jersey Homesteads. This meant that Ben would have to commute to Manhattan, but that presented no problem. What disturbed and upset him and his colleagues was the fact that the move to New York did not bring with it any hoped-for fundamental change in the policies of the organization. The material created in New York was treated in exactly the same way that the material and ideas had been treated in Washington. Almost everything was rejected by the boards and committees that controlled Design and Services from Washington.

Entrusted with fewer projects and therefore not fully occupied with their own work, Ben and his colleagues had time to offer their services to other war-related agencies, but once again they were rebuffed. Most of their creative output—not only posters, but design ideas, entire informational campaigns, even a mock-up for a proposed newsletter—were judged unacceptable.

The situation was untenable. The entire staff was demoralized. A group of energetic, dedicated, and gifted men and women were eager to offer their services, but were frustrated at every turn. Among these men and women were Golden, who was drafted into the Army soon after moving to New York, and Raymond Gordon, a very young and engaging graphic artist who soon afterward also found himself in the Army, with Golden and Lincoln Kirstein. Also a part of the staff were a Viennese Jewish refugee, Henry Koerner, a brilliant and extraordinarily prolific commercial artist who designed striking posters and gained the reputation of being the most even-tempered and pleasant of all the workers in the office, and David Stone Martin, a self-confident and talented graphic designer who was also a muralist and had been a staff artist with the Tennessee Valley Authority in Knoxville. Among the others were Bernard Perlin, an immensely gifted twenty-four-year-old painter who had also submitted a design for the Bronx Post Office mural and became a disciple of Ben's, and Irving Geis, a feisty and explosive idea man who had come to the OWI from *Fortune* magazine. Prominent among the women on the staff were Betty Chamberlain, a writer who had worked at Time, Inc., and Muriel Rukeyser, who became a distinguished poet but who, according to Perlin, wasn't quite sure what she was supposed to do at the OWI. She was delighted, however, when Perlin lettered her name on the glass door to her small office.

Though Hank Brennan, who rejected some of Ben's posters himself, was the titular head of the office, Ben soon asserted his own leadership. The most gifted artist on the staff, he impressed all of his colleagues not only with his talent but also with his charm and wit and his frequent acts of great generosity and kindness. His need to dominate was obvious, however. Geis characterized him as the resident guru, who was also the president of the Ben Shahn Fan Club, an unrivaled raconteur, and, Geis felt, his own best invention.

Though he admired Ben and enjoyed his friendship, Geis was unable to understand the pleasure he took in making fun of Hank Brennan, a good and bright man who had, when they first met, described himself to Ben as a "smiling" rather than a "fighting" Irishman. Many mornings, it seems, Ben would greet Brennan by mentioning something of no particular relevance, to which Brennan would respond by asking how Ben had learned whatever it was. Ben's answer was always the same. He would tell Brennan he had read it in *The New York Times,* sending him to look through the newspaper in a futile effort to locate an article Ben knew had never appeared there. Brennan apparently never caught on.

Whatever may be said about Ben's behavior, he was a dynamic creative force whose art exerted a strong influence on those who worked with him. Both he and his colleagues, however, were wasted in the labyrinth of cross-purposes that the OWI had become.

Morale at the New York office continued to deteriorate during the first months of 1943, and reached a new low with the hiring of two men who would take charge of the organization. One was William Lewis, a former vice president of the Columbia Broadcasting System; the other was James Allen, a former press agent and motion picture executive. Within a short time, these men initiated radical changes in the basic policy of the OWI. The writers, who had been allowed a measure of creative freedom in the past, were no longer permitted to think up their own ideas and develop them. Instead, they would work only to specifications given them by Lewis. To make matters even worse, Lewis and Allen—presumably at the suggestion of Gardner Cowles, Jr., director of the organization's domestic branch—hired Price Gilbert, a former vice president of Coca-Cola, to head the Bureau of Publications and Graphics. Gilbert took charge immediately. One of his first acts was to cancel the production of a Shahn poster claiming that the portrayal of Nazi brutality was too harsh and ugly to be displayed. He wanted posters that carried the same message as did Norman Rockwell's tranquil scenes of American life.

The artists and writers were enraged. On their own, Brennan, whom Price had replaced as head of the Graphics Bureau, and Shahn created a poster that they felt embodied their idea of Gilbert's requirements. It showed the Statue of Liberty, arm raised high to carry, instead of a torch, four frosty bottles of Coca-Cola, bearing the words "The War that Refreshes; the Four Delicious Freedoms."

On April 6, 1943, Brennan, now converted into a fighting Irishman, wrote Elmer Davis a letter of resignation. The advertising men, he charged,

> utilize every trick of the trade to make necessary civilian actions appear palatable, comfortable, and not quite as inconvenient as Guadalcanal. . . . To our shame, while American soldiers rotted in the desert heat, the Graphics Division was designing posters about ordering coal early. . . . Now, with the African campaign at its height we are instructed to produce more ancient graphic saws that will soon smile cheerfully from the billboards, saying: "I'm happy in my new war job," and "We'll have enough to eat this winter, won't we, Mother?"

With Alan Reitman, working for the CIO-PAC during the 1944 presidential campaign.

Both you and Mr. Cowles have said that some advertising techniques are valuable. If by that you mean the fairly simple job of getting messages printed, distributed, and read, I agree. But if you mean psychological approaches, content, and ideas, I most firmly do not agree. . . . Those techniques have done more toward dimming perception, suspending critical values, and spreading the sticky syrup of complacency over the people than almost any other factor.

A few days later, the writers made one final attempt to reestablish their influence. They threatened to resign unless they could report directly to Elmer Davis, who they believed would be fair and more sympathetic to their side of the struggle. But Davis's response was ambiguous and disappointing. He refused to give in to their specific demands and at the same time urged them to stay with the organization and fight. Rebuffed, fourteen writers, among them many who had given up good jobs to work for Davis and contribute to the war effort, issued an angry statement to the press: "The activities of the OWI on the home front are now dominated by high-pressure promoters who prefer slick salesmanship to honest information. . . . They are turning this OWI into an 'Office of War Bally-hoo.' The soap salesmen are in the saddle in the OWI."

It came as no surprise to Ben when, the following July, he received a letter from Elmer Davis informing him that, because of cuts in appropriations for 1944, the functions performed by Ben's office would be discontinued and his active service with the OWI terminated.

He was fed up with the OWI anyway. After July he was offered a few freelance government jobs and accepted some of them, but before long he realized that he was unable to work for the government in any capacity. He could, he believed, make a greater contribution to the war effort by returning to his home in Jersey Homesteads to plant a victory garden and can vegetables. More important, he could return to his own painting, through which he could most effectively express his pain at the horror and sadness of war.

CHAPTER TWENTY-FIVE

CIO-PAC:
A Crusade,
Not a Committee

BEN'S RETURN TO JERSEY HOMESTEADS SIGNALED THE BEGIN-
ning of an intense period of painting, which resulted in some of his
best work to date. These paintings included *Italian Landscape 1*,
Italian Landscape 2, *India*, *Cherubs and Children*, and *Girl Jumping Rope*, poignant, deeply moving scenes of the desolation and
loneliness of war, most of which would be shown at Ben's next
exhibition in 1944.

In early 1944, however, this productive period came to an end.
Ben received a call from Wilbur Hugh (Ping) Ferry, a teacher, journalist, writer, and public relations director, who offered him a job
directing the newly formed pictorial art division of the political
action committee (PAC) of the CIO.

The PAC was to act as the union's political arm, conducting an
educational program whose goal was to enlist the members of all
trade unions in the fight to reelect FDR and the rest of the Democratic administration in 1944. The CIO-PAC was also meant to
become a permanent political organization, promoting the candi-
dacy of all labor-supported candidates in future elections.

Ferry's offer, made on behalf of the powerful, dynamic labor
leader Sidney Hillman—director of the CIO-PAC, head of the

Amalgamated Clothing Workers of America, and a founder of the CIO—was too attractive to reject. In spite of his bitterness over the OWI fiasco, Shahn continued to believe deeply in FDR and felt that America's future depended upon his reelection.

The early days of PAC were colorfully, if somewhat effusively, described by Joseph Gaer, PAC's publications director:

> In no time at all, or so it seemed, a national office was established in New York, and regional offices sprang into being from coast to coast. People were considered, selected, hired for various jobs. The tasks were broken down. While the partitions in the offices were going up, various divisions began to take shape. A research division was first to appear, followed closely by a public relations division, a press relations division, a women's division, a publications division, a radio division, a youth division, a Negro section, to be followed shortly by a pictorial art division, a shipping department, a distribution committee, a speaker's bureau.
>
> They came into being with sleeves rolled up, so to speak, and impetuously busy. While the furniture was being moved in, people were already telephoning printers, telephoning artists and writers and radio script makers, telephoning Detroit, Los Angeles, St. Louis, Miami, setting up contacts, gathering data, sending out information. Men were at work preparing publications, posters, stickers, buttons, songs and slogans. Each division head worked late into the night devising plans—publications plans, radio plans, poster plans, field assistance plans—plans that had to be discussed, coordinated, sifted, and developed into what ultimately evolved as a unified program of activities.
>
> A constant stream of people kept flowing through the office. People with ideas. Office seekers. Job hunters. Men and women curious. Newspapermen. And all went away shaking their heads and wondering what it was that made the people working for PAC work with such zeal. One newspaperman exclaimed: "This isn't a Committee—this is a crusade!"

Ben did, in many ways, work like a crusader, leading his team of dedicated workers. His full-time assistants were Mary Collier, David Stone Martin, and James Grunbaum. Among his part-time workers were a number of freelance artists, including Abe Ajay and Ad Reinhardt.

Shahn was astounded at the amount of work that could be done in a short time because of the "complete unity of spiritual intentions" that permeated the organization. "We did fifty times as much work with one-fiftieth as much help," he said, referring to his experience at the OWI. "There were no opposition committees, no divisions on policy. When a design for a poster was ready, instead of equivocation we got the go-ahead signal immediately." Taking charge as soon as he entered the organization, Ben became not only the chief artist, but also the chief "idea man." Furthermore, his past experience as a printer enabled him to save the PAC large sums of money. At an art school symposium in Andover, Massachusetts, a few years later, he spoke of the education of the "communicative artist":

> There are numerous ways of reaching an audience. The easel painting is one which reaches a limited and highly select group, the mural a larger one. Posters and other media which can be mass-produced have, of course, the widest reach. It is important to the communicative artist to master the techniques of all these media. He ought to know printing processes and the differences in effectiveness and in cost between them.
>
> When I went to work for the Political Action Committee in 1944, I found that they were paying twenty-one cents each for two-color posters eight by eleven inches in size. That the posters were thoroughly ordinary and unimaginative in design was only one defect. In an office of seventy people, many of whom had, no doubt, taken "Art 117," or Art Appreciation, or [an] Art Practice course, there was no one who knew how to design or order a poster. An examination of the field made it possible for us soon to produce posters thirty by forty-six inches in size and in four colors for seven cents apiece. . . .
>
> You, if you expect to be the communicative sort of artist, ought to set yourself the task of learning the possibilities of every form of reproduction. You should know what can be done with silk screen, what should be done in offset, what in letterpress. You should know papers, their cost, weight, and standard sizes. You should know the degree of accuracy that can be expected of

the various media, the average press run for this or that process. You should be alert to every means of duplication, even to the multilith and photostat.

Thanks to Ben's skill and knowledge, the department under his supervision functioned with extraordinary efficiency. Prior to and during the 1944 campaign, the CIO-PAC issued sixteen different posters, some of them in several sizes, with a combined circulation of 417,307 copies. Some of these posters were based on photographs or cartoons. Ben used his own paintings as the basis for others. In all, five Shahn posters were printed during the 1944 campaign. They include *Register . . . The Ballot Is a Power in Your Hands, From Workers to Farmers . . . Thanks!, Here There Is No Poll Tax, Register, Vote,* and one, *Our Friend,* which is dominated by an image of FDR. Included in this group, too, is perhaps his most famous poster, based on a painting, *The Welders,* now in the collection of New York's Museum of Modern Art. Originally done for the OWI, it was rejected and then used by the CIO-PAC. On one side it shows the face and hands of a man who looks something like FDR, with goggles over his eyes and a helmet on his head. Standing next to him is a black man, also with a helmet on his head. Underneath the figures appear the words "For full employment after the war, REGISTER VOTE." Ben took pride in this poster; he felt the audience at which it was directed would be moved by it. Walter Abell, writing in *Magazine of Art* (October 1946), agreed: "Shahn's *Welders* can speak to a factory worker much as a *Holy Family* spoke to a medieval monk. It is of the tissue of his soul's experience; a symbol of his work and of his impulse toward a fuller life."

The right-wing press, however, responded angrily. The New York *Journal American* reproduced the poster full size, with one color, and commented that the white man "hiding" behind the glasses was Roosevelt, misleading the "colored" people to vote for him. The New York *Daily Mirror* of October 16, 1944, found that "this poster is plainly an appeal to racial prejudices." Actually, the "best friend the Negro has ever had," the editorial writer noted, "is the Republican Party"—this, because Lincoln was a Republican.

Final production of all of these posters [Abell explained]

involved problems of layout, supervision of printing, and scores of other practical details. In addition, cartoons were drawn and mats of them circulated to 1,500 labor newspapers throughout the country. Illustrations in a breezy, and sometimes very sophisticated, graphic style, were provided for some two score pamphlets, leaflets, and fliers which reached a combined circulation of approximately 78,000,000 copies. Miscellaneous items included designs for six different campaign badges, a sticker for envelopes, a colored post card showing Hoover and Dewey in the relation of Bergen to Charlie McCarthy. 528,000 of the latter cards spread their ironic humor from coast to coast."

Ben was completely committed to the PAC. He worked day and night and even enlisted the help of Bernarda, who contributed nineteen drawings for a pamphlet called "A Woman's Guide to Political Action," and twenty-three very witty drawings for the PAC's "Radio Handbook." Though Ben at first felt himself a strange phenomenon in an office peopled with hard-boiled union men and trained political scientists, he discovered he could work with them successfully and harmoniously. Sidney Hillman, who made policy from his small corner office, cooperated fully with Ben, occasionally coming to watch him work at his drawing board (Hillman had never before seen an artist at work) and even, from time to time, bringing a prominent visitor to observe the art department at work. Hillman's assistant, Calvin Benham (Beanie) Baldwin, who, though known for being indecisive, made day-to-day decisions, was a hardworking Southern liberal, an expert on agricultural matters, and a former head of the FSA; he was equally cooperative with Ben and his department.

Prominent among Shahn's other colleagues were Raymond Walsh, the director of research, and Walsh's assistant Frederick Palmer Weber, who would later succeed him. Walsh, a mild-mannered jovial man, a distinguished news commentator who had also taught at Harvard, had brought into the organization a small staff of writers, among them Ferry, Gaer, and Alan Reitman, a brilliant young editorial writer. Weber, admired for his profound knowledge of Congress, was an especially close friend of Ben's, for whom he felt genuine affection. Ben enjoyed teasing Weber, usually with no harm done. But Weber's fiancée, Gertrude, felt that on one occasion Shahn had crossed the line between humor and cruelty. Palmer was so poor during this period that he was forced to wear borrowed trousers, which were far too long for him. Ben remarked that if only Palmer had a bowler, he would look just like Charlie Chaplin's Little Tramp. He was so amused at the idea that he presented Palmer with a bowler. When Gertrude saw him wear it and learned that Ben had given it to him, she was furious. The gift was, she felt, an example of the vicious streak in Ben's character. Though Palmer didn't see it that way, for Gertrude the joke was clearly a form, and an ugly one, of abuse.

But Hilda Robbins, a secretary only two years out of Radcliffe who sat at a desk outside the adjoining offices of Ben and Palmer Weber, saw another side of Ben.

Though not familiar with the art world, she had heard of him because of her knowledge of the Sacco-Vanzetti case. Initially nervous at the thought of meeting such a distinguished artist, she was delighted to find that he was "a teddy bear, a simple, humane mensch," who, from the time of their first meeting, always made her feel comfortable and treated her as his equal. She remembers him fondly: grizzled, with thinning hair, his shirtsleeves rolled up, bending over a drawing board, an enthusiastic worker, always quick to laugh.

After the 1944 campaign, when Roosevelt was elected for an unprecedented fourth term (credit as well as bitter complaint came the CIO-PAC's way for its role in that victory), Ben's division was temporarily dissolved. This was actually a good thing for him. It enabled him to recuperate from the long hours and debilitating tensions of the last few months of the campaign and gave him a chance to return to work on his paintings, quietly, in his studio.

But the hiatus was not long. In the summer of 1945 he was asked to rejoin the CIO-PAC to help wage the 1946 congressional campaign which, following FDR's tragic death in April, was certain to be a difficult one. This time he was to be director of the Graphic Arts Division.

Shahn didn't need the job; in addition to the income he was now receiving from the sale of his paintings, he was earning enough money from freelance work as a graphic artist and illustrator to live comfortably. But he agreed to return, because he needed to work for and identify himself with the interests of labor. This time, however, he planned to devote only three days a week to the PAC. The rest of the time he would spend painting, with one day off for relaxation. Given his commitment to the cause, however, it is unlikely that he was able to maintain this divided schedule.

Ben's posters for PAC during this campaign were as brilliant and effective as the previous group. One of them, *Warning! Inflation Means Depression,* was based on a 1943 painting, which was in turn based on a photograph he took during a trip through Arkansas for the FSA. Another, *We Want Peace,* depicts a dark-eyed child, his hand outstretched, pleading desperately for peace. Based on his painting *Hunger,* it had originally been produced for and rejected by the OWI. Two more, done in 1946, bear the messages "Break Reaction's Grip" and "For all these rights we've just begun to fight." Both of these, as well as the other two created at the time, bear the words, "Register-Vote."

Ben undertook one additional job that summer of 1946, his first assignment for *Fortune* magazine. *Fortune* was planning to run an article on organized labor's drive to unionize the southern workers, particularly cotton workers. At the suggestion of two of the magazine's art editors, Leo Lionni and Deborah Calkins, both friends of his, Ben was asked to travel to the South to gather material on which to base his illustrations for the article.

He had asked Philip Murray, the president of the CIO, for a one-month leave, and got it. Though *Fortune* was the magazine of business, it had since its inception in 1930 published articles critical of business; Murray knew that any publicity for the union's efforts to organize the South would be useful to the CIO. He knew, too, that Ben was uniquely qualified to illustrate the article.

As for Ben, he was unconcerned about any conflict between his views and those of his corporate employer, as long as he was free to express those views. He profoundly believed what he wrote in a 1946 letter to the Chrysler Corporation, which wanted to commission for its art collection a painting that would, in some way, refer to the automobile. When he got the initial phone call, he shouted "No!" and slammed down the receiver. On further reflection, he wrote:

The business of painting, like that of music, prose writing or poetry is a matter of saying something with which the artist, musician or writer is keenly preoccupied. He will have thought about it for a long time, distilled it in his mind, and the result is this picture, that book or musical score. He has felt a need to present certain relationships, either abstract or human, and he has given you the answer in his own highly personal terms.

Unless there is, in the objective situation which he is about to paint, some element which, on the one hand, may offer him a challenge as to an aesthetic solution; or, unless there is a human or personal problem which he feels the need to present and interpret, there is little honest motive for making a painting. The value of any painting must, therefore, necessarily derive from the importance which the artist himself places on it. If he feels a powerful urgency in a situation, and if he has at his disposal the technical proficiency to realize that urgency truly, the resultant work of art will be one of value to himself and others. Therein lies its aesthetic value.

For an artist to make a painting which is without significance to himself is simply to commercialize his past achievement.

———

Ben was enthusiastic as he left for the South. His first stop was Durham, North Carolina; there, he was to meet the *Fortune* team, which had already started putting together material for the planned all-labor issue of the magazine. Instead of meeting a well-organized, large group of journalists, all possibly wearing red armbands that read "Fortune," Ben found Dero A. Saunders, a very tired reporter, and an even wearier woman researcher in a small room in Durham's Hotel Washington Duke. Ben and Dero worked well together. They spoke to the publishers of vicious hate sheets as well as the lawyers for the big southern mills, who were willing to reveal their strikebreaking techniques in hopes of getting their pictures or names in *Fortune*. Despite such encounters, Ben found far less anger and hatred in the South of 1946 than in that of the 1930s.

Back in New York, he worked day and night, Saturdays and Sundays, to complete the paintings and drawings he had conceived.

Labor Drives South depicted calm moments of day-to-day life—a man playing a guitar, a relaxed mill hand in a rocking chair, and men shaking hands outside a church—all meant to demonstrate that labor's drive to organize the South was peaceful. Only one drawing, that of a policeman, his back to the viewer, watching a group of half a dozen people who were in turn watching him, was unacceptable to the magazine's editors. It had an ominous quality, a feeling of tension; it conveyed the fear of an outbreak of violence.

By the time Ben returned to the CIO-PAC's New York office in September 1946, it was clear that the election was going badly for the Democratic party and, therefore, the PAC. In the first week of October, poll results were released that showed Truman, FDR's successor, with an approval rating of only 40 percent. A few weeks later, a short time before the congressional elections, that figure had fallen to 32 percent. The CIO-PAC staff was understandably demoralized, even more so since their powerful leader, Sidney Hillman, had died earlier in the summer.

The "crusade" was coming to an end; the mood in the office was changing; even Ben's posters were increasingly criticized as too innovative. They showed suffering and pain rather than the smiling, determined faces most labor leaders were accustomed to, and they were not acceptable. In spite of this, Ben continued to work hard and maintain at least a show of good spirits. Today his colleagues, especially those who worked for him, look back with nostalgia on their time spent with the PAC. One of them, Estelle Thompson Margolis, has especially vivid memories of Ben and the PAC office.

An inexperienced young woman at the time, working as a volunteer for the American Veterans Committee, Estelle went to the PAC office in the winter of 1946 in search of a job. Though she was warmly greeted by Ben, "a big jolly man" who spoke to her at great length, she was told that there was not enough money to hire her. She persisted, however, regularly returning to see the "funny, wonderful" man, for whom she was determined to work. In the course of one talk, Ben suggested that she might draw cartoons, as his friend Ad Reinhardt did, but she refused: she could do layout and typography, but not cartoons. In June, as the 1946 political campaign began to warm up, Ben was told that, regardless of the criticism of his work, he would be responsible for the preparation of leaflets and posters for the entire country. Help was essential; he finally hired Estelle, at $42 a week.

Estelle found that working for Ben was just as rewarding and stimulating as she had anticipated. In turn, her skill at doing mechanicals, layout, and typography enabled her to be of great help to Ben, and the two worked together for many hours at a time. Estelle also put together leaflets he or Bernarda had designed.

Estelle was a gifted artist with considerable potential; Ben became her mentor. It was a role he enjoyed, as he had in the past and would in the future with other promising young artists. He was generous with his time as well as his knowledge, and all he required in return was appreciation and respect. But once a student questioned or challenged Ben, the relationship almost always came to an end.

Estelle immensely appreciated and respected Ben. She enjoyed his wit and charm and keen intelligence, and the two lunched together frequently. The young woman, in awe of her boss-mentor-friend, often visited the Shahns in Jersey Homesteads, where she played the role of big sister to their three children. During these visits, too, she learned the place of a woman in the artist's home. While Ben and his male friends would hold long, serious discussions, Estelle and Bernarda were relegated to the kitchen to make seemingly endless pots of coffee.

=====

As anticipated, the results of the 1946 election were disastrous for the Democrats. Jack Kroll, who had been with the CIO in Washington, had come to New York as Hillman's replacement, but there was little Kroll (or even Hillman) could have done to change the outcome. A combination of inflation, labor unrest, and growing anti-union sentiment crushed CIO-backed candidates at the polls, and the Republicans gained control of both houses of Congress for the first time since 1930. The morning after election day, both Ben and Estelle found notes on their desks informing them that they had been fired. Ben was not as upset as he might have been. The CIO was becoming as bureaucratic as the OWI had been, and it was increasingly clear that his posters were considered too militant for the organization's purposes.

Shahn's major contribution to the 1948 Progressive Party campaign was this gouache, later reproduced as a poster, of Truman and Dewey.

Nonetheless, the news of their dismissal came as a surprise, and, at Ben's suggestion, the two ex-employees went for a walk. Ben told Estelle a story he felt was appropriate for the occasion: it is 1929. Two partners in a successful clothing business are told by their accountant that, because of the Crash, their business has gone bankrupt. The two of them, stunned, decide to take a walk. As they wait for the elevator, one turns to the other and wails, "Oy vey!" The other replies, "If you want to talk business, I'm going home." On that note, Ben and Estelle, also stunned, began their walk down Third Avenue and away from CIO-PAC.

Ben took his last office job in 1948, when Estelle asked him to work for Henry Wallace's Progressive Party, the dissident left-wing party that offered Ben and many other liberals an alternative to Truman and Dewey. Estelle had agreed to become its art director on the condition that she could ask Ben to join her in creating posters and leaflets for the campaign. Ben agreed but was soon disillusioned. Though he admired Wallace as a man and as a principled politician who shared his own ideals, he discovered that Wallace was no longer in charge. Instead, the Progressives were controlled by outside forces, largely hardline Communists who were using Wallace as a figurehead. This was a group whose ideas did not coincide with his. Unlike many of his colleagues, most from the CIO-PAC days, Ben did not leave the Progressive Party. But his heart was no longer in the Wallace campaign, and he worked with little enthusiasm. His single memorable contribution was a large caricature showing Truman at the piano with Dewey stretched out across its top. The sheet music on the piano includes such popular songs as "A Good Man Is Hard to Find," "Little White Lies," and "It Had to Be You." The poster parodied a well-publicized photo of President Truman accompanying Lauren Bacall as she serenades him, which was used extensively in the campaign. Ben was so proud of it that he donated the original to the Museum of Modern Art.

CHAPTER TWENTY-SIX

A Return
to Painting

BEN'S MURALS WERE NOW CONSIDERED AMONG THE FINEST
ever created in America. They brought him both fame and admiration. His strikingly effective, graphically innovative posters added
to the acclaim. Unfortunately, however, he had not had time to do
the work closest to his heart. He had completed relatively few
paintings over the last few years. In 1944, after several years spent
mostly in office work, he had again been able to devote much of his
time to painting. There was a special incentive as well: he had to
prepare for his first one-man show in New York since 1940. He was
back at Edith Halpert's Downtown Gallery (they had apparently
made up their quarrel), this time for three weeks beginning in
November 1944.

The exhibit consisted largely, but not exclusively, of war paintings—not scenes of battle or heroism, but pictures showing the
devastation of war and its effect on innocent people, the wanton
destruction of homes and towns and villages.

> During the war, [he wrote later,] I worked in the Office of War
> Information. We were supplied with a constant stream of mate-
> rial, photographic and other kinds of documentation of the dec-
> imation within enemy territory. There were the secret

confidential horrible facts of the cartloads of dead; Greece, India, Poland. There were the blurred pictures of bombed-out places, so many of which I knew well and cherished. There were the churches destroyed, the villages, the monasteries—Monte Cassino and Ravenna. At that time I painted only one theme, "Europa," you might call it. Particularly I painted Italy as I lamented it, or feared what it might have become.

These paintings mark a significant departure from his earlier work. Shahn described one of them, *The Red Stairway*, in a conversation with Henry Brandon of *The Sunday Times* of London.

It showed a crippled man walking up an endless stair, and then when he came to the top of that stair he went down again. And the whole thing was in a ruin of rubble and burned-out buildings. To me this is both the hope of man and the fate of man, you know. It's obvious almost, that he seems to recover from the

There is a sense of profound sadness and futility in The Red Stairway *(1944), which depicts a man on crutches making his way up a flight of stairs that leads only to a descending flight of stairs.*

THE SAINT LOUIS ART MUSEUM

most frightful wars, the most faithful plagues, and goes right on
again when he knows full well that he's going into another one;
but that's that eternal hope in the human being.

Shahn's gentle wit and deeply felt melancholy are combined in
other paintings that have nothing to do with the war. One example
is *Four-Piece Orchestra,* a portrait of three men playing four instruments (one plays the guitar and harmonica at once). Their faces
are expressionless, not relating to each other but looking off in different directions. The three men have been brought together by
this music, but the result is still loneliness and frustration. Another
work, *Fourth of July Orator,* combines satire and sadness. Three
men, politicians, occupy a raised platform in the midst of a large
barren field (in the background are the flat Bauhaus homes of Jersey Homesteads). One of the men is delivering a speech, but no
one is there to listen.

These paintings of the early 1940s reveal a maturity, a poetry,
and a psychological depth that surpass anything Ben had created
in the past. His anger is present in much of the work, but it is tem-
pered by a newfound compassion. Toward the end of the war his
technique changed as well, the application of translucent tones
over opaque passages giving his colors greater life and profundity.
The medium is almost always tempera, which he preferred, using
honey, oxgall, gum arabic, and sometimes egg yolk.

The change in Ben's work was recognized by the critics. Howard
Devree of *The New York Times* commented:

> He has risen above mere literal reflection of these times and,
> with subtler brushwork than heretofore, breathes a big spirit
> into these new paintings. By reason of his choice of subjects, his
> painting is static rather than dynamic, but he manages somehow
> to invest even his most purposeless scenes . . . with a truly ter-
> rific sense of the ominous and the foreboding.

Finally, in its summary of 1944, *Art News* listed Ben's exhibition
among the "Ten Outstanding One-Man Shows" of the year, praising the artist as "a skillful master of scale and clear focus, both in
paint and perception."

As was often the case, Ben himself summed up his work best.

The paintings which I made toward the close of the war—the *Liberation* picture, *The Red Stairway, Pacific Landscape, Cherubs and Children, Italian Landscape,* and quite a number of others—did not perhaps depart sharply in style or appearance from my earlier work, but they had become more private and more inward-looking. A symbolism which I might once have considered cryptic now became the only means by which I could formulate the sense of emptiness and waste that the war gave me, and the sense of the littleness of people trying to live on through the enormity of war. I think that at that time I was very little concerned with communication as a conscious objective. Formulation itself was enough of a problem—to formulate into images, into painted surfaces, feelings, which, if obscure, were at least strongly felt.

Ben, obviously pleased by the favorable response to his latest work, had another, and more important, reason to be gratified. Before the 1944 exhibition, his paintings had hung in relatively few museums: New York's Museum of Modern Art and Whitney Museum; the Wadsworth Atheneum, in Hartford; and the Walker Art Center, in Minneapolis. But the success of this most recent show generated sales to museums throughout the country, where his work could be seen by thousands of people. In the eyes of the public as well as the critics, he was now a major figure in the world of American art.

During the period when Ben was celebrating his greatest successes to date, both artistic and financial, he and Tillie were divorced. It was, of course, no surprise to anyone. On August 30, 1943, he had been refused a passport because of a letter from an attorney "saying that if he is permitted to leave the United States his wife and children would be left without support." That same year, the Bureau of Personnel Investigation of the United States Civil Service Commission ruled that he was "ineligible for employment on account of admitted adultery."

The divorce decree became final on October 9, 1944, with a court order "that the marriage heretofore existing between the plaintiff [Tillie] and the defendant [Ben] be dissolved by reason of the defendant's adultery, that plaintiff be freed from the obligations thereof, and that plaintiff be permitted to marry again, but

Shahn told James Thrall Soby that Liberation (1945) *was inspired by "the sight of his own and his neighbors' children swinging around a pole in half-comprehending but real glee after the news had come over the radio that France was at last free of the German occupation forces."*

THE MUSEUM OF MODERN ART, NEW YORK. JAMES THRALL SOBY BEQUEST

that defendant is forbidden to marry any person other than the plaintiff during the lifetime of the plaintiff except by express permission of the court." Tillie was granted custody of the couple's two children, and Ben was ordered to pay her $100 a month, half for her support and half for the support, maintenance, and education of the two children. (These payments would very often be late in arriving.)

It was around this time that Judy again saw her father after many years. She was sixteen years old and about to graduate from New York City's High School of Music and Art. The meeting had been arranged by Milton Friedman, the lawyer who had represented Tillie in the divorce proceedings. It was held in a restaurant on Third Avenue, with Friedman, Tillie, Ben, and Judy all present. Ben spoke of a drawing Judy had recently published in the *New Masses*. He was proud of what she had done, but he suggested that she use another last name if she were to become an artist. Though she now realizes that it was a logical and even protective suggestion, at the time she felt rejected and disinherited.

At that same meeting, it was suggested that Ben help pay for Judy's college. He refused, and Tillie decided to give her daughter the full $100 a month that Ben was to send.

Just before she left for college, Judy received a $25 check from her father. He enclosed a note asking that she use it not for anything she *needed*, but for some luxury. It was a difficult request to grant; it was hard to decide what was a luxury and what was a necessity; even necessities were luxuries for the young woman.

CHAPTER TWENTY-SEVEN

1947:
The MOMA
Retrospective

ON SEPTEMBER 30, 1947, A RETROSPECTIVE OF BEN SHAHN'S
work opened at New York's Museum of Modern Art. It was a great
honor for the artist. Barely forty-nine years old, he was at the time
the youngest American painter to be accorded such a distinction in
the history of the museum. Proof that he had arrived, it marked a
decisive turning point in his career.

The exhibition was a recognition of the unusual popularity he
had achieved in a relatively short time and after only four one-man
shows in New York. This popularity could be explained by his special appeal to a broad public. Part of this public consisted of art
lovers, those who regularly visited galleries and appreciated Ben's
great talent as an artist. The rest was made up of men and women
who never visited galleries or bought art, but who were drawn to
the artist's subject matter—his protest against injustice and his
compassion for human suffering—and were touched by his portrayal of it. Furthermore, and most important, Ben's popular success was the result of the courage and perspicacity of Edith
Halpert, who not only gave him exhibitions but also stubbornly
promoted his work to major museums throughout the country.
Finally, a great deal of credit belonged to officials of the Museum

of Modern Art, who were among the first to recognize Shahn's excellence as an artist.

Ben's relationship with the museum had been a long one, going back to the institution's earliest days. His work was shown in exhibitions in 1930 (less than a year after MOMA's opening in November 1929) and again in 1932. In 1938, *Six Witnesses Who Bought Eels from Vanzetti* was part of the first MOMA exhibition to tour Europe, and two years later he was represented in another MOMA exhibition, "*PM* Competition: The Artist as Reporter." In 1942, Shahn's *Governor Rolph of California* and *Bartolomeo Vanzetti and Nicola Sacco* were included in "Twentieth Century Portraits," an exhibition that included paintings by Eakins, Whistler, Renoir, Bonnard, Chagall, Modigliani, and Rivera. The following year, there were thirteen Shahn works in another MOMA exhibition, "Americans 1943: Realists and Magic Realists," and two paintings, *Pretty Girl Milking a Cow* and *W.P.A.*, were part of a somewhat reduced version of the same show. Finally, in 1947, his large panel *The Passion of Sacco and Vanzetti*, was shown in an exhibition called "Large-Scale Modern Paintings." In that same year, examples of Ben's work were included in an exhibition of recent American advertising art, which traveled both in the United States and in Europe.

In addition to taking part in these exhibitions, Shahn participated in several MOMA-sponsored activities. He spoke as part of "Photography and the Other Arts," an April 1944 program that also included talks by Charles Sheeler, Paul Strand, and Hyatt Mayor; and he took part in a symposium on *Guernica* with Stuart Davis, Jacques Lipchitz, Jerome Seckler, José Luis Sert, and Alfred Barr, Jr.

The idea for the Shahn retrospective undoubtedly originated with two men closely associated with MOMA: Barr, the museum's first director, who was responsible for its growth and who had long admired Shahn, and James Thrall Soby, Barr's close friend and colleague at MOMA.

A man of sensitivity and intelligence, Soby was descended from a wealthy Hartford, Connecticut, family. He showed a passion for art while still young, and in 1930 began assembling what became an outstanding collection. It consisted largely, but not exclusively, of Surrealist art. During the same period, he allied himself with MOMA, working there, paid and unpaid, in a number of capacities for many years.

He first saw Ben's work at the Julien Levy gallery in 1940 (for a time, Soby was a silent partner of Levy's). Impressed, he bought one of the artist's masterpieces, *Vacant Lot,* on behalf of his good friend A. Everett (Chick) Austin, the enterprising director of the Wadsworth Atheneum, where the painting hangs today. Shahn and Soby met briefly in the course of the exhibition, but their long and warm friendship did not begin until 1945, when Soby, who had by then purchased two more of Shahn's finest paintings—*Liberation* and *Fourth of July Orator*— began to gather material, photographs, and illustrations concerning Shahn for an unspecified future project, which was assumed to be a book.

(Left to right) Shahn, Soby, and Amédée Ozenfant at the members' opening of the retrospective at The Museum of Modern Art in New York, September 30, 1947.

The purpose behind Soby's endeavors was finally revealed on April 16, 1946, when the Museum of Modern Art's Exhibition Committee approved a one-man Shahn show, to be directed by Soby. Soby later confessed that he felt a sense of elation that never diminished from the beginning to closing day.

Ben worked closely with Soby. He helped select the works to be exhibited and checked the text of a small book that Soby was preparing in conjunction with the MOMA show. They both agreed (as did Barr, who also edited and corrected Soby's text) that the link between Shahn's photography and his paintings should not be heavily emphasized. Soby was concerned that too close an association between a painting and a photograph might diminish the importance of the art. In his book on Ben, he wrote that "while Shahn's painting often records a photographically arrested reality, its impact is quickened by the most exacting and imaginative painterly means."

There were very few problems. At one point, an elderly museum trustee, angered by the presence of the CIO-PAC posters in the show, demanded their removal. Soby was furious when he heard of this, and threatened to abandon the project if the posters were removed. Half an hour later, René d'Harnoncourt, the museum's director, relieved, reported to Soby that all had been settled.

In early June, Soby wrote Ben that the museum officials had even agreed that the artist could choose the wall colors for the show. Everything, he believed, should be done Ben's way. And in July, the dates were officially fixed: three full months at the end of the year.

The exhibition spanned the entire spectrum of the artist's work. There were illustrations from the *Haggadah;* works from the Sacco-Vanzetti series, the Tom Mooney series, and the Prohibition series; and a study for the ill-fated Rikers Island mural. There were seven posters, a generous selection of photographs, and forty easel paintings. There were, however, relatively few drawings—the medium in which Ben excelled. Ben had given so many away that it was difficult to find enough to show.

In conjunction with this exhibition, Penguin Books published Soby's book on Shahn in its series "The Penguin Modern Painters." Soby emphasized Ben's "relentless integrity" and characterized him as "one of the most gracious of modern American artists" as well as "one of the most varied of living American painters, not only as to pictorial discovery but in prevailing mood and expressive means." The summer issue of the *Bulletin of the Museum of Modern Art* became the catalogue of the exhibition. It revealed that distinguished figures such as Elmer Rice, S. J. Perelman, Mrs. Edward Rowan, Lincoln Kirstein, Roy Neuberger, and Heywood Hale Broun were among the private lenders. Institutional lenders included the Whitney Museum of American Art, the Wadsworth Atheneum of Hartford, the Pepsi-Cola Company, the Phillips Memorial Gallery of Washington, the Walker Art Center of Minneapolis, the City Art Museum of St. Louis, the U.S. Department of State, the OWI, the CIO-PAC, the Jewish Museum, and the Museum of the City of New York.

Critical response to the retrospective was mixed. A few critics were puzzled by Ben's style or styles; several complained that his work was difficult to understand or categorize; some even found it distasteful. But on the whole, Ben was assessed with respect as an important artist.

There is no record of what Ben thought of these reviews, though he usually paid little attention to what the critics had to say. He painted neither for art critics nor for any particular audience. He often said that he painted for only five (sometimes three or four) people. He never knew who the three or four or five people were, but art critics were clearly not among them. Nonetheless, there was one review that must have bothered him: a frequently condescending and often vicious attack in the November 1 issue of *The Nation,* by Clement Greenberg.

The review was disturbing not only because of its content but because of the power and reputation of its author. Greenberg, perhaps the most powerful figure in the art world of the 1940s, was a "starmaker" who believed that the future of American art was in the hands and brush of Jackson Pollock, whose abstractions—so different from Shahn's representational, narrative works—he had enthusiastically acclaimed and promoted.

According to Greenberg, Shahn's work—so obviously of "assignable definition"—was "rarely effective beyond a surface felicity. What his retrospective show at the Museum of Modern Art (through January 4) makes all too clear is how lacking his art is in density and resonance. These pictures are mere stitchings on the border of the cloth of painting, little flashes of talent that have to be shaded from the glare of high tradition lest they disappear from sight."

Greenberg did have a few kind words. Ben's gift was "indisputable," and he had managed to paint "some striking pictures." Furthermore, "on the whole Shahn's art seems to have improved with time. The later pictures become more sensitive and more painterly."

Nonetheless, in Greenberg's view Ben was more a photographer than a painter: he "feels only black and white, and is surest of himself when he orients his picture in terms of dark and light. All other chromatic effects tend to become artificial under his brush."

Greenberg's conclusion was devastating:

> This art is not important, is essentially beside the point as far as ambitious present-day painting is concerned, and is much more derivative than it seems at first glance. There is a poverty of culture and resources, a pinchedness, a resignation to the minor, a certain desire for "quick" acceptance—all of which the scale and cumulative evidence of the present show make more obvious.

Greenberg saw no place for Shahn in the future of American art. The Abstract Expressionists—a term first applied in 1946 to the work of a rather diverse group of artists, once known as the "New York painters," by Robert M. Coates in *The New Yorker*—constituted the wave of that future. In 1946 acrylic paint was first used by Pollock, Barnett Newman, Ad Reinhardt, and Morris Louis. The following year, that of Ben's MOMA show, Pollock created his first drip paintings, and the Abstract Expressionists gained formal recognition and prestige when one of them, William Baziotes, won the first prize at the Thirty-eighth Annual Exhibition at the Art Institute of Chicago. Ben was far removed from this movement, and to many critics his work appeared old-fashioned. His art, however, remained very much in demand. It seemed that there was a buyer as soon as each painting was finished and his prices were rising steadily. "I wonder," Bernarda told Betty Chamberlain of *Art News,* "when we can afford to own a Shahn painting."

CHAPTER TWENTY-EIGHT

Fame, a Mine Disaster, and the Hickman Family

SHORTLY AFTER THE CLOSE OF BEN'S MOMA RETROSPECTIVE, *Look* magazine published the results of a poll which confirmed that Ben, though on the way to becoming "unfashionable," remained one of the most popular contemporary painters in America.

Sixty-eight leading museum directors, curators, and art critics across the country were asked in confidence the following question: "Which ten painters now working in the United States, regardless of whether they are citizens, do you believe to be best?" Thirty-nine replied, and most often named these artists, in order: John Marin, Max Weber, Yasuo Kuniyoshi, Stuart Davis, Ben Shahn, Edward Hopper, Charles Burchfield, George Grosz, Franklin Watkins, and, tied for tenth place, Lyonel Feininger and Jack Levine. In a follow-up poll, the results of which were also published by *Look,* the winning artists, who had not yet learned of the results of the first poll, were asked the same question. Once again, Marin was at the top of the list. Otherwise, the artists chose men who had won the first poll: Grosz, Davis, Kuniyoshi, Shahn, and Weber. The artists differed from the critics by adding Max Beckmann, Philip Evergood, John Sloan, and Rufino Tamayo to this select list.

Now Ben had been formally accepted by professionals in his field and, at the same time, his popularity spread as the retrospective traveled throughout the country. Crowds in Boston, Baltimore, Northampton (Massachusetts), Minneapolis, Portland (Oregon), San Francisco, and Austin responded enthusiastically to the show. Because his art was so accessible, he was called "the people's painter." However, this very popularity, and his ability to communicate with unsophisticated viewers, made it easy to dismiss Shahn's painting as superficial and facile, and to ignore the fact that he was not only a highly skilled, honest artist of sensitivity and compassion, but perhaps the finest draftsman of his time.

The season of 1947–1948 was a successful one for Ben. According to a list prepared for him by the Downtown Gallery, during that period his work was shown at the Milwaukee Art Museum, the Fort Worth Art Museum, the University of Wisconsin, Columbia

Shahn and Alexander Calder, the artist whose company he enjoyed most, in Rome (Porta Portese).

University, Memphis's Brooks Museum of Art Gallery, the University of Indiana, the Carnegie Institute of Pittsburgh, Philadelphia's Pennsylvania Academy of the Fine Arts, the Detroit Institute of Art, the Virginia Museum of Fine Arts, the University of Iowa, the University of Nebraska, the Whitney Museum, the Des Moines Art Center, and the Art Institute of Chicago.

As his reputation grew, Ben's circle of friends and acquaintances inevitably widened well beyond the world of Jersey Homesteads (which had changed its name to Roosevelt following the death of FDR) and the world of progressive politics. He met Alexander Calder, one of the few artists who became a close, lifelong friend. They were compatible politically and in other ways. Calder disliked talking and theorizing about art as much as Ben did. He also enjoyed telling a good story. S. J. Perelman, a man who made a living from telling good stories, also became a friend and admirer. The two met through Philip Shan (Ben's brother, who had become a successful accountant, dropped the extra "h" for reasons not satisfactorily explained). Perelman had bought Ben's portrait of Governor Rolph of California, from the Mooney series: "When and wherever we do meet," he wrote to Ben, "you can be sure I will seize the opportunity to behave like one of Sinatra's more emotional fans confronted with his idol."

Some of America's most distinguished poets, too, admired Shahn. Archibald MacLeish, whom he had met while in Washington, became a very close friend, and Marianne Moore, to whom he sent his annual Christmas greetings—illustrated booklets of great charm, which he had printed in limited editions—became an enthusiastic fan. William Carlos Williams, a fellow New Jerseyan whose portrait he drew and whose poetry inspired him on one occasion to express in images what the poet had expressed in words, also became a friend.

The famous sought him out. From California Vera Stravinsky sent word that her husband, "a very great admirer of your work," would be coming to New York and would like to invite Shahn for a drink at his convenience. Ben, himself a celebrity now, thoroughly enjoyed the company of other celebrities.

Throughout the 1940s, Ben earned the family's living, and Bernarda took care of the house and, along with Ben, raised their three children. However, Bernarda's considerable talent as an artist was not completely wasted. She was able to work as an illustrator, integrating that with the upkeep of the household and the care of the children, as well as her frequent help on Ben's projects. *Harper's,* for instance, published her drawings, and it was through her dealings there that Ben was given his first assignment by a magazine. He was asked to illustrate an extraordinary article, the longest the magazine had published in many years. It exposed the story of a tragic mine disaster at Centralia, Illinois, which, because of ignorance, laziness, negligence, carelessness, and bureaucratic ineptitude, caused the death of one hundred and eleven miners. The author was a brilliant journalist, John Bartlow Martin, who shared Ben's passion for justice and his anger at the inequities he so often encountered. A tall, thin man with glasses and a collegiate crew cut, he was a powerful writer. He used simple, direct language to arouse a reader's deepest emotions—much as Ben used his simple, incisive, jagged line, which could, as Russell Lynes, his editor at *Harper's,* would later say, "draw blood but it can also draw tears." Shahn and Martin also shared a willingness to work for far less money than they could command elsewhere, given a cause in which they believed and a magazine, like *Harper's,* that they respected.

Lynes became a close, lifelong friend of Shahn. Their relationship began in late 1947, when Lynes sent Ben a manuscript copy of Martin's article. The editor apologetically told the artist how much *Harper's* could afford to pay for the job: only $200. He asked Ben to read the piece and decide just how many illustrations he felt would be necessary. Or, looking at it another way, how much work he would be willing to do for such a sum.

A few days later, Ben called Lynes at home to tell him the article was "wonderful." Lynes noted that when "Shahn says 'wonderful,' it sounds as though he means it. The first syllable takes three times as long as the other two." Ben also told the editor that he would bring some drawings to his office a few days later. Ben turned up at *Harper's* with sixty-four completed drawings—and assured Lynes that there were thirty more at home in case the editor couldn't find what he wanted among the first batch. Once he started work on these illustrations, he said, he just couldn't stop.

Lynes called the selection process heartbreaking. He wanted to use all of the pictures, but finally picked twenty-four to illustrate the twenty-eight-page text. They are among Ben's simplest and most compassionate drawings. Lynes had sent him news photos of the disaster; Ben also brought to the work his understanding of the miners he had known and photographed while working for the FSA years before, as well as his outrage at the violations of safety laws that created dangerous conditions in coal mines throughout the United States.

All of these illustrations, many of them portraits of the miners, are profoundly disturbing, but two stand out. One shows the doomed coal miners seated underground at the bottom of the shaft of the Centralia No. 5 mine, waiting for the time to go "on top" and home. The other is a heart-wrenching scene of a group of wives, seated beneath the clothes their husbands would put on after a day in the mines, waiting patiently but hopelessly for them to return.

Martin's article, "The Blast in Centralia No. 5: A Mine Disaster No One Stopped," was published in March 1948. Shortly thereafter, Lynes gave Ben a second assignment, to illustrate another of Martin's documentaries. He had only three weeks to do it and would be paid $250 for the job. No matter what the pay, Ben could not turn the assignment down.

Martin's piece documented the story of a hardworking, religious black man, James Hickman, who had left his life as a sharecropper in Mississippi to come to Chicago where he hoped to find a better life for his wife, himself, and their seven children. Hickman's search for an apartment led to a dreary attic in a tenement owned by another black man, David Coleman. Soon, Hickman and Coleman quarreled over Coleman's plan to evict all of his tenants and divide the building into a number of smaller apartments. If he didn't get his way, Coleman told Hickman, he would burn the building down.

During the night of January 16, 1947, the tenement did burn down, killing four of Hickman's children. Hickman, distraught and enraged, bought a pistol and killed his landlord. Tried for murder, Hickman was found guilty only of manslaughter and sentenced to two years' probation.

To write this story, Martin not only interviewed Hickman, his

wife, and a number of Coleman's relatives; he also studied histories of black people in America including Gunnar Myrdal's *An
American Dilemma,* a monumental study of America's racial problems. The result was another quietly told but emotionally forceful
plea for an end to injustice. It was not merely Hickman's story,
Martin said, but "a story about slums and housing and race discrimination, the plight of the Negroes in northern ghettos, the seg-
regation that keeps them there and generates explosions like this
fire and what came after it."

Before beginning work on his drawings, Ben questioned Martin
about Hickman, his wife, and their children, and he studied photos of them. He also asked Martin to help him by sketching the
tenement. The two men became friends (Martin wrote that Shahn
had "the kindest eyes" he had ever seen) as well as collaborators.

Ben's sixteen drawings were richer, more detailed, and less spare
than those he had done for the Centralia article. He portrayed the
Hickman shack in Mississippi and the ill-fated brick tenement in
Chicago. There are several portraits of sad-eyed James Hickman
and of his angelic children. There is a memorable image of four
children, intertwined and tragically bound together, captioned
"Fire was made to burn coal and rags, not people. People wasn't
made to burn." And there is the powerful image of an angry flame,
a crown that consumes the doomed tenement building.

Shahn and Martin worked together one more time on Martin's
"The Strangest Place in Chicago," the story of life in the Mecca, a
building constructed in 1891 on Chicago's South Side, which was
designed to be a luxury apartment house but had become what
Martin called "one of the most remarkable Negro slum exhibits in
the world." Their collaboration was published in the December
1950 issue of *Harper's,* which also included Bernarda's illustrations for a Katherine Anne Porter short story as well as illustrations
of a Max Steele story by the twenty-two-year-old Andy Warhol,
who later confirmed that his early work had been influenced by
Ben's.

A great deal has been written about his "incisive line," still
unmistakably recognizable as his own. Bernarda noted in an article published in *Image* in 1949 that it can cut "through the flesh of
his subject to expose his most unpleasant inner workings," but, she

Deeply moved by John Bartlow Martin's article, Shahn created Miners' Wives *(1948).*

insisted, "some of the most compassionate drawings I have seen have come from the brush of Ben Shahn."

Ben, however, believed that even these highly praised drawings fell short of expressing the depths of his feeling. In *The Biography of a Painting* he wrote: "One cannot, I think, crowd into drawings a really towering content of feeling. Drawings may be small, intimate revelations; they may be witty or biting, they may be fragmentary glimpses of great feelings or awesome situations, but I feel the immense idea asks for a full orchestration of color, texture, and form."

Although Ben underestimated the power of his magazine illustrations, they often served him as sketches for later, fully orchestrated paintings. Haunted by the circumstances of the Centralia disaster, Ben painted several new works, including *Miners' Wives, Mine Building, Mine Disaster,* and *Death of a Miner,* which grew out of his involvement with that disaster. Years later, he told Nadja Aisenberg, an interviewer:

> In one instance I had to do a series of illustrations on a mine disaster. I have been quite familiar with mines (my wife comes from mine country and I have been down mines). It was a relatively easy thing, although I had never done anything like it before, but I was really eager to do this assignment. Even when I sent my drawings off to the editor I continued to draw the subject because it intrigued me so much. Over the following two years I made at least six paintings based on this subject. I remember once being at a mine disaster and seeing two rather official-looking gentlemen. They looked like mine inspectors or something—sort of dark clothes. They might have been undertakers. Well, they entered the first painting, and they were in the second painting and they were in the third painting. But they got smaller and smaller, and finally in one painting they were just in the doorway, no bigger than three inches. Then they disappeared completely and never appeared again.

Concerning the Hickman drawings, some of which employed images that later recurred in paintings, he explained in *The Biography of a Painting:*

Sometimes, if one is particularly satisfied with a piece of work which he has completed, he may say to himself, "well done," and go on to something else. Not in this instance, however. I found that I could not dismiss the event about which I had made drawings—the so-called "Hickman Story." In the first place, there were the half-realized, the only intimated drawings in a symbolic direction which were lying around my studio; I would develop some of them a little further to see what might come of them. In the second place there was the fire itself; I had some curious sense of responsibility about it, a sort of personal involvement. I had still not fully expressed my sense of the enormity of the Hickman fire; I had not formulated it in its full proportions; perhaps it was that I felt that I owed something more to the victim himself.

In the end, it was his art that was of the greatest importance for Ben, and he told Aisenberg:

Painting can become, and has become for me, a way of life, so that inevitably I can express almost anything I feel better in that medium than in any other medium. And that would be equally true for anyone engaged in other fields. Of course, there are times when I wish I could sing, and I can't. There are times when I wish I could write, and I can't. Often I have started to write something and have abandoned it because of the insurmountable difficulties. I found I could say what I wanted to say much more effectively in a drawing or a painting. It is a way of life that is sometimes hard to make younger people understand. I am consulted constantly by students here about painting as a career. They think of it in terms of a livelihood or in terms of a profession, and I try to tell them about my feeling that painting covers every experience a human being can have. And consequently, . . . I have not felt that there was any other medium that I could use more effectively to express what I want to say, or what I feel in the world around me, or about my inner world, than the one I feel most at ease with.

CHAPTER TWENTY-NINE

Social Realism
to
Personal Realism

BEN'S FIRST ONE-MAN SHOW AFTER THE MOMA RETROSPEC-
tive was held at the Downtown Gallery in the fall of 1949. Most of
the works were new, and many of them had to be lent to the exhibition by such knowledgeable collectors as Nelson Rockefeller,
Walter Paepcke, Wright Ludington, Duncan Phillips, and the
Smith College Museum of Art, evidence that much of Ben's output
was purchased even before it was publicly exhibited.

The critical reception to Ben's work gave no indication that it
was no longer fashionable. Critics did, however, note a fact of great
significance: Ben was moving from what had been called social
realism to a personal realism, an observation previously made by
the artist himself. Howard Devree of *The New York Times*, while
pointing out Ben's "steady and striking advance as a colorist," also
commented that "for those who were once inclined to dismiss
Shahn as a social content painter, such a picture as *Summertime*
will be a revelation," as would several other paintings that demon-
strated the artist's gentle sense of humor and wit.

Thomas B. Hess, who would before long turn against Ben's work
as he became an avid admirer of the Abstract Expressionists, called
Ben "one of the very few living American painters of his generation

who is accepted as a major artist by almost our entire informed body of critical opinion."

In judging Ben's latest exhibition, Robert M. Coates of *The New Yorker* complained that the MOMA retrospective had been poorly timed, since it came during a period when the artist's style was changing radically, "giving an inconclusive impression of the man's career." Viewing the latest work, Coates was encouraged, however. He found some faults, which, he believed, "are those of excess, which are always better than those of caution," but he concluded his review on a positive note: "For all that, Shahn is still one of the few really talented American artists today."

Emily Genauer, writing in *Art Digest,* also noted the change in Ben's work; she, too, thought the retrospective should have been

In his second Harvard Lecture, "The Biography of a Painting," Shahn described the origins of Allegory *(1948).*

assembled somewhat later in the artist's career. She now found, for the first time, a freshness and lightness in some of his work, and she thoroughly approved of the change.

Among the canvases in this 1949 exhibition was one of Ben's most compelling works, *Allegory*. Its central image of a great red beast—part lion and part wolf—with its head encircled in angry flames, its body standing over the huddled, intertwined figures of four dead children, was, of course, derived from Ben's drawings for the Hickman story. It is a large, powerful, and disturbing painting.

Allegory had been seen once before, as part of the Whitney Museum's Annual Exhibition of Contemporary American Painting in November 1948. At that time, one critic, Henry McBride of *The New York Sun*, in the past a great admirer of Ben's work, took issue with the painting. His objections were not artistic but political. Though admitting that Shahn was one of his favorite American artists, "one of our half-dozen best," he complained that *Allegory* appeared to be against the "American way of life . . . and to be paying what looked very much like a subtle tribute to our quondam friend but present enemy, the Soviet Republic." McBride based this charge, in large part, on the color red that the artist employed.

"The political implications that cling to his work I have always thought to be the shadiest," he continued. "The shade often is red, and it is this time. His *Allegory* gives you a rampant lion painted so enthusiastically in red that it is positively subversive. This lion has chewed up several small people and is looking for more people to chew up and he is looking in this direction." In the end, however, McBride expressed the hope that Ben would be forgiven by the public:

> For myself I pay no attention to the politics or the morals of my artists. All I ask of them is to be good painters and in this way Ben Shahn certainly qualifies. There is a chuckling vivacity and a decorative beauty to his performances even when charged with dynamite as on the present occasion that so pleases me that I keep hoping the public attention will focus upon the art rather than upon the insinuation. I would certainly hate to see Ben Shahn boxed up with the Dean of Canterbury and sent away to wherever it is that they send disturbers of the peace.

Ben remembered the review—not too accurately, however, since he recalled that McBride recommended that he be deported, when the opposite was true. Nonetheless, he did accurately remember its angry tone; he even used the review as the starting point for *The Biography of a Painting*. This lecture, which he gave almost a decade later, contained a careful analysis of the painting meant to discover, in his words, "what really was in it, what sort of things go to make up a painting . . . to what extent I could trace the deeper origins, and the less conscious motivations."

Among these origins were the terrifying fires of his childhood, the flames that devoured the Hickman house many years later, a cat he had once owned who had eaten her own kittens, the feared wolf of Russian folklore, history, and literature, and the well-known Roman sculpture of Romulus and Remus being suckled by the she-wolf—who, Ben had long believed, was really about to destroy them. *Allegory*, the artist concluded, was "an idea painting . . . and also a highly emotional painting, primarily an image, a paint image."

Though admittedly "disconcerted" by McBride's words, Ben was not unduly surprised by his charges. It was not the first time, nor would it be the last, that a critic had completely misunderstood his work. In fact, in responding to McBride, he brushed aside the critic's far-fetched charge that the painting was politically moti vated and discussed it solely as he believed it had to be discussed: as a work of art.

CHAPTER THIRTY

Beginning
of a
Witch-hunt

IN SPITE OF WHAT CAN ONLY BE CALLED THE FOOLISHNESS OF his interpretation of *Allegory,* Henry McBride was a distinguished and widely respected critic, known for both his astute judgment and his graceful and inventive way of expressing himself. However, he seems to have felt the need to distance himself from Ben's politics—his association with leftist causes and with Rivera's mural— even as far back as 1932. Then, in a review of Shahn's *Sacco and Vanzetti* series, he wrote: "I am not a communist myself, and I thought the Sacco and Vanzetti trial was conducted fairly, but that does not prevent me from taking an unholy joy in Mr. Shahn's violent arguments to the contrary."

McBride's disavowal of any taint of Communism was certainly not unusual—especially in the late 1940s, when the United States was in the midst of a wave of anti-Communist hysteria. Relations with the Soviet Union had deteriorated in 1946, shortly after the war. At first, Americans feared Soviet military aggression; this was followed by an even greater fear of a Communist threat at home. It was a period of loyalty oaths and security checks, when leftist political sentiments were all too often confused with disloyalty. In the beginning, only government employees were affected. In time, however, the House Committee on Un-American Activities, charged with the task of keeping watch for any signs of Communist infiltration, was examining the influence of Communism in all segments of society, even the fine arts. Ben, who was outspoken in his espousal of progressive social causes (though he was too much an individualist to become much of a joiner), was naturally a target of the Red-hunters.

Ben's first brush with government censorship of the arts took place in 1947 when the State Department, in answer to the requests of several governments around the world, organized a two-part traveling exhibition (half for Europe, half for Latin America) of modern American art. "Advancing American Art" was meant to demonstrate the importance the American government placed on the arts as well as the excellence of that new American art, then little known outside the United States. It comprised seventy-nine paintings, for which the State Department had paid some $55,000. Among these were three of Ben's: *Renascence, Hunger,* and *The Clinic.*

The tour was an unexpectedly short one. Attacks by right-wing Republicans, as well as members of the press, both of whom cited the leftist politics of the artists, including Shahn, as well as the nature of the paintings (after seeing Kuniyoshi's *Circus Rider,* President Truman, no art lover, commented, "If that's art, I'm a Hottentot"), persuaded Secretary of State George Marshall to withdraw the exhibition. The paintings had up to that point been shown only in Haiti and Czechoslovakia. They were deemed "subversive" by the State Department and accused of projecting a false image of the United States; on May 6, 1947, Marshall announced that in the future no taxpayers' money would be spent on modern art. This abrupt cancellation was vigorously protested by a number of artists' organizations, but to no avail. The paintings were shown at the Whitney Museum for one month, after which the War Assets Administration sold the entire collection for a ridiculously low sum, little more than $5,000.

Two years later, the attack on modern art intensified. It was renewed by a Republican congressman from Michigan, George A. Dondero. He deplored government participation in what he called "radical, left-wing art" and derisively called attention to the small amount realized by the government from the sale of the paintings bought for the ill-fated 1947 tour. This was proof that "radical, left-wing art cannot survive of itself. It does not have merit, and its creators do not have the real talent to cause sufficient demand for their product from the public." The congressman deliberately distorted the facts by ignoring the special circumstances of the sale. The War Assets Administration had solicited bids; the winners totaled almost $80,000, far more than the "ten cents on the dollar" Dondero claimed. However, WAA rules required that tax-supported schools and museums get a 95 percent discount, and priority had to be given to bids from veterans' and totally tax-supported institutions. Consequently, many of the high bids were rejected.

Having in this way established modern art as worthless in the marketplace, Dondero went on to call his colleagues' attention to another shocking situation. Special art exhibitions, organized by a MOMA official, were being held for patients at the United States naval hospital in the St. Albans neighborhood of New York City. Among the works shown were paintings by "individuals of known radical affiliation." Ben, of course, was on the congressman's list. The organizations to which he had belonged and the causes which he had supported, according to Dondero, included the John Reed Club, the American Artist's Congress, the Artist's Union, the New Masses art auction, and the State Department show; also, he had been an "assistant to Diego Rivera on the Radio City mural later destroyed because of Lenin's figure."

Outraged that this group of "Communists" had been allowed to spread their message to a captive audience in a naval hospital at government expense, Dondero promised more to come. He assured the members of Congress that he would furnish them with additional facts that "will arouse your indignation as they have aroused mine, and instill in you an enlarged determination to see that these subversive movements are thwarted, and that Americanism is permitted to continue its healthy growth."

Dondero, who later called Joseph McCarthy "a man of moral courage," continued his relentless attack two weeks later. His subject was the "Communists' maneuver to control art in the United States"; his specific target was the Artists Equity Association and its board, which included Shahn. Repeating the list of Communist organizations to which Ben had belonged in the past, he declared that "right up to the present he has continued his revolutionary aim." "Modern" art was synonymous with Communist art, the congressman warned: "We are dealing with a subtle enemy. Let every citizen be on guard against this insidious menace to our way of life."

A few weeks later, Dondero again addressed the House on the subject of art. This time he attacked the American Contemporary Art Gallery as well as the majority of American art critics—most of whom, he declared, were Marxist. He assured his listeners that it was not his purpose "to suggest that newspapers should clap censorship on their art critics," but he also urged that "if this condition of overemphasis and an attempt to glorify the vulgar, the distorted and the perverted has come about due to neglect and lack of proper supervision, then it is high time that some of our newspapers start cleaning house in the smaller compartments of their organizations."

Much of Dondero's next speech complained of European artists, who had either lived in America or influenced American artists. The "isms," as he calls them, were to blame. These "instruments of destruction" included Futurism, Cubism, Dadaism, Expressionism, "abstractionism," and Surrealism. He took potshots at Paul Klee, Joan Miró, Henry Moore, Max Ernst, Marcel Duchamp . . . and finally zeroed in on the Museum of Modern Art. One of that museum's crimes was to have published a book on Shahn,

> that proponent of social protest in art, whom we have tagged as a Communist-fronter and member of the John Reed Club, in a previous address. Shahn would seem to be one of the pets of the Museum of Modern Art. Does the museum approve, as well, of the company he keeps? Ben Shahn, Diego Rivera, José Clemente Orozco, and David A. Siqueiros are among the most outstanding proponents of social protest in art in North America. The three last named are Mexican Communists, but all have been active in the United States. As I have previously stated, Shahn aided Rivera in painting the murals at Rockefeller Center, which were removed as Communist, and unacceptable.

Orozco and Siqueiros were delegates to the American Artists Congress—cited as Communist created and controlled—and Shahn was a signer of the call for that same congress. Orozco and Siqueiros read papers before the Congress meeting at the New School for Social Research in February of 1936.

Dondero's irresponsible charges did not go unanswered. The editors of *Art News* and *Art Digest* responded angrily, as did Emily Genauer in *Harper's* and James Thrall Soby in the *Saturday Review of Literature*. Soby found a silver lining to Dondero's attack: "Indeed, almost the only encouraging factor in the current witch hunt is that it has united American art circles in protest as I have never seen them united before. Those of us who believe that freedom of expression is not a helpful condition but an absolute requirement of art *must* stand together against reactionary irresponsibility."

Ben himself did not respond publicly at the time. He neither changed his way of living nor his artistic and political affiliations. His art continued unequivocally to express his anger. However, in one of his Harvard lectures delivered almost ten years later he took aim at the congressman from Michigan and the danger he represented. The lecture was called "On Nonconformity":

> Art has not yet come in for its official purgation, although it is understood to be on the docket. Nevertheless it has had its own ordeal of conformity. And it has its own Congressional scourge in the person of a Midwestern Congressman who provides the *Congressional Record* with periodic messages under the heading: "Extension of Remarks by Congressman Dondero." In the shelter of his privilege he has recorded a list of artists whom he has designated as "international art thugs," "art vermin," "subversives of art," and so on. To museums and museum directors, that is, those interested in contemporary art, he has attributed reprehensible motives and practices. He regards modern art forms as a disguised plot to undermine our morals and our "glorious American art." Such are the bludgeons of conformity.
>
> So alerted, some sections of the public have felt that the call was for them, and have rallied to the cause of watchfulness. Civic groups or veterans' groups—all sorts of organizations and

their committees and their auxiliaries have assumed the solemn duties of the judging and screening of art. Crusades have developed in a number of places with some work of art as their subject. A mural in the process of execution in a federal building just barely survived a campaign to have it removed because it contained a portrait of Roosevelt. Another just barely survived because someone thought it failed to express American ideals. On a sail in a painting of a regatta a city councilman professed to have discovered a Communist symbol, and he sought to close the exhibition of which the painting was a part. (The symbol turned out to be that of a Los Angeles yachting club.) Another large painting was vetoed because it contained nudes.

Congressman Dondero continued to complain about "the Red art termites" until he left the House of Representatives in 1957, still convinced that far too many artists and museums continued to be "used" to "present American art as Moscow would like it to be."

CHAPTER THIRTY-ONE

A Premature Biography and a Premature Death

BEN'S FIRST RETROSPECTIVE, AT THE MUSEUM OF MODERN Art, had been held when he was not yet fifty years old and was in the middle of his career; he was the subject of a biography published when he was only fifty-two. The book was *Portrait of the Artist as an American: Ben Shahn, a Biography with Pictures,* and the author was Selden Rodman, a writer, editor, and art critic. In the 1930s, he edited a political magazine exploring American alternatives to Marxism, and in 1947 he wrote a biography of the American naïve painter Horace Pippin. He was best known, however, for his pioneering studies of "popular" painting in Haiti, and was for a time codirector of the Centre d'Art in Port-au-Prince. Author of *Renaissance in Haiti,* he also initiated and supervised the painting of the apse and transepts of the Cathedral of St. Trinité in Port-au-Prince.

It was through his profound admiration for these naïve Haitian artists that Rodman developed his interest in Shahn. Was there, he had wondered, an American artist who was giving as true an account of himself and his civilization as these Haitians were of what he believed to be their less complex environment? His answer, arrived at after much study, was yes: Ben Shahn was just such an artist. Shahn, he believed, "consciously, out of a painful apprenticeship to the centuries of Western painting, had managed to devise an expert means of simple communication," one that the masters of Haitian art had arrived at by instinct. Rodman wanted not only to tell the story of Shahn's life but also explain how this American artist had managed to achieve the directness of these Haitians.

The book, published by Harper & Brothers in the fall of 1951, was widely reviewed and, for the most part, enthusiastically praised as an important contribution to the literature of American art. Attesting not only to the importance of the book but, even more, to the importance of its subject, *The New York Times Book Review* devoted the first page of its October 21 issue to what the reviewer, the distinguished art historian James Thomas Flexner, praised as "this story of a meaningful life, evoked in all its complexity . . . a work of art in itself."

Some critics had one major complaint: Rodman's reverse chronology. The narrative begins in 1949 and moves backward. The last section describes Shahn's birth, and the last sentence is, "He was born in Kovno the morning of September 12, 1898." This device was not merely irritating; it was frequently confusing.

Rodman, however, was pleased with the biography. After reading the proofs he wrote Ben that he considered it "the most interesting if not the best that has been written about an American artist," adding that Ben deserved no less than that. Ben apparently agreed that Rodman had done a good job; he wrote an editor at Harper & Brothers that the "great beauty of the work lies in its critical and philosophic outlook." Whether he approved of Rodman's approach to his subject—he knew in advance that the book was to end with his birth—or of all his ideas is unclear, but while the book was being researched and written, the biographer and his subject established a warm relationship. Rodman's wife, the writer Maia Wojciechowska, became especially fond of Ben, though they disagreed completely about politics as well as many other matters. One argument centered on Ben's assertion that the Polish people, in general, were anti-Semitic. Wojciechowska disagreed; only the Polish peasant class was anti-Semitic, she responded. To prove her point, she introduced Ben to a Polish friend who was obviously not a "peasant." To her dismay and surprise, her friend did make comments that were clearly anti-Semitic. The next time Ben saw Maia he presented her with a small drawing. It showed a rabbi, with a menorah, entering a synagogue; underneath it were the words "Maia, do you remember?" When her Polish friends saw the drawing they would conclude that she was Jewish, Ben told her; from that time on she most certainly would notice a change in their attitude toward her.

As far as Rodman was concerned, Ben was in one way the ideal subject for a biography, since he cooperated fully with his biographer. He accompanied Rodman on a visit to Brooklyn, pointing out the places where he spent his childhood, granted him lengthy and frequent interviews, and urged his friends and associates to help him whenever they were called upon to do so. Ben firmly believed that Rodman alone was responsible for the contents of the book, and he was determined not to interfere. Nonetheless, he asked to read the finished manuscript and suggest changes. Rodman agreed. Furthermore, in response to the inevitable questions posed by the publisher's attorney, Ben took the opportunity to clarify, once and for all, his political opinions and affiliations. He had never been a member of the John Reed Club, he asserted. Furthermore, he was not a Communist; indeed, since the very early 1930s he had been an opponent of Communist activities. Nor was he a Marxist; nor had he ever claimed to be one. Finally, he wanted to be certain that any criticism of Mrs. Rockefeller, who had befriended him and was a devoted patron of the arts, be eliminated from the book. In every way he could, he was eager that this biography answer all accusations of subversive, radical activity that had been and were still being raised against him.

After receiving Ben's suggestions, Rodman replied that he had made the corrections and that the book was now "tidied up, politically speaking, the way you wanted it, and if you're now mistaken for a good 'liberal,' or even an anti-Stalinist that Clement Greenberg would approve of, don't blame me!"

Ben asked for one other change. It regarded Rodman's portrayal of Tillie as a rather dull, convention-bound housewife, rather than the spirited, intelligent woman she was. He asked Rodman, who had interviewed Tillie, to delete any uncalled-for mention of "horn-rimmed spectacles," as well as a statement that she "looked a little like a peasant." He found Rodman's references to Tillie throughout the book unnecessarily harsh and could not see that they served any purpose in being so—"and even if they did," he added, "I would object."

＝＝＝

Sadly, Tillie never had a chance to read Rodman's biography. In September 1951, just before the book was published, she died in a hospital on Cape Cod, near her small house in Truro. She had gone to Truro to spend the Labor Day weekend with Judy, who had recently finished college in Mexico.

The cause of Tillie's death was a cerebral hemorrhage. She was fifty-four years old. Her life since Ben left her had been a very difficult one. As a single mother, she had struggled for many years to support her two children and herself. Helped only by Ben's erratic $100-per-month child support payments, she was forced to take a full-time job whenever she could find one. Her last job, which she had held since November 1941, was at the Institute of Pacific Relations, a nonprofit research organization that published the journal *Pacific Affairs*. On her salary as office manager and book-keeper, she was able to rent a small apartment at 59 West Twelfth Street in Manhattan. In late 1950 or early 1951, she lost that job because of office rivalries, scandals, and personal matters with which she was really not involved but to which she had inadvertently become privy. Presumably because she was so good at her work—she was known as a superb organizer—Tillie was allowed to remain at the institute at half pay until she found another job. Finding employment, however, was not easy. In desperation, she even tried to improve her chances by taking a few years off her age on her résumé. This was of no avail, however, and at the time of her death she was unemployed.

When Tillie was brought to the hospital in Hyannis, the doctors urged Judy to notify Tillie's other relatives (she had, of course, been in touch with Ezra). Judy phoned her uncle Philip Shan, who in turn would contact Tillie's sisters. He asked Judy whether he should tell Ben of Tillie's imminent death. Though Judy was opposed to the idea, Phil took matters into his own hands and telephoned his brother.

Ben arrived in Hyannis as soon as possible, shortly after Tillie's death. He immediately took charge of the situation: he arranged for the funeral service and the burial in a local cemetery, and he consoled Judy. Although Tillie's Orthodox Jewish relatives expected Judy to join them in Brooklyn to sit shivah, Ben protested: he decided, and Judy agreed, that the two of them should take a trip together through New England. During the past few years, Judy had seen her father from time to time. She had slowly grown closer to him. He had critiqued her painting (she was at the beginning of a successful career), and she found it easy to talk to him. The time they spent together during this trip in 1951 was the beginning of a genuine adult closeness between father and daughter.

CHAPTER THIRTY-TWO

Integrity
and
Commercial Art

EVEN WHEN THE ECONOMY WAS PROSPERING, THE WORK OF
few American artists sold well enough to support the artist. To
make a living, artists (including Shahn) had to work at jobs unre-
lated to their art, engage in commercial work (advertising or magazine illustration), or find a teaching position.

Ben chose commercial art because for him there was little distinction between that and fine art, and he declared his intention to
do his own art in his own way, no matter the context. He also chose
teaching, because it gave him the opportunity to leave the seclu-
sion of his studio and make contact with people whose company
stimulated him.

His views on commercial art versus fine art were explained in a
speech given at the Franklin School in New York City in 1950. If
artists approached their commercial art with the same standards
and care that they applied to their fine art, he believed, there was
really no line of demarcation between the two; commercial art was
no less important than was fine art. Craftsmanship, he felt, was an
essential element in commercial art. Commercial artists had to
know their tools, their media, and the methods of reproduction.
They should be experts in lettering and familiar with typefaces as

well as with production problems and costs. Ideally, in fact, a commercial artist should be a production manager as well as an artist.

There was one rule, however. Commercial art, to be of real value, had to reflect the ideas and integrity of the artist who was the innovator, inventor, and originator. The commercial artist—and this was a point Ben emphasized—must not give in to the whims or wishes of the art director or the client. Absolute integrity was essential, the only condition under which an artist could successfully work. Commercial art, Ben told Selden Rodman in the late 1940s, was "something I'd never undertake under my own steam, but something I am now in a position to do on my own terms and which offers a challenge to my ingenuity in what I conceive to be the primary function of art: communication."

Maintaining his integrity as an artist was never a problem for Ben, nor would it ever be. He was not only unwilling to compromise in order to satisfy a client or an art director; he was, most probably, unable to do so. He was willing to offer an entirely new work to a client rather than alter in any way something he believed was already satisfactory. Ben's respect for his commercial art is evident in the results of his efforts. Everything he did reveals not only his great technical skill, but also his unfailing honesty, compassion, and, at times, wit.

In 1943 he was introduced to Charles Coiner, the art director and vice president of Philadelphia's N. W. Ayer and Son, the oldest and, at the time, the fourth largest advertising agency in the United States. Coiner and Shahn were a perfect match. The former in no way fit the stereotype of an advertising executive. Tall and lean, with a cropped gray mustache, he habitually came to work wearing a battered hat and what could at best be described as "casual" clothes, belying the importance of his position. His demeanor was equally surprising for a man of his profession. Neither aggressive nor pretentious, he dominated business conferences by the quiet force of his personality and because he knew exactly what he wanted and why. He was widely acknowledged as the advertising art director who first, and most successfully, bridged the gap between fine art and advertising art. Just as N. W. Ayer was known to use novelists and poets to write copy for their ads, Coiner delighted in employing "serious" artists, with no experience in commercial work, to design and create paintings for use in his advertisements.

Because Ben's taste and standards resembled Coiner's, the two men were able to work in harmony for many years. Among the Ayer clients for whom Shahn prepared advertisements were the Lederle Laboratory, the Hawaiian Pineapple Company, and Capehart. For Capehart, he was asked to produce an advertisement for a recording of *Peter and the Wolf*. The result became one of his most reproduced works: a painting showing two children, each masked—one as Peter and one as the wolf—face to face in the woods, attempting to frighten each other. In spite of the excellence of this small painting, Capehart rejected it on the grounds that a detail on the sneaker of one boy was inaccurately depicted. Shahn firmly refused to make even this minor change—as Capehart had been told in advance he would do. He took the painting back and brought it to the Downtown Gallery, where it was almost immediately bought by the distinguished art critic Aline Louchheim.

Coiner learned from the very beginning that the fewer instructions Ben got, the better the results. "The usual procedure in constructing an advertisement is for the agency sketch-artist to rough out a layout showing how the text is to be illustrated," he wrote in John D. Morse's excellent anthology of writings about and by Shahn.

This is submitted to the client for approval before negotiations begin with the artist who is to do the final work. If approved, this artist "finished" the art, not deviating from the basic idea of the sketch. In the case of Shahn we submitted the *artist* to the client, saying that it would be ridiculous for him to follow a sketch-artist's work. The idea was well received, and Shahn then made a finished work. He said that if his work was not approved he would like to have it back, and there would be no charge. . . . Shahn's approach to advertising art was similar to that of some of the great French painters. If the price is right and they are given carte blanche on execution, most will accept a commission for a painting or design for industrial use—display advertising, posters, or even fabric design. Shahn proved that in this country, too, fine art can be used in advertising to the advantage of both the advertiser and the artist.

Ben's most distinguished work in the field of advertising was done for one of Ayer's most interesting and forward-thinking clients, the Chicago-based Container Corporation of America. He established a close relationship with Walter Paepcke, the company's president, as well as with Egbert Jacobson, its art director, both of whom appreciated Ben's art as well as his technical skill in adapting that art to the company's needs. In 1945, Ben, Leo Lionni, and Coiner traveled to Chicago together to attend the opening of an exhibit of Container art, "Modern Art in Advertising," held at the Art Institute of Chicago.

Ben and Lionni spent hours wandering through the city, including its stockyards and the Lithuanian section; Ben especially admired the costumes of the Lithuanian residents. Together, too, they joined a distinguished group of artists—among them Fernand Léger, Willem de Kooning, and Man Ray—at a gala dinner preceding the opening of the exhibition. And Ben's association with the CCA continued a few years later when he and Lionni both attended a prestigious CCA-sponsored design conference held at Aspen, Colorado. Lionni, who became a successful designer as well as a prolific author of enormously popular children's books, greatly admired Ben's skills. He believes to this day that Shahn exerted and still exerts a strong influence on graphic artists all over the world.

Ben's participation in these CCA events identified him as a member of the "team" that was, in many ways, changing the face of advertising in the United States. Largely thanks to Paepcke's vision and through his efforts, the Container Corporation of America in 1950 launched a daring, innovative campaign that established it as more than merely a manufacturer of boxes: the "Great Ideas of Western Man" series. Each ad contained a very brief quotation from the work of a Western writer, illustrated by a distinguished artist's interpretation of that quotation. There was never any sales copy. The purpose of these ads was not to sell any particular product—no product was ever mentioned—but to familiarize the public with CCA and its high standards of quality. The copy read simply: "Great Ideas of Western Man . . . one of a series." Somewhere on the page the words "Container Corporation of America" appeared, together with a drawing of a box, the company's symbol.

The ideas expressed in these short quotations fell into three categories: moral, philosophical, and political. The distinguished philosopher, writer, and educator Mortimer Adler of the University of Chicago did the initial research for the quotations; a small committee made the final selection. Their choices included ideas expressed by the greatest thinkers of all time, from Henry Adams to Emile Zola, from Aristotle to Alfred North Whitehead; later, non-Western thinkers were added.

Among the artists selected to interpret these quotations were René Magritte, Philip Guston, Herbert Bayer, Man Ray, Joseph Cornell, Jacob Lawrence, and Milton Glaser, as well as Ben. They were given no instructions or directions. The sole stipulation was that the design must be in some way related to the quotation. These were ideal working conditions for Ben; he would never even be asked to compromise his principles.

In July 1950, Bernarda was asked by N. W. Ayer to illustrate a passage by Thucydides. She had continued working whenever possible but now had to refuse to compromise in advance. Though the time allotted as well as the pay were satisfactory, she found the quotation offensive and refused to associate herself with it. "It is the very essence of the credo behind authoritarian government," she believed, "the thing that's expected of the Communist citizen and of the Fascist citizen."

Ben, fortunately, was never confronted with a similar problem. The three ideas he was asked to interpret did not in any way conflict with his own: one was "John Locke on the Purpose of Government"; "John Stuart Mill on the Training of Men"; and John, Viscount Morley's "You have not converted a man because you have silenced him."

Ben's individualistic approach to commercial art was also manifested in his work for the Columbia Broadcasting System. He worked there on and off for several years, showing clearly that his strength lay in institutional advertising rather than advertising meant to sell a product.

In his early years there, he made a number of distinguished drawings for brochures meant to attract advertisers to the network. He did so together with William Golden, his old friend from the OWI, who had become the network's art director and would soon create the "eye" logo that still identifies CBS today.

The subject of the first CBS brochure, produced in 1947, was the growing problem of juvenile delinquency in the United States. It was to be used in the promotion of a radio program, to be called "The Eagle's Brood." Golden knew it was useless to make any attempt to give his old friend any guidelines, or even suggestions. He merely showed him the material at hand and explained how it was to be used for the radio broadcast. Deeply moved by it, Ben created a drawing that expressed the compassion and outrage he felt. Golden's use of the drawing, Ben believed, effectively enhanced it, and from that time on the two men collaborated with unfailing success at CBS. The second brochure, equally moving, introduced a radio documentary called "Fear Begins at Forty," which dealt with the problems of aging.

In 1948, Ben made a drawing for a brochure pointing out the enormous and complex work done by CBS employees between programs, after the performers had gone home. The drawing, *The Empty Studio,* shows an orchestra pit without musicians, only an expanse of empty music stands and chairs. It became one of Ben's most frequently reproduced drawings and he often joked that the real title was *Local 802* (the musicians' union) *on Strike.*

In 1949, Ben once again conveyed the compassion he displayed in his "serious" art by creating drawings for a brochure promoting a broadcast, "Mind in the Shadow," whose theme was mental illness. The cover of this booklet is characteristic Shahn: the brick walls so often used by the artist, surrounding a locked gate of a prisonlike institution, the sign above it reading "Men's Violent." Inside the brochure are tragic figures of men and women, bent over in emotional agony, made painfully disturbing by the artist's simple, jagged line.

Because of the success of his institutional advertisements, Ben was soon—and frequently—called upon to provide illustrations for a number of magazine articles, as he had done for the John Bartlow Martin pieces for *Harper's.*

His reputation grew; neither his integrity nor the suitability of his illustrations in illuminating the texts assigned to him was ever questioned. The range of subject matter was vast. He made drawings for "U.S. Anti-Semitism Today," by Bruce Bliven, "The Producer Pens a Memo," by Ring Lardner, Jr., and "Test for the

Steelworkers," by Michael Straight, all of which appeared in the *New Republic*. For *Fortune*, he illustrated "Container Corporation of America Gasoline Travels in Paper Packages" and "Honorable Discharge" by George P. Hunt; and he drew several covers for *Business Magazine*. In addition, he illustrated articles and stories for *Seventeen* and *Charm*, as well as pieces for *Masses and Mainstream* and articles by and about Albert Einstein for *Scientific American*.

CHAPTER THIRTY-THREE

The
Teacher

BEN URGED ANY WOULD-BE PAINTER TO OBTAIN A SOLID, DIVER-
sified education, both formal and informal. Although he often
expressed his disdain for formal art schools, he felt they might be
of some limited use. Once, asked by a student which school he
would recommend, he replied that it should be one that had a good
art museum you had to pass through in order to reach. He believed
that drawing anything and at any time was essential to the development of an artist. A job, any kind of job, was important, he felt,
as was reading: artists ought to read all they could about art, by
anyone except art critics. He also advised them to read Sophocles,
Euripides, Dante, Proust, the Bible, Hume, and "Pogo." Poetry of
all kinds was on his list. Math, economics, logic, and, above all,
history were important, as was knowledge of foreign languages,
one of which should be French. Look at and listen to everything;
travel; go to galleries and museums, and to artists' studios when
possible, he told students. He believed a student of art must work
in many mediums and must never be afraid to become embroiled
in art or life or politics. "Never be afraid to learn to draw or paint
better than you already do; and never be afraid to undertake any
kind of art at all, however exalted or however common, but do it
with distinction," he advised.

However, teaching at an art school to make a living was danger-ous for an artist, Ben felt. At a symposium in Andover, Massachu-setts, in 1949, he warned that after an artist turns to teaching, he is in danger of losing his identity as an artist. "I think that the artist as teacher pours so much of his thinking and so much of his energy into other people that he saps his own creative springs at the source," he noted.

In spite of his reservations, Ben taught—and lectured—on sev-eral occasions, and not only to make a living. Obviously, he was unable to resist the opportunity to speak before audiences who were obliged to listen to his often-told anecdotes as well as his often-repeated advice. Frequently didactic and pontifical in social gatherings, he now had license to be so in front of a number of eager students. He spoke slowly and deliberately, enjoying himself, and his listeners were charmed by the expertly delivered words of a warm, genial, intelligent, and articulate painter.

His first job as a teacher came in the summer of 1947, the sum-mer before his MOMA retrospective, when he agreed to head the painting classes at the Boston Museum of Fine Arts summer school, held at the Berkshire Museum in Pittsfield, Massachu-setts. Predictably, a problem arose between Ben and the museum's director. Bud Stillman, a reporter for the *Berkshire Eagle*, remem-bers being asked by Ben to join him at a meeting with the director, who had come to Pittsfield to discuss the matter of giving grades. Ben was strongly opposed to the idea; giving grades to painters, he believed, was degrading. The museum's director remained firm. If Ben wanted to receive a salary, he would have to give grades. Ben's solution was simple: he gave all his students As.

Two years later, Ben taught again, for one week at the University of Wisconsin in Madison. The following year, 1950, he agreed to teach at the summer session of the University of Colorado in Boul-der for ten weeks. He later commented on the attitude of these students:

Whenever I found one who was merely pursuing a hobby, I let it go at that. With the abler students, I was much harder. On sev-eral occasions my criticism was met with this curious rejoinder (which illustrates again some misconceptions about commercial art): "But Mr. Shahn, I'm only going in for commercial art anyway." Of course I would answer, "Oh no you're not—at least not until you learn to draw!"

The students seemed to be under the impression that in commercial art one needs only to be abreast of a current set of tricks. It was my painful duty to point out that if one is painting for oneself alone, for one's own pleasure and no one else's, he might get on without craftsmanship. But in commercial art it is a *sine qua non*. Without it the young aspirant may as well put down his pens and brushes and try something else. Commercial art, contrary to the general conception, is an unyielding taskmaster, a hard school. It is also an excellent school for any artist, *provided it is not abused*.

The year 1951 was an especially busy one for Shahn the teacher. At the beginning of the year, he was hired to replace Max Beckmann, who had recently died, as an instructor for the spring term of the Brooklyn Museum Art School. The school's faculty was a distinguished one. Among its members were Edwin Dickenson, Gabor Peterdi, and Isaac Soyer. Ben was to teach a course in advanced painting and drawing. On the first day of the class, he examined the latest work of his students and was disappointed. Most of it was imitation Beckmann.

One of his first announcements startled the students: he wanted them to work without a model. About eight of them left immediately. Then, Ben, leaning against the model stand, began to talk for what even he considered a very long time. At the end, a student stood up and informed the teacher, with some contempt, that he had come there to study painting and not philosophy. That was all Ben needed to continue. He described the experience:

> I felt good and leaned back on the model stand and asked which of the one hundred and one ways do you want me to teach? I've developed a new technique where you put the canvas on the ceiling and throw the paint this way, you see and it drips down very slowly, so that when you finally mount it on a stretcher these things come out at you. I said, I don't know. I can't teach you how to paint. I vowed when I was a student that

I would never touch anybody's canvas, as my teachers had done. Well, he walked away, and whenever I came around to do a criticism he disappeared. But after a month or so he came over and apologized and said that he had been studying for seven years, and the criticism had always been "you aren't getting that feeling," you know. "Move this over a bit." He had never run into anyone before who talked about the relation of the artist to society. I have been asked this question before: what is the role of the artist in society? The role of the artist *is in* society.

After Brooklyn, Ben traveled to Ohio State University for a week of seminars. His duties there included one formal prepared lecture and a series of seminars—"Painting as a Profession," "Problems and Pitfalls of the Oil Medium," and "Problems and Pitfalls of the Watercolor Medium"—for both graduate and undergraduate students. In addition to these encounters with students, which he enjoyed, there were even more than the usual number of cocktail parties, luncheons, and receptions, which he liked far less.

All of these teaching jobs kept Ben's name before the public and were, to some extent, stimulating. One teaching assignment, however, at Black Mountain College, came to mean more than all the others.

CHAPTER THIRTY-FOUR

Black
Mountain

BEN STAYED AT BLACK MOUNTAIN FOR ONLY FOUR WEEKS, BUT this period was a crucial one which both disturbed and stimulated him and tangibly affected his work. He had a good deal of time to paint and, equally important, to think. His academic obligations were minimal, taking up a few hours a week. After his first meeting with his class, he realized that Black Mountain students were so different from those he had previously taught that it would be useless to hold formal classes. Instead, he decided to devote a set number of hours to his students, leaving a notepad on the door of his studio on which each student could indicate exactly when he or she would like to see the instructor. Given the diversity of the college's small student body, and the independence of each student, it is not surprising that some young artists came to see Ben often, while others never showed up at all.

Ben found himself in a completely unfamiliar and totally undisciplined milieu. Nevertheless, in spite of feeling somewhat uncomfortable in an atmosphere so foreign to him, he began to question his own work and the direction it was taking. He had been profoundly disturbed by the charges of critics like Greenberg who found that he had become old-fashioned and irrelevant, and Black

Mountain allowed him a period of introspection. This proved to be of profound importance in his progress as an artist.

Black Mountain College was a unique experiment in American education. Set in a peaceful small valley in the western part of North Carolina, eighteen miles from Asheville, the college was founded in 1933 by John Andrew Rice, an iconoclastic educator whose dream was to create a community as well as an innovative educational institution. The arts were to be at the core of the curriculum, and most responsibilities were to be shared by the faculty and the students.

Under the leadership of Josef Albers, the German painter and designer who had both studied and taught at the Bauhaus before emigrating to the United States in 1933, Black Mountain flourished. For nearly sixteen years the faculty included some of the most progressive and influential artists of the time: Willem de Kooning, Lyonel Feininger, Franz Kline, Jacob Lawrence, Robert Motherwell, Jack Tworkov, and Philip Guston. Walter Gropius also taught there as did Buckminster Fuller, John Cage, Merce Cunningham, Roger Sessions, and Charles Olson.

But—as Martin Duberman, author of a definitive history of the college, has pointed out –the story of Black Mountain is more than merely a recitation of famous names:

> It is the story of a small group of men and women—ranging through time from a dozen to a hundred, most of them anonymous as judged by standard measurements of achievement—who attempted to find some consonance between their ideas and their lives, who risked the intimacy and exposure that most of us emotionally yearn for and rhetorically defend, but in practice shun.

Of course, Ben welcomed the opportunity to work with such an unconventional group of students and faculty, although many were certain to be younger avant-garde artists and writers who considered his own work passé. Most important, however, he accepted the offer because of the presence at the college of Charles Olson, then the school's rector, a brilliant historian, Melville scholar, and poet whose postmodern poetry influenced the work of many younger poets of his time.

Ben and Olson had become close friends in Washington during the war, when both worked for the OWI. While in the capital, they collaborated on at least one project: Ben did the layout, design, and a photo montage for "Spanish Speaking Americans in the War," a pamphlet Olson had written eulogizing the Spanish-speaking members of the U.S. forces in the Pacific.

They were similar in many ways. They both resigned from the OWI at the same time, distressed that the agency was being taken over by the world of advertising. Each was able to fill a room with his dynamic energy and forceful personality. Physically, too, both were imposing figures; Olson, more than six feet seven inches tall, weighing 240 pounds, resembled an extended, blown-up version of Shahn. But there were other, more basic and not altogether praiseworthy similarities, and a description of Olson by his biographer Tom Clark could, with astonishing accuracy, also describe his friend Shahn:

> He took great ostentatious delight in the company of down-to-earth working people, waitresses, fishermen, truck drivers, and cooks, yet actually spent far more time cultivating the rich and powerful, persons of worldly influence and success in art, politics, business and public life. An unconscious snobbery, whether bred of class insecurity or a natural aristocracy of taste, showed itself in both the earnest climbing and the democratic stooping.

When Ben, Bernarda, and their children arrived at Black Mountain in the early summer of 1951, Olson was emerging as the new leader of an institution which, along with the usual problems of readjustments to administrative and academic changes, was suffering from severe financial problems. The summer was characterized by Wesley Huss, its administrator, as a "three-ring circus."

That summer, Harry Callahan, Arthur Siegel, and Aaron Siskind taught photography; Katherine Litz, who had danced with the Humphrey-Weidman and José Limón modern dance groups and had performed on Broadway in *Carousel* and *Oklahoma!*, taught dance and worked on her own projects; and Lou Harrison, a composer, and David Tudor, a pianist and organist, ran the music department. In addition, there were classes in weaving and woodworking; most important, there was Olson's eccentric and stimulating class in literature.

Black Mountain's students that summer, about sixty of them, included many young men and women who would in later years make their mark on American culture. Robert Rauschenberg was among those who studied painting; Francine du Plessix Gray, who had come to study painting, instead studied writing under Olson. So did Jonathan Williams, who gained prominence as a poet in the years following his summer at Black Mountain. Also present was Suzi Gablik, who later became a well-known painter and a writer and lecturer on the arts.

Neither Ben nor Bernarda enjoyed their month at Black Mountain. She found the college stifling. The endless discussions of aesthetics, she believed, were fruitless, and she was too hard-headed and uncompromising to enjoy them. Both the faculty and the students—with few exceptions—were far too analytical and self involved. When she complained to a poet that no one ever visited the interesting areas around the school, the somewhat condescending reply was, "We're not very folksy around here."

The couple's stay at Black Mountain was undoubtedly colored by disturbing news given them by a local doctor only two weeks after their arrival: Bernarda, the physician informed them, had breast cancer, and it was essential that she undergo a biopsy the following day. Despondent, Ben turned to Olson, his only friend at the college. Sobbing so deeply that his words were difficult to understand, he informed him of the diagnosis. (That diagnosis proved to be incorrect. Laboratory tests showed that the tumor was not malignant.)

Olson's reaction to what seemed to be tragic news, given to him by a man he cared for, was confusing. In a letter written on July 15 to the poet Robert Creeley—though never mailed—he declared that it was time to hold Ben's hand, not only because of Bernarda's illness, but also because Ben was suffering from the presence of "all these little shit painters" at the college. Yet in the next paragraph, he unexpectedly lashed out at Ben, complaining that his art had stood still for more than three years, because he was unable to make the next step, and repeatedly used the same mythologies for years. (To add to the confusion, in a subsequent letter he stated that Shahn is "the only American painter who has ever interested me.")

The rest of the letter was even more puzzling. In it, he complained angrily of Ben's determination to find him in order to share his grief "in that goddamned restless eating nervous unhappy way that great Jews [he was here referring to his mentor Edward Dahlberg] have always dogged my tail." Following an attack on the whole Judeo-Christian humanist tradition, Olson returned to the subject of Shahn, admitting that though his friend troubled him with the intensity of his emotions, Ben remained the source of Olson's greatest satisfaction during the artist's month at Black Mountain.

Ben's last days at Black Mountain were further unsettled by the arrival of Robert Motherwell, who was to take over his painting class for the second half of the summer. Neither artist made any effort to disguise the contempt in which he held the other. In almost every way, they were opposites. Motherwell, the intellectual of the Abstract Expressionists, educated at Stanford, Harvard, and Columbia, represented, for many, the "new art." His style, his ideas, and his philosophy were diametrically opposed to Ben's. Their personalities contrasted sharply as well. Ben delighted and entertained his students with his colorful anecdotes; Motherwell was colder, analyzing works of art with immense intelligence and precision but with none of Ben's charm and wit. Their many disagreements had been aired in public a few years earlier, at a conference sponsored by MOMA. Motherwell had initiated the battle with uncommonly offensive (and, considering his intelligence, somewhat foolish) words about Shahn, labeling him "the leading Communist modern artist in America" and concluding that "his art contains no feeling for real humanity and its capacity for self-realization."

Though these were words that he could never forget, Ben did not respond publicly. But Motherwell came to represent for him all that was wrong with Abstract Expressionism, and his name disappeared from Ben's vocabulary.

Perhaps Motherwell's presence at the college was behind the extraordinary rudeness and insensitivity with which Ben treated another painter whose ideas and art differed radically from his own. That painter was the twenty-six-year-old Robert Rauschenberg, who had been at Black Mountain the previous year. Rauschenberg was not one of Olson's favorites. He was not, the poet believed, "destined for fame."

In spite of Olson's opinion, Ben asked the young painter and his then wife, Susan Weil, if he could come to their apartment to see their work. The two artists, at the beginning of their careers, were eager for Ben's visit. They respected him as a man and admired him as an artist. They cleaned their apartment, prepared dinner, and hung their art on the walls. Ben arrived, ate his meal, but made no comment about the art until it came time to leave. He then turned to his children Susanna, Jonathan, and Abby, who had accompanied him, showed them the paintings, and said, "I just wanted to show you what some people are doing in New York. This is the kind of work you should avoid."

Ben's treatment of Rauschenberg was not an isolated example of his response to highly promising young artists. Certainly, neither Black Mountain nor Motherwell's presence there could excuse or explain his treatment of another young artist a few years later. This time, however, the artist, Bernard Perlin, had been a friend; more than that, Ben had been a mentor and father figure to him ever since they had met when both worked at the OWI.

The incident which destroyed their relationship took place in 1955, when Perlin's paintings were shown at the Catherine Viviano Gallery in New York. It was an important show for Perlin, his first following a long stay in Italy. Toward the end of the opening, Ben called Perlin to ask if he could come to see the show. Although it was late and everyone else had already left, Perlin didn't hesitate. He was overjoyed that a painter who had so greatly influenced him was coming to see his latest work.

When Ben arrived at the gallery, he greeted Perlin warmly, after which the younger painter, eager to spare Ben the embarrassment of having him tag along while he viewed the paintings, tactfully left Ben alone in the gallery. After about ten minutes, Perlin emerged from his hideout in the gallery's office to receive Ben's judgment and say good-bye. To his great surprise, however, Ben was already at the elevator, waiting to open the door and leave. When he saw Perlin approaching, he had only a few words to say: "Well, so long, Bernie." (Perlin hated to be called Bernie, as Ben knew.) He made no comment and offered no criticism. Those were the last words he ever spoke to his "protégé." It was, Perlin remembers, "quiet, gentle murder."

Perlin was crushed and also puzzled by Ben's cruelty. For years, he thought his mentor might have been offended by his use of pebbles—similar to those in Ben's *Pacific Landscape*—in one of his own paintings. It was Ben who had taught him how to paint pebbles many years before. Only recently, he has come to believe that Ben felt he had been betrayed because Perlin's paintings in no way reflected "social content," or "the human condition," but were only unpolitical "pretty" pictures of Italy.

Ben was more than eager to leave Black Mountain. He had had enough of the suffocating atmosphere of the college and enough of most of the people there. Nonetheless, he left on a positive note, since the last few days were, to some extent, a celebration of and a tribute to his stay there.

First, as a member of the old guard, he was praised for his participation in a thoroughly avant-garde mixed-media event, held in the college's dining hall shortly before his departure. It all began when Olson, who had recently returned from a long visit to Mexico where he studied Mayan glyphs (double images most often carved from stone), presented Ben a poem called "A Glyph." In return, Ben gave Olson a drawing inspired by the concept of the glyph. At this point, the scope of the production grew. Olson's poem inspired a dance choreographed and performed by Katherine Litz to modern music written by Lou Harrison, who had studied with Arnold Schoenberg and worked with John Cage. One section of the score, for prepared piano, required "someone's pressing firmly against all the low strings, & at a 'nodal angle,' a heavy piece of wood, as perhaps, 2" × 2", on the sharp edge."

Ben's role was to create paintings that would serve as backdrops for the spectacle, as well as a drawing to be placed on the body of Nick Cernovich, a young dancer. Olson described the drawing in a letter to Robert Creeley as a "combo of a Mayan glyph and a Chinese written charactor."

The two backdrops were long figures, about eight feet by two feet, one called *Nicholas C.* and the other *Downfall*. These works are the first of what Ben referred to as his "palimpsest paintings." These are paintings in which he left traces of preliminary work, corrections and all, which are visible through the painted surface

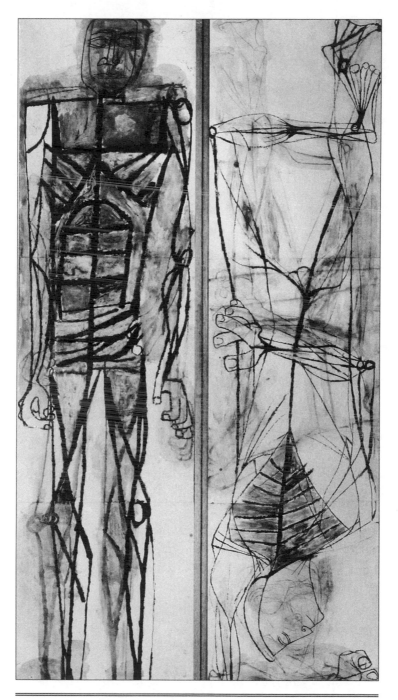

The two backdrops, Nicholas C *and* Downfall, *that he created at Black Mountain College in 1951, are examples of what Shahn called his "palimpsest paintings."*

of the finished work. These faint shadows of earlier, tentative forms give a time dimension to the work. Ben expanded on this several years later in an interview printed in the *Review of Existential Psychology and Psychiatry:* "I have sometimes found myself beginning a picture with an image and coming up with an entirely different one—and I even like the trace of the first that may remain visible within the second—for search and dissatisfaction are real within us, and their shadow may be a telling image."

The Glyph, as Litz called her solo dance, puzzled some members of the audience but pleased others, who applauded it with enthusiasm. It can be assumed that Ben was among the silent ones. A few nights later, Litz performed four of her dances in Ben's honor. Finally, on July 29, Ben gave his final lecture at Black Mountain, "Aspects of Realism." Well-reasoned, perceptive, and thoroughly intelligent, it answered the question "What is realism?"

Realism was not easily defined. "Let's say I make a painting of this room with all its people exactly, minutely as I see them from here," he said. "That would take care of realism for a great many people. But what egotism! Because I would be making the room in perspective—perspective, a strictly personal, limited, one-sided view of the material."

Each object has, he contended, a different perspective for each observer. "The Cubists broke the dogma that perspective is truth and produced their own." A botanist, he suggested, would think the artist's representation of a tree a superficial one. He would say, "You've got to show us how the tree functions, how sap is carried to the leaves, chlorophyll manufactured—how growth occurs." A physicist would demand to know how the painter would deal with the reality of the tree's complex atomic structure.

Ben mused at the thought of how a political, class-conscious friend would look at a painting of a tree, whether botanical, atomic, or Cubist. He ventured that he would probably remark, contemptuously, "The only realistic art is that which advances the class struggle, and aids man in his crusade for economic betterment."

A psychologist, Ben continued, believes that Surrealism is the correct approach to reality. A philosopher contends that Ben's paintings show only aspects of reality. Their greatest fault is that

they are lacking "values." For a priest, these paintings are mecha-
nistic, giving no hint of the "unfolding of Divine Law," which is
reality. And a critic informs Ben that he is simply "out of the swim,"
that the trend is toward the nonobjective.

Realism, you may conclude, may be anything to anybody. Perhaps the meaning has truly been rubbed off the word, and, as a
word, it no longer has any constant properties. . . . Let's look
back. In each of my bootless efforts to paint, there was one constant factor—the search for some sort of truth. That is the
beginning of an attitude toward realism. To the academician,
realism closes with the one-sided perspective view of things. His
mind also closes there. But in a highly subjective person there is
the landscape of inner imaginings which is also reality. Shall we
rule out one reality and admit another?

As someone suggested, it all depends upon your frame of reference. That is probably about the sum of what you are as a person—your capacities, competence, cultural perspective—your
values . . .

If I may at this point come up with a tentative definition, I
would say, then, that Realism is an earnest search for truth
within the framework of one's own values.

So far as I personally am concerned, my frame of reference is
a highly humanistic one. I am unwilling to regard man as of use
value. To me the human being is ultimate value; the arts, its
prime manifestation.

In this connection I want to digress for a moment. Art, we pre-
sume, creates and *is* value. But value is no absolute; it requires
an evaluator. The only evaluator that I've heard of so far is man.

I know that I am in a stronghold of anti-humanists, and I am
greatly puzzled as to why anyone should seek to produce value
on the one hand, and to outlaw the evaluator on the other. . . .

I said above that real life is essential to the artist—that it is the
museum of man's effects, the source of authentic particulars. If
I may be allowed this small bit of presumption, I'll continue that
out of such particulars stems the philosophical particular into
the universal.

The great painters have been the great symbolic philoso-
phers—unlisted in your who's who of philosophy. The Christ

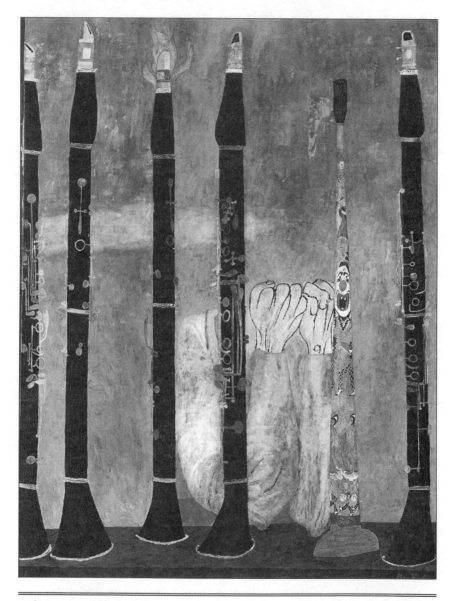

Soby wrote: "Shahn almost always knew what to leave out, as in this fine Composition for Clarinets and Tin Horn *(1951), where he realized that the face of the man behind the instruments would have proved a distracting element, and therefore showed only his arms and hands."*

that you know is the Christ that Leonardo painted. Ancient sculptors turned man into symbols of power; into symbols of terror. Perhaps it was Praxiteles who first gave us the human form as a symbol of beauty. All this is comment by the artist upon life. And it is the creation of values.

I like to look at a great deal of abstract art, and I think it has discovered a new and tremendously significant world of form. I like to look at some non-objective art. Yet I think this has not brought us much beyond what the abstractionist has already brought us. In all the profuse yield of non-objective art, I cannot recall more than a handful of what might be called lasting symbols.

The human population—1951—is no longer popularly regarded as an aggregate of individual persons. It now comprises statistical segments for use—whether as consumers, as labor, or what have you. Collectivization is not confined to Russia—we can probably still show her some tricks.

So I deeply regret to see artists join in the repudiation of human values. It appears to me that there is still a hell of a lot of stimulus for art left in the human race. In fact, I think it's a bit craven of us to join the statisticians in wiping out that which is individual, that which is particular, and that which is human.

Ben had been uneasy during his month at Black Mountain. It had been a period of questioning, of self-doubt. He came to believe that he was capable of a broader range than his work had previously shown. In 1949 and 1950, he had moved away from his political works, and his artistic vocabulary turned to allegory, classical references, and symbolic images, which had not concerned him in the past. At Black Mountain, his work approached the abstract, and his style changed markedly.

Two of his paintings illustrate the new direction his art was taking. One, *Composition for Clarinets and Tin Horn,* shows four clarinets, a bright menacing fire behind them, and alongside them a tin horn on which are painted the tragic face of a clown as well as minstrels and Spanish dancers. Behind these instruments are two tightly clenched fists. Ben commented on this ominous painting in a speech given before a meeting of the American Society for Aesthetics:

It contained no singers whatsoever, but only tortured hands covering a face which is half-hidden behind a playful array of clarinets. I discovered, after considerable struggle, that it was an *emotional* image that I wanted to symbolize, rather than the literal one of the singers. The emotional image, for me at least, is caught and held in the painting. Such is the game of hide-and-seek that one must play with his own images.

He also described a second painting of this period.

So, [in] this picture that I called *Epoch* . . . there is a little creature balancing himself precariously on some acrobatic cyclists, each of whom have in their hand a little sign of some kind—one which says "No" and one which says "Yes." They, themselves, are in a very precarious position but they're professionals, they'll come through. But the character that is balancing himself on them is really in a dangerous position. I set the whole scene, as it was, in a circus-like or country-fair-like atmosphere. It does have a kind of a depressing look—an abandoned kind of a look, if you wish—for I was disturbed by the world situation, by our own national situation—that was at the beginning of the high point of this endless suspicion of one toward the other for one's own security, for the national security—one's loyalty, and so on . . . those words were so much used that they ceased to have any meaning. There was I balancing myself between these "Yeses" and these "Noes"—and it wasn't only I, it was all of my friends, it was everyone I knew or cared to talk to who were in this same precarious position. I don't think I feel any more secure now except that I am getting used to precariousness. The two characters—the professional cyclists—who are carrying us, as it were, through this time, I think are rather sinister, they're almost inhuman. The character that represents me, or represents you, isn't much more human, except that in his fright he does look human; his clothes are rumpled, his expression, his pallor is very apparent.

Epoch *(1950) is an intriguing work, both witty and puzzling.*

CHAPTER THIRTY-FIVE

The 1950s

THROUGHOUT THE 1950S, THE NEW YORK SCHOOL, THE Abstract Expressionists, and finally the exponents of Pop Art had become increasingly fashionable. Shahn became, instead, a celebrity. He was more than just a popular painter; he was an immensely popular figure: a writer, lecturer, illustrator, and television star as well as an artist. His articles appeared in a number of magazines, and the ideas he expressed were widely discussed; his lectures, from one end of the country to another, were well attended and enthusiastically received; his brilliant illustrations and scratchy line became instantly recognizable as the work of Ben Shahn; and he was a witty, charming, and articulate guest on both serious and less than serious television programs. For a time, he was so sought after as a speaker that he was offered—and accepted—the representation of a high-powered lecture manager, Harold Shaw. Before long, however, Ben realized that his lectures were taking valuable time that would have been better used for painting. "If I keep on speaking," he replied to one request, "I won't be able to paint, and if I stop painting, you won't want me to speak."

His work was being exhibited more than ever before. During the 1950s, one-man shows and group exhibitions in which he participated were held throughout the country—in Chicago, Los Angeles, Boston, Santa Barbara, San Francisco, Detroit, Houston, Louisville, and Milwaukee. In a *New York Times* review of his 1951 exhibition at the Downtown Gallery, Aline Louchheim noted that "only a great artist can make line at once intrinsically beautiful and an instrument of summarized description which creates images, space, illusion, and emotion. Such an artist is Ben Shahn." The following year Stuart Preston wrote a discerning review of a Downtown Gallery exhibition of watercolors and temperas. His controversial subject matter, according to Preston, has "unfairly obscured the most important fact about him, that he is intensely an artist, one whose primary values are, as they must be, aesthetic values." In 1955, commenting on an exhibition celebrating the twenty-fifth anniversary of his first exhibition at Halpert's gallery, a writer for *Time* took note of the change in the artist's work: "In the past quarter century, the art of burly Ben Shahn has bellowed and broadened with the man. The bristling dark mustache of his fiery youth has faded to white, and it now screens more smiles than scowls. At 56, after many storms, Shahn seems to have entered a calm sea."

Ben was becoming known and appreciated outside the United States as well. He won a prize in São Paulo and showed his work in Calcutta. He exhibited and lectured in London several times, and six of his works were part of a circulating exhibition under MOMA's auspices, which visited Paris, Zurich, Düsseldorf, Stockholm, Helsinki, and Oslo. Most important of all, he and Willem de Kooning represented the United States in the 1954 Venice Biennale.

His greatest successes abroad, however, came in Italy—through well-received exhibitions in Rome; the publication of a book devoted to his life and work by Mirella Bentivoglio (the first book about Shahn written in a foreign language); and, especially, through his participation in 1958 at Gian Carlo Menotti's Festival of Two Worlds in Spoleto, for which he designed sets and a poster for the Jerome Robbins ballet *New York Export—Opus Jazz*. Robbins had, since 1952, hoped that he and Ben might one day work together, and their collaboration in Spoleto proved to be a harmonious fusion of two major talents, during what was for both Ben and Bernarda a relaxed and carefree summer.

During the 1950s, Ben also became known for his superb book

Ben and Bernarda thoroughly enjoyed their visits to Italy, where Ben worked on the sets for Jerome Robbins's ballets at Spoleto and at Cesenatico in 1956.

illustrations, two of which were done in collaboration with modern poets. The first, with Edward Dahlberg, a distinguished essayist and novelist as well as poet, was doomed from the beginning. Though gifted, Dahlberg was emotionally unstable, and his erratic behavior disturbed and unsettled Ben. Even more important, the two men were unable to conceal their contempt for each other's work.

They were brought together in March 1955 by the art historian Sir Herbert Read, who wrote to Ben asking that he illustrate Dahlberg's newest book, *The Sorrows of Priapus*. The idea had come to Read after he had seen Ben's drawings at an exhibition in São Paulo. Dahlberg, he believed, was a genius, but something had to be added to his new book so that it might attract a wider audience.

After reading the manuscript, Ben not only agreed that it was not salable; he also believed the book was unworthy of being sold. "It is neither honest nor innocent but is a weary effort to capitalize on the public fancy," he wrote Read, unequivocally rejecting the idea of linking his name with the poet's erratic and frequently incomprehensible re-creation of biblical and Greek myth and the literature of other ancient cultures.

Dahlberg was furious. He wrote to Ben, whose art he had already characterized as "drawings on the walls of a jake": "Damn your departed bones, and your falsehood"—words unlikely to convince any artist to embark upon a collaboration.

Yet Dahlberg's friends continued to plead his case. Among these were men Ben respected: James Laughlin, the courageous publisher of New Directions, and William Carlos Williams. Ben had met Williams in 1950, and he esteemed both the man and his poetry to such a degree that it was impossible to ignore his plea. As a result, Ben relented and created forty-two drawings, largely line or wash, for a book he thoroughly disliked, written by a man he disliked even more.

Williams expressed his gratitude by writing in a review that Ben's illustrations were "one of the book's outstanding features." Dahlberg, on the other hand, complained (incorrectly) that Ben's name was more prominently placed than his own on the title page. "Who was Ben Shahn," he asked later, "and what cause had he either to be born or to inhabit this pustular globe?"

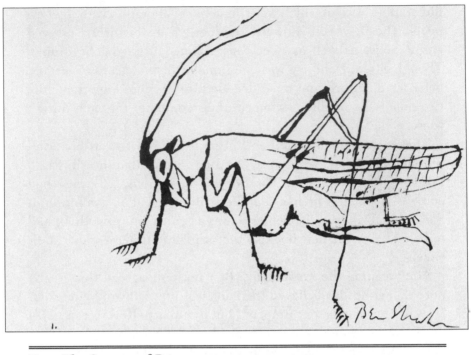

From The Sorrows of Priapus.

Ben's experience with John Berryman, another brilliant but emotionally disturbed poet, was altogether different. At Princeton, where Berryman was teaching, they quickly became friends. Ben had heard a reading of the poet's long work *Homage to Mistress Bradstreet,* and he needed no urging when asked to illustrate the poem for a new edition. First published in *Partisan Review,* it had been praised by Edmund Wilson, who called it "the most distinguished long poem by an American since *The Waste Land.*" There was no reason to believe that it would not again be acclaimed when it appeared for the first time in book form, with Ben's illustrations, in 1956.

Ben's ten illustrations of houses, flowers, trees, a Puritan, and a delightful Indian cupid did, as he had hoped, add charm to a handsomely designed and well-produced volume. "They are *beautiful,*" wrote the appreciative author. "Concise, wonderfully imaginative, and complete . . ."

Two other books of the period are examples of Ben's remarkable ability to enter into the spirit of diverse authors with stunning results. *Ounce Dice Trice,* the work of a young Scottish poet named Alastair Reid, was a collection of sounds and the words that grew from them. Ben's task was both to design the book and to translate Reid's words into visual images. Ben's delightful pictures, about a hundred of them, display a wit and whimsical charm seldom found in his other work. They are unfailingly entertaining. The volume, originally meant for children, was of equal interest to adults, who were delighted by the artist's interpretation of "tirrivee," "gongoozler," "joskin," "gognomony," and "cloaf," among many other "words."

Undoubtedly the most significant and, for him, the most gratifying book Ben illustrated during the fifties was *The Alphabet of Creation,* first published in a limited edition in 1954 and reprinted in a trade edition later the same year. An introduction to the letters of the Hebrew alphabet, the text is an adaptation of an ancient Gnostic legend from the *Sefer Ha-Zohar,* or *Book of Splendor,* presumably written in Aramaic by Moses de León, a thirteenth-century Spanish scholar who claimed that it was not his own but had been revealed centuries earlier to another Jewish mystic, Rabbi Simeon ben Yohai. The chance to illustrate this text, which told of God's creation of the world through the letters of the alphabet, was a daunting challenge, but it gave Ben a chance to pursue his fascination with letters and lettering.

Since the artist's knowledge of Hebrew was limited, he frequently turned to Morris (Moshe) Bressler, a Hebrew scholar, folklorist, and insurance man, who was a neighbor of his in Roosevelt and who had originated the idea. Shahn also consulted the distinguished rabbi Louis Finkelstein of the Jewish Theological Seminary of America to make certain that his Hebrew text was accurate.

In addition to his bold interpretations of the Hebrew alphabet, Ben provided the volume with more than twenty drawings, powerful and witty, playful and threatening, in themselves a work of art.

CHAPTER THIRTY-SIX

The FBI,
HUAC, and
the Blacklist

GIVEN HIS ACTIVE PARTICIPATION IN A LARGE NUMBER OF PRO-
gressive political and social organizations and his never-ending
battle against injustice, it was obvious that Ben could not emerge
unscathed from the Red scare that swept the country during the
first half of the decade to which Ben had referred in his painting
Epoch. This witch-hunt, fueled by Wisconsin's Senator Joseph
McCarthy, was spearheaded not only by the Federal Bureau of
Investigation and the House Un-American Activities Committee
(HUAC), but by a number of private organizations that devoted
their energies and their resources to the destruction of subversive
elements, real or imagined.

Ben had been a subject of FBI investigations for many years,
long before HUAC had come into existence and before Senator
McCarthy gained power, and he remained so for several years
longer. A September 1952 FBI report summarized the case against
him:

> A review of the Bureau's files reflects a long history of Com-
> munist Party front activity on the part of the subject, continuing
> to the present time. It is observed that the subject has been iden-
> tified with the following Communist Party front groups, among

others: Southern Conference for Human Welfare in 1947; the publication "Jewish Life" in 1948; Civil Rights Congress in 1948; National Council of Arts, Sciences, and Professions in 1948 and 1950; Scientific Cultural Conference for World Peace in 1949; Young Progressives of America in 1949; American Labor Party in 1950; New Jersey Committee for Peaceful Alternatives in 1951 and 1952.

Only a few months later, at the end of February 1953, special agents of the Bureau visited the Shahn home in Roosevelt, as they had done frequently in the past. Ben decided to make them feel welcome. He talked endlessly about every conceivable subject, making it impossible for them to leave (though they were unable to hide their restlessness). When Abby, the Shahns' youngest child, came home from school, Ben introduced her to them, explaining that these were the "real" FBI and not the "television" FBI. Next, he offered them a drink, which they refused, and then lunch, which they also refused.

Understandably, the FBI agents were both confused and impressed. Ben was very "courteous to the interviewing agents and talked freely," it was reported. He told them that he had never been a member of the Communist Party, but felt he might belong to seven or eight organizations that had been cited by the U.S. Attorney General as subversive. He was, he added, interested in peace and would offer his help to any group he thought was working for a good cause. Furthermore, he gently but unequivocally refused to name anyone whom he believed to be Communist. In spite of this, the interviewing agents felt they should interview the couple again in the near future, because there was still a chance that they might furnish valuable information.

It took the FBI ten years to give up. A request by an agent to interview Ben again was, for the first time, denied by the director on September 25, 1963. "In view of the facts that no information has been developed indicating Communist Party membership on the part of the subject . . . and that his association with Communist front groups took place some years ago, it would appear that little information of value could be gained from such an interview," the director declared. Furthermore—and this is an astounding admission as well as a surprising show of good judgment—the statement included a warning that "subject is employed as an artist-writer by profession and might possibly exploit an attempted interview in an effort to embarrass the Bureau."

Before then, in 1959, Ben had been called to testify before the House Un-American Activities Committee in Washington. One of his paintings, *Parable*, was to be included in an exhibition of American art to be shown in the Soviet Union in exchange for a selection of Soviet art to be shown in the United States. A vigilant congressman, Francis E. Walter of Pennsylvania, had somehow learned that more than half of the sixty-seven American paintings and sculptures to be sent to Moscow had been created by artists with records of affiliation with Communist fronts and causes. HUAC intended to question Ben concerning the participation of American artists in the Communist Party.

Ben; his lawyer, Philip Wittenberg; and Philip Evergood, another artist suspected of subversion, arrived in Washington on July 1, 1959. Ben refused to answer any of the questions put to him, pleading the First, Fifth, Ninth, and Tenth Amendments to the Constitution. Instead, he read a statement he had written for *Art News* in 1953, defining his political position at the time.

> The Liberal of today—the Altruist—the Humanitarian—any citizen who feels his responsibility toward the public good— finds himself caught midway between two malignant forces.
>
> To the right of him stands the force of reaction that has always opposed reform or progress and that will always oppose reform or progress with whatever weapons it can lay its hands upon, including slander and calumny.
>
> To the left of the Liberal is the Communist contingent, ever alert to move in upon his good works, always ready to supply him with its little shopworn packages of dogma, to misappropriate his words, his acts and his intentions. The Liberal has long suffered this Communist invasion of his organizations. It has been his cross and it has, over a period of years, thoroughly demoralized the great American liberal tradition.
>
> Together, these two forces have constituted an unholy team: The accusation of communism is the most powerful scourge that has fallen into the hands of Reaction since heresy ceased to be a public crime.

But Communism and the far right were not the only targets of Ben's scorn.

> Whatever this Committee may succeed in dragging out of the remote past of any artist it interviews, I believe that its chief purpose is not to serve this democracy or the public welfare, but that it is to vilify and humiliate a certain group of artists whose work is in the vanguard, and whose thinking is fresh and experimental.
>
> Whatever its temporary successes at home, the *world* effect of the Un-American Activities Committee has been more than once to turn us into an international laughing-stock, to lose us respect and friendship on every hand, to earn us the reputation of being a Philistine nation—which we are not.
>
> The artists whom it is about to crucify are, on the other hand, among our greatest international assets. Their names are known and honored in every country in Europe. Their works are coveted, their approach and understanding of art is studied. Just how, and to what extent will the present interrogation serve the National interest?

The session ended on a note of irony. Ben showed the Committee a recent issue of *Amerika*, a Russian-language magazine distributed in the Soviet Union by the U.S. Information Agency. It contained a translation of Ben's lecture "On Nonconformity," which he had delivered at Harvard University in 1957.

As dangerous and destructive as the FBI and HUAC investigations and interrogations were during these years, nothing was more threatening to the freedom of American writers, actors, musicians, and artists than *Counterattack*. This infamous hate sheet was first published in 1947, at the beginning of the witch-hunt. Founded by three former FBI agents backed by a number of reactionary businessmen, it had a sole purpose: to uncover and make public the names not only of Communists but also of all men and women who had ever, even inadvertently, showed the slightest sympathy toward what *Counterattack* called "Communist front" organizations—groups that under the pretense of serving humanitarian goals actually did their best to promote the cause of Communism in the United States.

The newsletter encouraged the public to protest to radio and
television companies, as well as to the sponsors who employed
these "subversives," and demand that the controversial employees
be dismissed from their jobs and placed on a blacklist which would
prevent them from finding further work. The blacklists were
tremendously effective, since the employers themselves were
threatened with boycotts if they did not rid their organizations of
"Reds."

Ben's experience with *Counterattack* was a perfect example of
the power of this scurrilous newsletter. The campaign against him
and, simultaneously against CBS, Ben's employer and the most
liberal of the radio and television networks, was launched with the
July 25, 1952, issue. It was relentlessly logical. CBS had run an ad
promoting its coverage of the Republican and Democratic conventions; the programs covering the conventions were sponsored by
the huge Westinghouse Electric Corporation; and, finally, the
illustration used in the advertisement had been drawn by Ben
Shahn. The charges leveled against Ben were the usual ones. He
had contributed artwork to a number of Communist magazines
and newspapers. He had backed many front organizations. . . .

There was more. Ben had drawn illustrations attacking the gov-
ernment's refusal to issue passports to Paul Robeson and the writer
Howard Fast. He had defended, through his illustrations, the
"Hollywood Ten," prominent screenwriters who had been denied
work because of their alleged affiliation with the Communist
Party; he had drawn the cover illustration for a recent issue of *The
Nation* that "smeared" the United States, claiming that it was one
step from Fascism. Finally, he designed posters for the Progressive
Party that made fun of both the Democratic and Republican par-
ties.

Obviously, *Counterattack* reasoned, both CBS (which had hired
Shahn and prepared the advertisement) and Westinghouse (which
had paid part of the cost of the ad), were, in hiring Shahn, guilty of
aiding the Communist cause. As a consequence, the editors urged
readers to write to the presidents of CBS and Westinghouse, asking if they could "justify their firm's carelessness in helping to
finance a leading, continual supporter of Communist Party
causes."

CBS's president, Jack Van Volenburg, wrote a letter responding to *Counterattack*'s charges. Van Volenburg not only defended the use of Shahn but praised him as being "universally recognized as one of the greatest living painters." The purpose of the CBS ad, he declared, was to build "maximum audiences" for conventions and to help "a free people reach independent decisions on the basis of what they have seen with their own eyes." The implication, according to *Counterattack,* was that "as long as CBS is working for a noble cause, it doesn't matter that a fronter gets a big sum of money from CBS."

In spite of Van Volenburg's support, *Counterattack* prevailed in the end. After the publication's warning that a number of companies would withdraw their ads from CBS if the network continued to use Shahn's art, Ben's close friend William Golden, CBS's art director, relayed orders from above that Shahn's work would be withdrawn from future ads; in addition, Golden hired a replacement to make reasonably accurate copies of Ben's work.

What many of Ben's friends viewed as a shocking betrayal by Golden (Ben did not see it that way) was soon countered by another of Ben's longtime friends: Leo Lionni, then art director of *Fortune* who asked him to create a cover drawing for a forthcoming issue. This was only the first of several assignments Ben got from *Fortune* and *Time* (both of which were published by Henry Luce, hardly a Communist sympathizer) after CBS decided to stop using his work.

CBS didn't use Ben again until March 1954, but he managed to survive. In addition to the occasional assignments from *Time* and *Fortune,* he received commissions from *Harper's, The Nation, Scientific American, Esquire,* and *Charm.* He increased the number of serigraphs he made, so he could sell more of his works to a larger audience at a lower cost. In spite of his need for more work—his income diminished considerably with the loss of CBS—he remained faithful to his principles. Asked to illustrate an article for *Nation's Business,* a publication of the U.S. Chamber of Commerce, he read the piece and then refused, on the grounds that he could not be associated with ideas so foreign to his own way of thinking.

CBS's blacklisting of Ben came to an end in 1954 when Fred Friendly and Edward R. Murrow, two of the network's most talented employees, demanded (they were sufficiently powerful to demand rather than request) that he work with them on their highly praised series *See It Now*. It was an occasion for celebration at CBS as well as throughout the country, for the March 9 installment of *See It Now* was devoted to an enormously effective exposé of Senator McCarthy, which was so widely seen and applauded that it became the first step in the decline and fall of the senator from Wisconsin.

Though he was not involved with that historic telecast (he was asked to design an ad for it but was unable to because he was out of town), Ben was so impressed by the brilliance, courage, and efficacy of the program that he made two drawings, which he presented to Murrow and Friendly. One showed David slaying Goliath and the other depicted St. George slaying the Dragon. The faces of Goliath and the Dragon belonged, unmistakably, to Senator McCarthy.

CHAPTER THIRTY-SEVEN

Shahn at Harvard, and at Roosevelt, a Place to Come Back To

IN EARLY 1956, IN THE MIDDLE OF THE WITCH-HUNTS AND blacklists, Ben received an enormously welcome request from McGeorge Bundy, dean of the faculty of arts and sciences at Harvard University: would he serve as the Charles Eliot Norton Professor of Poetry for the academic year 1956–57? Poetry in this context meant "all poetic expression in language, music, or the fine arts." Earlier holders of the chair included e. e. cummings, Robert Frost, T. S. Eliot, Thornton Wilder, Sir Herbert Read, Erwin Panofsky, Paul Hindemith, and Igor Stravinsky. The Norton chair was, Bundy wrote, "our most distinguished appointment for visiting scholars in the field of the humanities." This honor would, of course, enhance Ben's reputation, though his friend S. J. Perelman kidded him about it. "This puts Harvard into a new league," he wrote him, "and I predict a distinguished future for what has hitherto been a small, local academy with a very dubious reputation." The FBI apparently felt the same way. Ben, they stated, was "reported to be teaching presently, name of school unknown, in the State of Massachusetts."

Ben was to have few duties. He was appointed for one year but he was asked to be in residence only from October 1 to Christmas and from February 1 to May 1. He was to deliver not less than six lectures and was obliged to have these lectures published by the Harvard University Press. Because the Charles Eliot Norton professor had to be paid the same salary as the highest-paid professor at Harvard, his salary would be a generous $18,000.

As flattering as the offer was, Ben hesitated before accepting it. He worried that he had already spent too much time speaking and teaching at colleges and universities. In addition, he wondered how his work would fare if he spent such a long time in an academic atmosphere; and he was afraid that he might fall into dilettantism in such a critical milieu, or that his art might not survive so professionally analytical an environment.

On the other hand, he could not resist the honor bestowed upon him or the prestige it would bring him. This was Harvard, where he would be living among his peers, not Black Mountain where he felt himself a stranger. Furthermore, after he had written so many speeches and published so many articles, the lectures at Harvard would give him a unique opportunity to summarize his ideas about art, ask himself questions, and examine his own methods and motivations. These lectures would constitute his credo as an artist and as a man.

Ben made the right decision. Both he and Bernarda felt completely at home; they flourished at the university and in Cambridge. Ben was a star among stars, as he had never been before. His engagement book for the academic year includes time spent with McGeorge Bundy; James Johnson Sweeney, the director of the Guggenheim; the art critic and museum administrator Paul Sachs; the literary critic Harry Levin; the historian Perry Miller; the literary critic I. A. Richards; Jerome Weisner, the president of MIT; and his old friend Archibald MacLeish, who, as Boylston Professor of Rhetoric and Oratory, was chairman of the committee that chose the Charles Eliot Norton professor.

Wanting to protect Shahn from unwelcome visitors—for the most part students—who might interrupt his concentration, MacLeish found him a studio reachable only by climbing up back stairs and passing through crooked corridors. In Roosevelt, he would often greet visitors to his studio with a paintbrush in his mouth, signifying that he was at work and did not want to be disturbed. This tactic, it seems, was unnecessary at Harvard. A star-tled MacLeish wrote: "He accomplished his great work, not by his lectures . . . but by taking over a studio at the top of the Fogg Museum, nailing the door open, and starting to work. You know how undergraduates smell? I've been up there on winter days when you could smell them two floors down, they were so thick in that room!"

While at Harvard, Ben helped mount an exhibition of his art to open at the Fogg in December. He worked on the Berryman and Dahlberg books, as well as on *Thirteen Poems by Wilfred Owen,* a collaboration with Leonard Baskin. He designed and supervised the execution and installation of his first mosaic mural, for the William E. Grady Vocational High School in Brooklyn, and he designed a number of book jackets, one especially charming one for his friend Perelman's *The Road to Miltown.* He also completed several paintings, including *When the Saints . . . ,* a large work he sold to Fred Friendly for $3,000, and *Goyescas,* which was first a drawing, then a watercolor, and then a watercolor with gouache. Of this he wrote, referring to an artist's retreat to academia:

> I am plagued by an exasperating notion: What if Goya, for instance, had been granted a Guggenheim, and then, complet-ing that, had stepped into a respectable and cozy teaching job in some small—but advanced!—New England college, and had thus been spared the agonies of the Spanish Insurrection? The unavoidable conclusion is that we would never had had "Los Caprichos" or "Los Desastres de la Guerra." The world would not have been called upon to mourn for the tortured woman of the drawing inscribed 'Because She Was a Liberal!' Nor would it have been stirred by Goya's pained cry, 'Everywhere It Is The Same!' Neither would it have been shocked by his cruel depic-tions of human bestiality, nor warned—so graphically, so unfor-gettably—that fanaticism is man's most abominable trait.

Ben's time at Harvard was in every way fruitful, but his most sig-nificant achievements were the six lectures he delivered there. With these, he accomplished what he set out to do: he summarized his ideas about art while, at the same time, providing his audience with insights into his own development as an artist and as a man.

The six lectures were titled "Artists in Colleges," "The Biography of a Painting," "The Shape of Content," "On Nonconformity," "Modern Evaluations," and "The Education of an Artist." They deal forcefully and cogently with a number of subjects: the role of the artist in an academic setting, nonconformity in art ("All art is based upon nonconformity," he declared), the importance of content in a work of art ("Form is the visible shape of content"), and wise, enthusiastic advice to the beginning student of art. Published under the title *The Shape of Content*, the lectures constitute an exhilarating, incisive statement of one artist's credo, written with rare clarity and intelligence. Some of Ben's relatives and friends maintain that although the ideas were Ben's, these lectures were actually written by Bernarda, a stylist of considerable ability. Bernarda herself counters that she was Ben's typist, and in typing the manuscript made only what she felt were minor changes. Whatever the case, *The Shape of Content* has been widely read since its first publication. Many readers agreed with Frank Getlein of *The New Republic,* who wrote at the time that the collection of lectures was "the clearest, most forceful statement on art by an artist of our time that I have read."

After his invigorating stay at Harvard, Ben returned to Roosevelt. He always returned there and continued to do so for the rest of his life. But although the town is so closely linked to him—the words "Roosevelt, New Jersey" almost always bring the response "Ben Shahn lived there, didn't he?"—he was never really a part of it. He had a house there, he was comfortable there, and it was his legal residence, but, as Edwin Rosskam, Ben's friend and author of an illuminating but controversial study of Roosevelt, has written (after its publication, "Ed didn't dare walk out of the house for three months," according to Bernarda), the town became for Ben "not so much a place to live in as a place to come back to."

As much time as Ben and Bernarda spent in Roosevelt between their many trips, they were only sporadically a part of the town. Visitors to their home, many of whom came to pay homage, included distinguished figures from the worlds of art, music, and literature, as well as theater, film, radio, and television celebrities.

These visits separated the Shahn family from the rest of the community, whose composition was changing. No longer were most of the residents immigrants from Eastern Europe; increasingly, they were young people drawn to the town because of the low cost of housing. Though not unfriendly, while in Roosevelt Ben and Bernarda felt superior and occasionally showed it. It was joked that Bernarda (undeniably a lady), when addressed by a stranger as "Lady," murmured: "I'm the only person in this town you could address as that."

When Ben was there, he was an affable, familiar figure. Every morning he would walk over to the Roosevelt post office and chat with fellow townspeople. After a hard day's work, he would have dinner at home and then go visiting. People in Roosevelt didn't lock their doors (many still don't), and Ben, though not invited, would often open the door to a neighbor's home and begin talking until late in the night, regaling his hosts with stories they probably had already heard numerous times and did not care to hear again.

Though he was a completely accessible citizen when not working, Ben was either liked or hated—or both—by most of the local population. One man, quoted anonymously in Rosskam's book *Roosevelt, New Jersey*, was confounded by the division between Shahn's public and private behavior. In his studio, he was a warm, generous, decent man, whose works of art only a truly compassionate man could create. After hours, in the living room, he was a performer who obsessively bored his listeners with the usual anecdotes. He dominated the conversation at all times. He was tense and caused tension; he was a tyrant capable of great kindness.

The problems he had with adults rarely surfaced with young people, especially those who showed promise as artists (when and if they fulfilled that promise, he was no longer interested in their art, he admitted). He was both friend and mentor to many of them, generously sharing his knowledge of and passion for art. Charlotte Safir, Pearl Hecht Seligman, and Ani Rosskam, who were among his students, all agree that he was a superb teacher, and all three think of him with unqualified affection.

Ani, Ed and Louise Rosskam's daughter, remembers Ben allowing her, when she was only twelve years old, to arrange his books on his bookshelf, and she also remembers him tearing off a piece of paper from the bottom of one of his own drawings and giving it to her, so she could draw a portrait of him.

Pearl has never forgotten his warmth, understanding, and kindness to her over a period of many years. When she was a teenager, she baby-sat the Shahns' children and became a part of their home. Later she became a close friend, who eventually served as a secretary and assistant to Ben when he and Bernarda were away. Both Shahns were people she could talk to about matters she could never discuss with her own family: literature, politics, and ideas. When she was seventeen, Ben encouraged her to attend art school; she was elated. For the first time in her life, she had evidence that someone (and that someone was a famous painter) believed that she had something to offer to the world.

Charlotte, too, remembers Ben as a warm mentor, who especially appreciated her sense of humor.

Ed Rosskam, who moved to Roosevelt at Ben and Bernarda's urging in 1957, was probably Ben's closest friend in the town. His picture of Ben is a balanced one; he was able to see both Ben Shahns and justify the negative elements of his friend's character because of the power of his art. In his book he wrote:

> Making pictures mattered to Ben more than anything; the cantankerous vanity that made it necessary for him to bathe in the approval he was getting was incidental: it was part of the same drive, I'm sure, that compelled him to make pictures, make pictures up to the very moment when he died. . . .
>
> Ben could be immensely arrogant, rude, self-centered, irritating; he could also be kind, helpful, brilliant, stimulating. His friends (and I specifically include myself) accepted his idiosyncrasies, they didn't need to forgive him anything, no matter how annoyed they were with him at times. It was all made right on the day—which came every once in a while—when he phoned and his voice was tense with a peculiar excitement and said: "Come on over, I've got something to show you." And you'd go to his house and the door to the studio stood open, and there was his latest work, still wet, propped up and he beside it, uncertain and hopeful as a child: here was a new picture, a newborn thing that had not existed before, and you didn't know what to say, you were speechless before it.

The artist in his studio at Roosevelt, 1967.

CHAPTER THIRTY-EIGHT

The Far East, France, and a Spiritually Enriching Project

OF ALL BEN AND BERNARDA'S FOREIGN TRIPS, TWO WERE OF special interest. One involved travel to countries they had never before visited. It came about because of an invitation from their close friends Dorothy and Sydney Spivack, to join them on a trip around the world, an offer too exciting to turn down. The two couples left New York for San Francisco at the beginning of 1960. From California they were off to Australia and New Zealand; they then planned to travel through Asia, the Soviet Union, and Warsaw, and across Western Europe, returning home in the middle of July.

The highlight turned out to be the eighth-century city of Kyoto, the cultural heart of Japan, where they remained more than a week. For Ben, the city was a living museum of Japanese art, with its splendid gardens, its ancient Buddhist temples, and the tombs of many notable figures in the history of the country. The Shahns discovered what is called the "total aesthetic," which, Bernarda explained, meant that "wherever one looks, whatever one holds in his hand—objects, houses, plantings of trees, mortarless fitted stone walls, arrays of fruits, a window displaying combs—every vista is conceived in terms of shape and texture, of muted colors and grace in line and contrast." Ben was surprised at the innateness of art, the integration of art with life, wherever they traveled in Asia, but it was Kyoto that fascinated him most and reminded him of the Paris of his youth. It was inexpensive, beautiful, and sophisticated, alive with poets and painters, a stimulating city in which to walk or merely contemplate. Ben felt a deep affinity for this completely foreign culture, particularly for the graceful, expressive Japanese calligraphy, which influenced his own. It inspired him to design a seal of Hebrew letters with which he stamped some of his works.

The behavior of the Japanese people charmed him as well. Once Bernarda spontaneously entered what appeared to be an unusually interesting art gallery. Ben followed and began a conversation with the gallery owner, who punctuated their discussion by frequently bowing down deeply to her American visitor. After they left, Bernarda, embarrassed by this display of subservience, asked Ben if he too were disturbed by it. Not at all, he assured her. Actually, he rather liked it.

One difference between this trip and the many others Ben had taken was that, for the first time in many years, he had his camera with him for his own pleasure. In spite of his efforts, however, he was not the average tourist. He photographed monuments and temples; he recorded many of the sculptures and sculptural details that intrigued him. However, he took no pictures of colorfully costumed local people or sad-eyed, ill-dressed children whose poverty tugged at the heart. His ability to photograph people had disappeared. "I found it was gone, you know," he told an interviewer. "It happens to people. A certain interest leaves them. I still love to look at photographs of people, but I couldn't make them myself."

There was one negative note in what was otherwise a perfect trip. It happened on February 22 in Bangkok, at about five in the morning. Ben awoke with a severe burning pain in his chest. The pain lasted for about an hour, leaving him weak and dizzy. Alarmed, he called a doctor, who arranged to meet him at the hospital at once. Ben volunteered that he had had a similar pain about three years earlier; two years ago, he had also felt an unusually severe pain. At that time, he was hospitalized and given a thorough checkup with no significant findings. That attack had been the last, up until the present time.

Ben, characterized as "a well-developed, slightly obese gentleman appearing anxious," was told by the physician, an American, that he probably had a gastrointestinal problem. Given his history, however, the doctor suggested that Ben remain in the hospital for two days of tests. Ben agreed, and after a thorough examination, the doctor determined that the pain was not cardiac but most likely gastrointestinal or neurogenic. Stressing that Ben was extremely anxious, the physician prescribed a sedative and dismissed him. The incident behind them, Ben and Bernarda continued their travels. In light of what was to happen in the future, it seems entirely possible that these episodes were really precursors of more serious attacks to come.

In April, Ben and Bernarda abruptly decided to go home directly from Japan, canceling their visits to India and the Soviet Union. Ben's reason was that he had had enough. "How much can you digest in one meal?" he wrote Halpert. Besides, he had been away too long and was eager to return to his work.

═══

An earlier and even more significant trip, to France, took place in April 1958. While on a sightseeing tour of Burgundy, Ben, Bernarda, and their three children—Susie, Abby, and Jonathan—stopped for the night at a small inn, the Hotel de l'Ecu near Dijon. At dinnertime, they noticed a small bearded man and a very attractive young woman, who seemed to be speaking English. As the meal came to an end, the young man approached the Shahns and introduced himself as Arnold Fawcus who, in spite of his unmistakably British accent, identified himself as an American. Fawcus, recognizing Ben's name, invited the family to visit the twelfth-century, four-towered château in nearby Villers, which he and his wife, Julie, had recently bought and were in the midst of restoring.

The following morning, when the Shahns arrived at the magnificent château, Fawcus revealed that he was a publisher of art books and, especially, facsimile editions. Intrigued, Ben promised that when the Shahns returned to Paris he would look at the books Fawcus's Trianon Press had published.

Trianon's office, on the Avenue du Maine, close to Montparnasse, was a modest one, reached by climbing a flight of narrow stairs at the rear of a small, dreary courtyard. But looking through

Trianon's books, Shahn was no longer merely intrigued; he was profoundly impressed. The reproductions of drawings by Chagall, engravings by Rouault and Piranesi, and watercolors by Cézanne— and, above all, the remarkable accuracy and impeccable quality of the facsimiles of William Blake's illuminated books—all testified to Fawcus's taste and craftsmanship and to the extraordinary care he gave the production of each volume. Obviously, this elfin, excitable, and energetic man of forty-one was responsible for some of the finest books being published anywhere in the world. It was only natural that he and Ben had already started to think of ways in which they could work together. Indeed, this was the beginning of an uneasy and, in the end, hostile partnership that, miraculously, resulted in some of both men's finest work.

Fawcus was born in India in 1917, the only son of a British father and an American mother. He spent his early years with his mother in San Francisco; when he was nine years old he was sent to school in England. He completed his formal education at Trinity College, Cambridge, where he distinguished himself as a skier and helped make skiing an acceptable sport. Following Cambridge, he returned to America where he organized skiing activities at Yosemite National Park. He then traveled to Mexico City where he entered the world of publishing, helping to edit an English-language magazine. After the United States entered the war, he joined the Army and was sent to Camp Hale, Colorado, to organize a training unit for mountain troops (skiing was, of course, included in the training). He also helped to write the first draft of the *American Military Ski Manual*, which was later revised into a successful commercial book, *Swing into Skiing*.

In 1943, Fawcus was again on the move, this time to Europe. He volunteered for counterintelligence work, accompanying the American forces as they advanced through Italy and southern France.

At the end of the war, in Paris, he met and joined forces with a small French publisher. Fawcus published his first book, a deluxe edition of Paul Eluard's *Le Dur Désir de Durer*, illustrated by Marc Chagall, with him.

In 1947, when his partner left the world of limited editions, Fawcus established the Trianon Press. Through Trianon, Fawcus met Sir Geoffrey Keynes, a Blake scholar, who was so taken with Arnold's work (and the comparatively low prices he charged for it) that he commissioned him to produce a facsimile of William Blake's *Jerusalem*. This was published in 1951. The astounding accuracy of the reproductions led to the establishment of the William Blake Trust, for which Arnold was to publish facsimiles of all of Blake's illustrated books. Trianon also began to publish a number of other books, by and about Marcel Duchamp and Georges Rouault, among others.

In the winter of 1958–59, while staying in New York, Arnold went to Roosevelt to see Ben. They spent a long day considering ideas they might develop together, until Ben mentioned the set of illustrations for the *Haggadah* he had done in 1930, which had never been published. A Shahn *Haggadah,* they believed, would be an excellent way of initiating their collaboration. They envisioned few obstacles. Of Ben's twelve original watercolors, eleven had found their way to the Jewish Museum in New York, and they could certainly be borrowed for the purpose of reproduction. Ben would work on the twelfth illustration, which he had failed to complete so many years earlier. In addition to these illustrations, which would be the volume's main attraction, Ben agreed to design and hand-letter the text of the *Haggadah,* both in English and in Hebrew. An outstanding scholar would be found to provide the volume with an introduction and notes.

Because Shahn and Fawcus were in complete agreement about the project, they moved quickly to produce the first book in what they both believed would be a long and fruitful collaboration. Trianon would publish both a Blake series and a Shahn series. Ben was in excellent company.

Though both men embarked on the collaboration with great enthusiasm, Julie Fawcus suspected that the relationship was doomed from the beginning: each partner wanted something that the other was unable to supply. According to Julie, Ben wanted Arnold to enhance his international reputation. Though well known and fêted at home, he was almost unknown in most of Europe. He assumed that Arnold—with his upper-class British education (and accent), his two châteaux (in addition to the one in Burgundy, he owned a château in the Jura, near Switzerland), and his house in Paris, to say nothing of his distinguished benefactors Paul Mellon and Lessing Rosenwald, whom Ben mistakenly believed had also become Arnold's personal friends—must be in a position to promote his art throughout Europe.

What Arnold wanted from Ben, Julie speculated, was unequivocal acceptance and admiration. Having had a poor relationship with his own father, he sought other father figures. He already had two when he met Ben: the Abbé Breuil, a French archeologist whose books he published, and Sir Geoffrey Keynes, neither of whom ever let him down. He now seemed to want a similar relationship with Ben.

If Arnold became disillusioned because Ben could not give him the emotional support he needed, Ben was equally disappointed to find that Arnold was not and had never been the rich and confident publisher he seemed to be. Indeed, he had been able to finance his business only through the generosity of friends, who either lent or gave him money. Julie had paid for the two châteaux, and an elderly friend had helped him buy the house in Paris. Arnold's success was due to his personal charm as well as to his high standards, tireless energy, imagination, remarkable eye, and determination to do the best work possible. In spite of these qualities, he was in no position to give Ben what he wanted, and as a result the artist came to feel betrayed. "What I find really strange is that they kept trying to work together, long after they realized that it was impossible," Julie wrote, "as if they were defending a kind of dream."

Nevertheless, the collaboration began on an optimistic note. In late April 1959, the original *Haggadah* illustrations arrived in Paris. Two months later, the paper was ordered, a major step forward. During the summer of 1959, Arnold and Ben turned their attention to the *Haggadah* text. Ben insisted that the right man be chosen to translate the Hebrew text into English and to furnish notes and an introduction. Arnold's first suggestion was Meyer Levin, a popular novelist who wrote with sensitivity of American Jews and set many of his novels in Palestine or Israel, but Ben disagreed, suggesting that Edmund Wilson undertake the task.

In early 1960, the first six *Haggadah* plates were finished. The results were superb. Under Arnold's careful supervision, two

meticulous craftsmen named Crampe and Hourdebaigt had produced a miracle: facsimile reproductions that so resembled the
original watercolors as to be practically indistinguishable from
them. The processes used to reproduce these watercolors are collotype and *pochoir,* or stencil. Collotype, though rarely used today,
gives wonderfully accurate results when used for small numbers of
reproductions, such as those printed for Trianon. Like lithography,
it is a planographic process and uses the water-absorbent qualities
of a light-sensitive gelatin emulsion spread on a glass plate. After
exposure to light, the plates that have received the least light
absorb the most water and when inked will take the least ink. The
greatest value of collotype is that the image is not screened, so that
very faithful replicas are possible, even of difficult subjects like
faint pencil drawings.

After Hourdebaigt had completed his job of printing the repro-

Shahn, in Paris in 1965, working with Crampe, pochoiriste, *on the plates
for the Trianon Press edition of* Ecclesiastes.

ductions in collotype, it was the turn of Crampe in his *pochoir* atelier to complete the work. *Pochoir* is an enormously demanding process, which calls for exceptional skill on the craftsman who practices it. The watercolor medium—the same medium as the original work—is applied through an infinite number of stencils made of thin zinc sheets. After the sheets had been cut to the proper size, Crampe began his difficult task. Working with the original watercolors, he analyzed the gradients, tints, and tonalities of their constituent colors. After that, Crampe cut a stencil for each color, using a specially printed guide sheet with the colored areas marked on it. For the *Haggadah,* an average of thirty-four colors were applied by hand through stencils for each plate. Arnold enjoyed referring to Crampe as "my captive genius." "Genius," he said, "because there is no one else who has comparable standards of perfection or the fineness of hand to execute it; captive because I would go to any length whatever to keep someone from taking him away from me."

The mood of euphoria continued in Paris and in New Jersey. Arnold, charged with energy, was so pleased that he was already thinking in terms of a trade edition of the book, a volume with a far larger print run, whose price would make it accessible to a larger public. Before that, however, the deluxe edition had to be finished, and a few important decisions still had to be made. Edmund Wilson had rejected the offer to translate the *Haggadah,* suggesting that Arnold contact Dr. Cecil Roth, a noted Hebrew scholar who had already done a very successful translation of the Seder service. Arnold agreed and sent off a letter to Roth asking that Trianon be given permission to use his translation and that Roth add a text and notes to the new volume. At that point, a more potentially dangerous problem arose. Ben, Arnold learned, was making his own dummy of the book, incorporating material they had never discussed. He was also making efforts to sell the book without consulting Arnold. In spite of his feeling that Ben was wrong to undertake a task that should be done by the publisher, Arnold professed to be "thrilled" when Shahn's dummy arrived in Paris. "It is going to be one of the books of the century," he wrote the artist.

In November, Cecil Roth entered the picture. He gave Arnold permission to use his translation and agreed to add an introduction and notes; but after receiving the dummy, he also began making unsolicited criticisms of the book itself. He had a few complaints, all of them concerning the artist's contributions to the volume (he was obviously not a great admirer of Ben's work). For one, since Roth wanted the book to be primarily a useful aid to the Seder and not an art book, he was disturbed to find Ben's handwritten text, his "creative lettering and alphabet," both unattractive and difficult to read. He suggested that it be replaced with legible typography. He was also unhappy about Ben's Hebrew, which he thought was awful. Furthermore, he thought that ten drawings Ben had added to illustrate the words to "An Only Kid" gave too much prominence to that playful song, which usually concludes the Seder. Instead, he suggested that other passages, of greater importance to the service, should be illustrated. Arnold, perhaps intimidated by Roth's reputation, agreed to many of the suggested changes. Thus, the book would become primarily a scholarly volume with detailed notes and explanations instead of simply a beautifully illustrated *Haggadah*.

Roth's criticisms, some of them useful, were only one of Arnold's worries at the time. He was also having trouble finding Hebrew type in Paris and, furthermore, he had been unable to find the money to help finance a trade edition of the book, which he could not produce without the aid of an American distributor.

At this point—it's difficult to know what Shahn and Fawcus had been waiting for—they decided to make some kind of contract concerning the publication of the *Haggadah*. That "contract," hardly a legal document, was no more than a letter, undated and handwritten by Ben while Arnold was in Roosevelt. Ben granted Trianon Press reproduction rights for both the deluxe and trade editions of the *Haggadah* for $5,500. It was understood, Ben wrote, that one thousand dollars was payable on request and the balance as soon as the project permitted. Also, if the total project was a success financially, Faucus would pay whatever his conscience permitted. In conclusion, he wrote: "It is further understood that neither of us will be greatly enriched financially by this project but will be enriched spiritually."

CHAPTER THIRTY-NINE

Shahn and Fawcus: An Uneasy Relationship

LONG BEFORE THE *HAGGADAH* WAS FINISHED, ARNOLD WAS already thinking of future volumes in the Ben Shahn collection. These included reproductions of the series of Dreyfus watercolors that Ben had done at Truro many years before, together with an appropriate text; reproductions of several delightful drawings of Louis Armstrong that Ben had done for CBS; and an illustrated Ecclesiastes, which had been suggested to Ben and Arnold by Joseph Blumenthal of the Spiral Press, a noted American typographer who wanted to print the text that would accompany Ben's illustrations. Later, Trianon would publish a facsimile of Ben's early illustrations for De Quincey's "Levana."

In the meantime, Trianon Press was in a state of chaos, which was not unusual. Arnold's success was often due to his ability to pull things together at the last moment, and the last moment had not yet come.

Nonetheless, in spite of misunderstandings and delays (Arnold's inability to organize his work was most often responsible for these), the personal relationship between Ben and Arnold apparently remained warm. Arnold had even found the ideal country house for the Shahns, near his own château, and he very much hoped that Ben might buy it.

Now Arnold arranged to have the original Dreyfus watercolors sent from New York to Paris, where Crampe and Hourdebaigt could start working on them, at the same time beginning the Ecclesiastes. This meant that three Shahn/Trianon books would soon be in various stages of preparation, with a strong possibility of a fourth, "Levana," to follow; all this without a formal agreement between the principals.

The year 1964 was a crucial one. In February Roth was angry. "I am really getting fed up with this one-sided correspondence," he wrote Arnold, reminding him that he had completed most of his work on the project five years earlier. Roth was undoubtedly placated to some extent the next month, when Arnold wrote him that the problem of the Hebrew type had been solved. He still complained, however, that he had no material—sample texts or layouts—with which to work. Why, Roth wondered, couldn't the planning have been done with all interested parties seated around a table, exchanging ideas? (He did not realize that that was not the Trianon way of working.) In any case, he wished he had been consulted more frequently. In September, Roth finally received proofs of his texts, but before he had a chance to finish reading and correcting them, he suffered a heart attack while on a visit to Jerusalem. Fortunately for Arnold's peace of mind, Mrs. Roth wrote him that it was not the strain of working with Trianon that caused her husband's heart attack.

On the business side there was very good news. In January, Arnold told Ben that the distinguished and powerful Boston publishing house, Little, Brown, was showing serious interest in distributing the trade edition of the *Haggadah*. Though Arnold was, of course, very pleased—this would assure the financing of the book—Ben was far from enthusiastic. Surprisingly, both he and Bernarda preferred that the book be sold to a small New York publisher, but Arnold, having had a bad experience with that publisher, paid no attention to their wishes. Instead, at the end of February, he accepted an offer from Little, Brown to take 15,000 copies of the *Haggadah*. (The offer was later changed to 20,000 copies, at a lower per copy price.)

Arnold proceeded to prepare the trade edition, while Little, Brown accepted all delays and changes with equanimity. There was only one problem, and it was a serious one: Arnold had not kept Ben informed of the progress of the negotiations, nor did he let him know when the contract was signed. This was legally correct—their agreement gave Arnold the right to sell the American rights to the trade edition to whomever he chose—but Ben was understandably offended at having been kept in the dark over such an important matter.

As Arnold must have feared—and perhaps this is why he delayed telling Ben about the Little, Brown contract—the artist erupted upon hearing the news. He felt betrayed, and the friendship between the two men came abruptly to an end. Ignoring the advantages of a financial agreement with a powerful, reliable American publisher that would pay its bills on time, Ben no longer looked upon the venture as one that would yield only "spiritual enrichment." It became a matter of doing business with a man he could not trust.

At the beginning of the year, Ben had finally hired a lawyer to protect his interests. The lawyer was Martin Bressler, son of Ben's friend Moshe Bressler. Young Bressler was inexperienced, but he was bright and could be trusted.

Ben was dealing with several publishers in addition to Trianon; Bressler's first task was to put everything in order, which he managed to do efficiently. In fact, there were no complications until he came to Ben's dealings with Trianon, which were too confused for an inexperienced attorney. The basic problem, he found, was that no formal, comprehensive contract had ever been drawn up between his client and Trianon. In August, he wrote to Arnold, introducing himself as Ben's attorney and asking Fawcus to enter into a formal agreement concerning the publication and sale of the *Haggadah*. Many questions had not been covered in the earlier written agreement; Bressler offered to send Arnold a new, complete contract covering such essential matters as royalties and foreign rights. Shortly afterward, he also wrote to Little, Brown, whose executives had been both gentlemanly and correct in their dealings in this matter, saying that Ben was unhappy. Little, Brown wisely hired an attorney to meet with Bressler at once.

The quarrels between Ben and Arnold multiplied. While visiting New York, Fawcus was told that the artist was making a will, providing for his children; this supposedly explained his latest and unexpected demand for a 10 percent royalty, about double what had been planned. Arnold, with good reason, felt he was being unfairly pressured; he complained that no progress was being made. At the end of the meeting, Bressler insisted that another meeting be held the following day, and ordered Arnold to remain in New York "or else." Outraged and bewildered, Arnold disobeyed. He already had a reservation on a plane for Paris, and he left— without seeing Ben's attorney.

There no longer seemed any possibility of an amicable solution. Ben was angry; he neither liked nor trusted Arnold anymore, and he neither could nor wanted to hide his feelings. Arnold, on the other hand, found it impossible to understand why his relationship with Ben had deteriorated. He stubbornly refused to give up. Frustrated and hurt, he sent a handwritten letter in which he begged Ben to trust him once again, to remember that he wanted to do what was best for Bernarda and the children, and that his goal was to publish the best possible *Ben Shahn* books.

This plea was useless, however. There had been too much acrimony for Ben and Arnold to regain the spirit of the past. Finally resigned, Arnold turned over all Shahn correspondence to his meticulous and thoroughly efficient editor, Mary Laing. Face-to-face encounters, however, were inevitable, but now the two men, barely speaking to each other, would have to have an impartial mediator when they were together.

Because of the hostility between the principals, progress at these meetings was painfully slow. Ben had become increasingly exasperated by the confusion that reigned in the Trianon office. Arnold, for his part, was hurt and puzzled by Ben's increasing arrogance. Fawcus was unusually short because he had been afflicted with rickets as a child in India; he had been bullied throughout his childhood, and now he felt that Ben, towering over him, intimidating and treating him with disdain, was one more bully.

In any case, there remained many issues to resolve. Among these was the question of the disposition of the extra copies of the frontispiece, a glowing seven-branched menorah, and the title page of the *Haggadah*. There were a few possible solutions. These prints could all be destroyed, thereby maintaining the value of those in the book. Or Ben could sign them, then sell them at a price to be determined by the author and the publisher. Or he could sign them and then sell a number of them to Trianon; or, finally, Trianon could divide them with Shahn, artist and publisher agreeing when they would be sold and at what price.

There was a more serious issue concerning the publication of *Ecclesiastes,* which was to be the second Shahn/Trianon book. Without giving Trianon any advance notice, Joe Blumenfeld had published his own Shahn *Ecclesiastes.* With a few black-and-white illustrations, it was in no way comparable to the projected Trianon version. Yet the publication of the two books at the same time was certain to confuse booksellers and cut into Trianon's sales. This was not, Arnold knew, Blumenthal's fault; the original idea was his, and he had every right to publish it. Even Ben had a right to do Blumenthal's book, but it was his obligation to notify Arnold of its publication. In any case, it was agreed that publication of the Trianon *Ecclesiastes* would have to be postponed.

There were a variety of other problems. Contracts had to be worked out and dates of publication established for all of these books. Arnold agreed that the Little, Brown contract should be changed, with royalties being sent directly to Ben and not through Trianon as had been previously stipulated; but no one knew just what to do with the Dreyfus plates, which had already been printed.

At one point, because of a misunderstanding, Ben even accused Arnold of producing and selling erotic Japanese prints, with the art books presumably no more than a front for this pornography business. This false accusation threatened to terminate all relations between the two men.

After Ben received his first copy of the deluxe *Haggadah,* however, there was a period of tranquility. It was a magnificent book, superbly printed on fine paper and enclosed in a parchment box with silver-gilt clasps: a remarkable achievement. The artist was obviously moved. He graciously wrote to Arnold, "Whatever fury may have flown back and forth between us has not dimmed in the least degree the flawless perfection of the finished *Haggadah.*"

This welcome interlude was short-lived. The battle resumed. A climax of sorts was reached at a meeting, attended by a mediator friendly to both men, at the Yale Club in New York. It was morning and the club's vast living room was quiet. The argument between the two men was particularly bitter. Arnold was, as always, excited and tense, ready to explode at any moment; Ben was—and this was obviously frustrating to Arnold—calm and quiet, completely in control while he presented his case slowly and deliberately. The subject was, as it most frequently was, money, and the underlying problem was that Ben was still firmly convinced that Arnold was a wealthy man with an endless supply of funds, furnished to him by a number of affluent benefactors. In reality, Trianon Press was, as it almost always was, on the verge of financial collapse.

At one point Arnold did explode. His face reddening, he rose and bitterly accused Ben of being a hypocrite who only pretended to care for the poor and oppressed, while he was really a greedy man who was doing all he could to squeeze the last penny out of a needy publisher whose sole concern was not money but the publication of fine books. "Ben Shahn, man of the people," he concluded, before he fell to the floor, somehow landing beard up and muttering, "Water, water . . ."

The horrified mediator looked about the room for someone to bring a glass of water, but no one was in sight. He headed for the bar, where he was sure to find help, but Ben stopped him. He asked him, calmly, to wait a minute: the incident reminded him of a wonderful story . . . that he was eager to tell.

CHAPTER FORTY

"The Old Master Is Masterly": The *Lucky Dragon*

DURING THE 1960S, OFFERS CONTINUED TO BE MADE AND honors bestowed on Ben from every part of the country; his position as one of America's best-known and loved artists was secure, in spite of the red-baiting of the previous decade. In 1962, he was asked to do covers for Capitol Records and to execute designs for a number of off-Broadway theatrical productions. He was invited to participate as a juror in the C&C Super Cola Arts Grants-in-Aid selection at the New York City Board of Education, to be featured speaker at the Pacific Arts Association Conference in Seattle, to lecture at Orange Coast College in Costa Mesa, California, and to conduct a workshop for the Arts Council of Coral Gables, Florida. He was appointed by the Museum of Fine Arts in Boston to serve as "Visitor" to the museum school, and he was requested by the department of art and archeology at Stanford to assist in a search for full professors and an administrative head of the department. He was also invited to lecture at the University of Louisville, contribute a painting for a Mogen David kosher wine brochure, and speak at the First Presbyterian Church in Freehold, New Jersey, at Idaho State College in Pocatello, and at the University of Utah in Salt Lake City.

Among the academic honors conferred upon him, the one that surely pleased him most came from Harvard which, in 1967, gave him the honorary degree of doctor of arts, with this citation: "Pathos, protest, wit and wisdom shape the content of this lively artist's telling work." This came five years after the honorary degree of doctor of fine arts given to him by Princeton. Yale, though it granted Ben no academic honors, did request, in 1965, that he serve on its University Council's Committee on the Humanities.

Other degrees came from Pratt Institute in Brooklyn, Rutgers, and the Hebrew Union College in Cincinnati, and he was awarded medals by the National Institute of Arts and Letters and the Art Directors' Club. One achievement was a source of special pride to him. In 1945, shortly after the death of FDR, Ben had thought it would be appropriate for the town of Roosevelt—Jersey Homesteads had recently changed its name—to erect a monument in honor of the late president. Not until seventeen years later was enough money raised. The monument, a massive powerful bronze bust executed by Ben's son Jonathan, was installed in a small park near Roosevelt's school. In a memorable photo Ben, beaming with pride, is seen seated next to Eleanor Roosevelt, who joined Adlai Stevenson and Anne Bancroft in speaking at the ceremony.

His most remarkable achievement had originated a few years earlier, however. It was his forceful answer to the critics who complained that he had in recent years lost his passion for justice, that he was no longer able to express through his art his anger and sadness at the plight of innocent human beings.

In September 1957, Russell Lynes commissioned Ben to undertake another assignment for *Harper's*, the magazine that had published his powerful illustrations for John Bartlow Martin's articles. This time he was asked to illustrate a series of articles by an atomic physicist, Ralph E. Lapp. "The Voyage of the Lucky Dragon" dealt with the fate of the crew of a small Japanese fishing boat (ironically called the *Lucky Dragon*) who had been caught in the fallout of radioactive ash that followed the March 1, 1954, American hydrogen bomb test at Bikini Atoll in the Pacific, about eighty-five miles from their boat. After their return to Japan, the twenty-three ailing crewmen were hospitalized and soon diagnosed as victims of

radiation poisoning. One of them, Aikichi Kuboyama, a radio operator and the best-educated and most highly esteemed member of
the crew, died after a long and painful illness. The story was
reported in newspapers all over the world. Panic swept through
Japan: had fish, the staple diet, been contaminated? The Japanese
feared that the entire economy of their country was threatened.

Lapp spent almost a year in Japan. He spoke to members of the
crew, to their families and doctors, to the Japanese scientists who
first suspected that the cause of the illness might be hydrogen
bomb fallout, and to American officials who at first denied that the
United States was in any way involved in the tragedy. The result
was a knowledgeable, informative, and intelligent text. Inspired by
the tragic injustice of Kuboyama's death and the terrifying implications of the bomb and the consequences of a nuclear war, Ben
once again executed far more drawings than the magazine
required; they contributed an element of human warmth and bitter sadness to Lapp's somewhat dry, scientific text.

"The Voyage of the Lucky Dragon" was published in the December 1957 and January and February 1958 issues of *Harper's*. In the
meantime, Ben had become obsessed with nuclear warfare and the
absolute necessity of disarmament. He wanted to create a drama
in paintings, he told Bernarda, and he would turn every facet of
the test and its results into a human experience. After several years
of calm, he had again found a cause for which he could fight with
both passion and compassion. He created eleven paintings as well
as numerous drawings: works that would surpass his two earlier
such series of emotion-charged works. He explained how the
method and scope of the *Lucky Dragon* series differed from those
of the past:

> When I did the Sacco and Vanzetti series and also the Mooney
> series, I was very careful to document my work with newspaper
> photographs and clippings, but with the Japanese paintings I no
> longer felt the need of such documentation. The radio operator
> on the fishing boat, who subsequently died of radiation poison-
> ing, was a man like you and me. I now felt it was unnecessary to
> paint him, but to paint us. The man consoling the wife of the
> radio operator was a man consoling a woman in agony. The radio
> operator playing with his child was any father playing with his

child. The Japanese Nobel Prize–winning physicist who first suspected the truth was a scientist. He might have been any scientist. I no longer felt the need to document him specifically. The terror of the beast . . . is the terror that now haunts all of us.

In late 1961, these paintings, along with several ink drawings, were shown at the Downtown Gallery. They tell the story from the day of the fishing boat's departure to the day of Kuboyama's funeral. A wild, fire-belching dragon hovers threateningly over a large number of these paintings, a warning of what the future could hold for all of mankind.

The first picture shows Kuboyama sitting stiffly on the edge of his hospital bed. His painfully emaciated body is red from radiation, and his bald head, in profile, stares at an unidentified beast. On his lap the sick man holds a sheet with lettering in Shahn's folk alphabet summarizing the story in spare, unembellished language. It reads:

> I AM A FISHERMAN
> AIKICHI KUBOYAMA
> BY NAME. ON THE
> FIRST OF MARCH
> 1954 OUR FISHING
> BOAT THE LUCKY
> DRAGON WANDERED
> UNDER AN ATOMIC CLOUD
> 80 MILES FROM
> BIKINI. I AND MY FRIENDS
> WERE BURNED.
> WE DID NOT KNOW
> WHAT HAPPENED TO US.
> ON SEPTEMBER 23 OF THAT YEAR
> I DIED OF ATOMIC BURN.

The paintings that follow are as moving and disturbing as those found in any of Ben's work. They include *I Never Dared to Dream,* a heartbreaking portrait of Kuboyama and his wife, clinging to one another, anticipating the radio operator's death; *We Did Not Know What Happened to Us,* a terrifying view of the blast itself, the monster's head emerging from the clouds above; *It's No Use to Do Any*

More, a dying Kuboyama in a white hospital bed, isolated and alone, observed from afar by two men, presumably doctors; and, finally, *Why?,* a stark, simple view of the urn containing Kuboyama's ashes, which had been placed in a marble vault in the mountainside above his native Yaizu; one white chrysanthemum, placed above the urn, posing the question, "*why?*"

These paintings represent a significant step forward in Ben's career. Perhaps he had mellowed. Certainly his knife had become less sharp—yet it cut deeper than his sharper knives, reaching to the very heart of Ben's subjects. The results are considerably more poignant, tender, and lyrical than any of his earlier series of protests—indeed, than any of his earlier works. According to Bernarda, the *Lucky Dragon* paintings were to Ben pretty much "a consummation of what he wanted to say in paint. Intellectually, emotionally, and in the material-visual sense they were gratifying to him. More than any other of his works, grouped or singly, they established him in his work, expressed his relationship to it, told the role that he wanted to play in it."

The exhibition was received enthusiastically. "The old master is masterly. . . ." wrote Brian O'Doherty of *The New York Times.* "To see Mr. Shahn's exhibition becomes almost a duty. For in one of the superb services that art can perform, and rarely does, he takes the inhuman energies that threaten to destroy us and simply puts them in human perspectives. It is impossible to contemplate The Bomb. At the Downtown Galleries one does."

In the fall 1961 issue of *Art in America,* Ben himself wrote perceptively of these works, which he considered his finest achievement as an artist.

> I have, during the past year, been mainly absorbed in seeking to formulate the possible coming cataclysm. If tragedy is universal, this imminent tragedy is simply total. In this most recent group of pictures I find that I have returned to the very early device of focusing upon the particular in order to illuminate the universal; but at the same time I have drawn strongly upon an almost primordial symbol, fusing the two to express something that I feel with overwhelming oppressiveness. The incidents of the *Lucky Dragon* are the particular—the actual real agony which happened and which will happen. The symbol, the dragon, is the

Suzuki Kuboyama, the widow of the radio operator, visiting an exhibition of the Lucky Dragon *pictures in Japan.*

ineffable, the unspeakable tragedy toward which the world's people are moving.

Following the exhibition, Ben's *Lucky Dragon* series were not dispersed into a number of museums and the homes of collectors throughout the country, as might have been the case. Instead, the paintings were reproduced together and preserved in book form thanks to the effort of an enthusiastic writer and a perceptive publisher.

The author was Richard Hudson, founder and editor of an anti-war journal called *War/Peace Report*. Hudson had written a bitter, sarcastic editorial during the period when Americans were frantically building fallout shelters, suggesting that the lucky citizens were those who died quickly outside the shelters rather than those who, in their shelters, suffered for a long time the painful effects of radiation. Ben, on the mailing list of *War/Peace Report* (he must

The Beast of the Atoll

have contributed money) was enthusiastic about the editorial, reading it aloud to his Roosevelt neighbors. As a result, he did a cover and several illustrations for the small journal, as did his friend Alexander Calder.

Shortly afterward, Hudson visited the Downtown Gallery to see the *Lucky Dragon* paintings. Profoundly impressed, he returned with Thomas Yosselof, who ran a small publishing house, and suggested that Yosselof publish them in book form. Yosselof agreed and asked Hudson to write the text.

Ben and Hudson met only a few times; a "collaboration" was not necessary, and Ben was not asked for help with the text, nor did he offer any. Clear, concise, and well-written, *Kuboyama and the Saga of the Lucky Dragon* was published in 1965. Other books (including the Trianon volumes) of Ben's were more beautiful—notably, the marvelous, celebratory *Love and Joy about Letters*—yet none rivaled in impact the dramatic *Saga of The Lucky Dragon.*

CHAPTER FORTY-ONE

The Termination of a Dealer-Artist Relationship

IN JANUARY 1968, BEN WROTE TO EDITH HALPERT, TELLING her that he was forced to terminate their long dealer-artist relationship. It was a painful step, he noted, but the ill-feeling between them over the past few years had made it almost impossible for him to paint.

After informing her that Martin Bressler would take the necessary legal steps leading to the dissolution of their relationship, including the return to Ben of all his works at the gallery or on loan elsewhere, he concluded that "only the most extreme circumstances could have pushed me to the point of a break, but this has, alas, become unavoidable."

The differences between Ben and Edith had surfaced many years earlier, when his popularity began to grow and he began to do commercial work. The major problem was Halpert's contention that she should receive a commission on any work sold, whether through the gallery or not. Ben disagreed and refused to pay her a commission on money he earned from assignments she had had no part in obtaining. Halpert was insistent. This was the gallery's policy; why shouldn't Ben follow it when her other artists—Stuart Davis, Charles Sheeler, and Georgia O'Keeffe, for example—did?

She had conscientiously promoted Shahn's art, and it was because of these efforts that he had been offered outside work. To her, it seemed only fair that she be compensated for all she had done, even indirectly, for him.

Ben reacted angrily to her implication that he would be nowhere without her promotional efforts. "If I ever came to a belief that my own reputation exceeded my abilities," he wrote, "I would throw all the paint I own into the nearest river."

In spite of Edith's protests, Ben never gave in to her demands. Nor did he ever satisfactorily respond to her complaint that he frequently kept her in the dark about work he had produced but did not give to the gallery. It was embarrassing, Halpert contended, to receive inquiries about efforts of his that she, his representative, knew nothing about.

In addition, and perhaps even more seriously, she protested that outside activities consumed too much of his time and dissipated his creative energies. He consigned fewer and fewer paintings to her, and getting new works of his for her annual group exhibitions was becoming increasingly difficult. It was hard to establish a reputation, she explained, but even harder to maintain it.

In June 1962, Edith accused him of "gallery evasion" and warned him that everything must be done in the "normal" way during the next season. She also reminded him of the endless battles she had fought over the past ten years to keep figurative art alive while "non-objective, abstract expressionism, crushed cars, etc." dominated the art market. In his reply, he restated his position, which had not changed, and added a major complaint of his own. It had come to his attention that she had frequently tried to undermine him and his work, that she had been rude to people who came to see it, and that, on one occasion, she had suggested to someone who had wanted to offer him a commission that it might be better to look for a younger artist.

Ever since their quarrel began, both Ben and Edith had repeatedly suggested that they meet to settle their differences. "You're a big boy and I'm a big girl," Edith had written, "so let's get this thing over with as soon as possible." However, there was no meeting then or at any time, just a continuing series of complaints, leading, a few years before their final break, to an angry letter from Ben in which he made his first threat: "Your unpleasant remarks about me, your complaints and gossip about me amount to efforts to damage my reputation. . . . I must ask you to stop that, and again let me assure you that if you find our association intolerable and wish to terminate it, I dare say that I can find another dealer."

In 1964, for the first time, Ben took concrete steps in that direction. He asked his friend Betty Chamberlain to make discreet inquiries about other dealers. Chamberlain reported back with some suggestions: Pierre Matisse (a "gentleman" dealer), Marion Willard, Cordier and Ekstrom, Borgenicht, and Saidenberg. However, Ben made no move until January 1968, when he wrote the letter ending his relationship with Edith. It was a desperate move. He was, Bernarda told Bressler (as Ben had written Halpert), so depressed that he was no longer able to work, and she asked the lawyer to do his best to extricate him from his ties to the Downtown Gallery. Bressler's first step was to arrange a meeting with Halpert.

That meeting was a painful experience for all concerned. It was made less so by Philip Wittenberg, Ben's old friend and former lawyer, who represented Halpert in the discussions and managed to reduce the tension in the room. Edith, however, was a very sick woman, physically and emotionally. During their long talk, she swallowed pills, drank coffee (most likely with alcohol in it), and chain-smoked in spite of her emphysema. Bressler was afraid she might even become so ill that she would have to end the conference.

A few months later, Edith Halpert issued a release announcing that she would no longer act as exclusive representative of Ben Shahn, Abraham Rattner, Georgia O'Keeffe, and the estates of Stuart Davis, John Marin, and Max Weber. Her last years were sad and lonely. Those who knew her during that period remember a pathetic, sick woman, more often drunk than not, not at all the vibrant, attractive art dealer who helped further the careers of some of the most important artists of this century. She died on October 7, 1970.

CHAPTER FORTY-TWO

The
Family Man

IN THE MID-1960s, BEN CREATED A NUMBER OF MOSAIC murals—for synagogues in Nashville, Buffalo, and New Haven; for Le Moyne College in Memphis; and for his friends the Spivacks in Far Hills, New Jersey. He also completed two larger works. One was a mural commissioned by the Zim Navigation Company for its luxury ocean liner, the S.S. *Shalom;* the ship was soon sold and the two panels of the mural are now in the New Jersey State Museum in Trenton. The other was a mural, executed in mosaic, based on the Sacco-Vanzetti case, which had been commissioned by Syracuse University. He also created a large number of prints, most of them serigraphs. These he did not sell through the Downtown Gallery; many were offered through his close friend George Nakashima, a brilliant woodworker who lived and worked in nearby Bucks County and had remodeled the Shahn home in Roosevelt. However, Shahn completed very few paintings during this period.

This slowdown was not completely due to the Halpert dispute. He was, and it was apparent to all, not a well man. He was tense and gray; he lacked his customary exuberance and seemed devoid of energy. At the end of 1966, he had to stop working altogether.

From time to time before this, he had suffered pain in his chest, but now it spread to his arms and shoulders. Finally, it became so severe that he had to be admitted to Princeton Hospital for tests. There he learned that he had suffered a mild heart attack and would have to cut down his activities and, above all, avoid stress.

It was impossible to obey the doctor's orders for very long. The following May, their daughter Susie called from England, where she had been living for several years, to say that she was not well and had been taken to a London hospital. Because Ben was far too weak to travel, Bernarda went alone.

It was said by many that Susie had gone to England, where she found work as a folksinger, to escape from her father's clutches. (Ben had opposed the move, and Bernarda had paid her way.) Other neighbors in Roosevelt believed that she had left because she saw herself as an ugly duckling, stared at and ridiculed by strangers who were disturbed by her unusual appearance. Susanna was somewhat deformed at birth; her chin jutted out, one leg was thinner than the other, and one hip was higher than the other. Even worse, she had been born with only one kidney, and had been told she could survive only by following a rigid diet and taking medicine. She had failed to do either, however.

On her arrival in London, Bernarda was met by Susie's husband, Tony Watts. When she reached the hospital she immediately realized that her daughter was near death. Horrified by the terrible conditions—she described the hospital as a bedlam—Bernarda contacted an English doctor whom she knew and who said that he would have Susie moved. It was useless. In spite of the doctor's intervention, there was no chance of overcoming the red tape of the country's National Health system. On May 8, 1967, Susanna Shahn Watts died. She was flown to the United States and buried in the Roosevelt cemetery.

Ben and Bernarda were devastated. They, their friends, and their other children agreed that Susie had been special—bright and spirited, with a radiant charm that made all who met her forget her physical irregularities at once. She was, it has been said, the glue that held a complicated, often troubled, family together. According to her sister Abby, she was "in touch with the straightforward human emotions, rare in that family." It was essential that she leave home, yet she never really detached herself. Her letters to her family effervesce with that joy and enthusiasm that were uniquely hers.

Throughout the funeral service Ben's face was agonizing to see; one observer described it as looking like a scream. Ed Rosskam believed that Ben himself started dying with the death of his beloved daughter.

As he wept over her death, Ben must have wept too for his own failures as a parent, and his inability to experience fully the joy of being a father.

"Every creative person is a prisoner of the work that he does," Ben told Tony Schwartz, who taped a series of interviews with him in the early 1960s. "Everything else is very unimportant—family and everything else. . . . I had a feeling that I must do something with the kids, but very little. I was too involved all these years, you know, and they grew up, and it's too bad I must have lost contact with some of them on this." On another occasion when he and Bernarda were being interviewed in connection with a CBS educational program, "This Is Ben Shahn," Ben was even more casual. "I've never brought up children in my life," he told an interviewer. "They—they grew up. We came to an understanding very early. If they'll let us alone, we'll let them alone, and that was the extent of it." Continuing in the same vein, he declared that their system must have worked since the children all left home very early. "They became independent really very early, all of them. I tried togetherness for a while, but it didn't work. . . . They're very nice, of course they are, but they're strong characters, all of them."

Under the circumstances, they were forced to be. Though their father could be warm and loving, each child suffered in a different way.

Both Ezra, a scientist, teacher, and the family's only nonartist, and Judy, who became a successful painter, had been abandoned at an early age. Ben left home when his son was one and a half years old and never really reentered his life. Ezra estimates that he saw his father no more than two hundred times, and those included the years he spent at nearby Princeton where he did his graduate studies. Judy, five years older, had a different experience: she knew and loved her father before he left home. She became bitter not only because of what he had done to her but even more because of the pain he had inflicted on her mother. Nonetheless, after Tillie's death, Judy and her father slowly regained a degree of closeness. Today, she retains loving feelings toward him and bears no grudge.

The three children who grew up with Ben were not physically abandoned, yet they may well have felt emotionally deprived. Abby, like her sister Susie, left home relatively early. An independent, determined woman, she was more able to defy her father than were the other children. After leaving Reed College in Oregon, she moved to San Francisco, where she attended art school; she was sufficiently talented to have an exhibition at City Lights Books. Her father objected to her remaining in San Francisco and in time persuaded her to return to the East Coast, where he felt all artists belonged. But Abby never again lived at home. Though aware of her father's shortcomings, she believes he was always there for his children when needed.

Jonathan, a gifted sculptor, was, by all accounts, closer to his father than were the other children. Keenly intelligent and witty, he has none of his father's pomposity or ego. Though he bears a striking physical resemblance to Ben, he is much the more gentle and affectionate of the two. Ben was proud of him, proclaiming that he was "one of the most learned people I know," and he was not ashamed to say so; he was also unafraid to belittle and ridicule him both privately and in public. Jonathan, too, left home at an early age, but, after living in Boston and, for many years, in Italy, he returned to Roosevelt with his wife and son.

Toward the end of 1967, Martin Bressler, who had been doing his best to set Ben's business and personal affairs in order since taking over as his lawyer, made a surprising discovery: Ben and Bernarda had never bothered to get married. When the lawyer asked Bernarda why, she replied that she had mentioned it casually to Ben several times, but that he had refused (and she herself was somewhat loath to marry). After that, they just never got around to it. Bressler was alarmed. This was a serious matter; Ben's health had been steadily deteriorating, and it was absolutely essential for legal reasons that he and Bernarda marry as soon as possible.

With the help of Bressler's sister-in-law, a municipal court judge was found and the couple were married in the nearby town of Cranbury on November 24, 1967. Following the ceremony, Ben, Bernarda, Bressler, and Bressler's law partner Bernard Meislin drove to the Shahn home where they drank a bottle of champagne to "celebrate" the long-delayed wedding.

Nothing changed with the legalization of their union: Ben and Bernarda had been together for more than thirty years. When asked how she would characterize their marriage, Bernarda immediately answered, "Frightening." After a few moments' pause, she changed her mind and said it had been "wonderful." It had probably been both. They fought frequently and angrily— so much so, that Abby and Susie made up a game in which one of them played Ben, angrily and imperiously shouting, "*Bernarda!*" while the other daughter, playing the role of Bernarda, would respond meekly and in a small voice, "Ben, Ben."

Ben's temper was monumental and unpredictable. To Bernarda's dismay, he often cruelly made fun of people. He held grudges far too long as well. As one example, he and Ad Reinhardt, once close friends, stopped talking to each other for years following a stormy disagreement. When they finally reconciled, it was almost too late—the reconciliation came one week before Reinhardt's death.

The relationship between Ben and Bernarda was frequently troubled. Bernarda, a strong woman of extraordinary intelligence and wit, as well as an artist of considerable talent, found it difficult and sometimes impossible to play the role of the meek, dutiful servant that Ben assigned to her. Though she never stopped working, she spent most of her time taking care of the children, the home, and, above all, Ben—thereby giving up a career of her own, though not her financial independence. (Because of Ben's reluctance to give her money, she kept her earnings in a separate bank account.)

There were, however, compensations. At his best, Ben could be the most charming of men, the perfect companion. He was, Bernarda felt, the most "entertaining" man she had ever met. They were intellectually compatible and thoroughly enjoyed each other's company. They could, according to Bernarda, sit around the breakfast table talking until four o'clock in the morning and then not speak to each other for four weeks. Though Bernarda had, on at least two occasions, left Ben, he had begged her to return, and they remained together until the end of his life. At her angriest, Bernarda never lost love and respect for the man and his unfailing integrity. At her angriest, too, she could look at his paintings and feel that in them she was seeing the real Ben Shahn.

CHAPTER FORTY-THREE

The
Death
of an Artist

BY 1968, IT WAS OBVIOUS THAT BEN WAS A DYING MAN. HE WAS weak and tired; according to one visitor, he resembled a sick bird, and his newly sprouted white beard was his feathers. He was in and out of the hospital, undergoing more and more tests, some of which indicated that he was developing diabetes. His right leg had caused him trouble for some time, and he walked with great difficulty, using a cane.

He continued working when he could, designing advertisements condemning the war in Vietnam—still protesting what he believed to be injustice wherever he found it. He also had the time and strength to help in the preparations for a large retrospective exhibition to be held at the Kennedy Galleries in New York in late 1968.

After the final break with Halpert, Ben had chosen Kennedy to represent him for a few reasons. It was a well-established, highly esteemed gallery, showing some of the most distinguished American artists, among them Hopper, Marin, and Charles Burchfield. Furthermore, Lawrence Fleischman, the gallery's owner and director, was a man Shahn admired and respected; Fleischman had founded the Archives of American Art and, as a discerning collector, had been buying Shahn's paintings for his own collection for many years.

The exhibition was an important one, celebrating the artist's seventieth birthday and showing a comprehensive selection of forty years of his work, from a 1928 self-portrait to *Skowhegan Parade* of 1968. Ben was pleased. He inscribed a catalogue of the exhibition to Fleischman with the words, "Remember, remember, remember," and his dealer reciprocated by presenting him with a paintbrush. The gallery was crowded; the line of Ben's admirers awaiting their turn to see the exhibition stretched outside the building. Ben, it seemed, was more popular than ever. The following day he appeared on three television programs—*The Dick Cavett Show, Today,* and Skitch Henderson's show. Very rarely did any of these give time to serious artists.

Not surprisingly, however, much of the press remained unenthusiastic. Critics were looking for something new, and Ben was old hat to many of them. Of all the reviews, one, written by Hilton Kramer for *The New York Times,* was the most hostile. According to Fleischman, it wounded Ben. Kramer called Ben "the classic case of an artist who needed a certain political atmosphere to sustain his talents. These talents, I believe, were rather modest and have remained what they always were: the talents of an illustrator peculiarly dependent on current history for his inspiration." The conclusion of his review was devastating.

> Mr. Shahn's true accomplishments were always in the realm of graphic art—the medium, par excellence, for direct visual statement. . . . No account of the thirties would be complete without attention to these accomplishments, but the history of American art since that period will not, I think, accord his work more than a passing, baffled reference.

A few months later, Ben was in the Princeton hospital again for more tests. It was decided that he should be moved to New York's Mount Sinai Hospital for surgery. After an exploratory operation, the pain that he had earlier felt was gone. In a state of euphoria, he phoned Martin Bressler and asked him to come to the hospital as soon as possible and bring with him a black Conté crayon. Bressler was a member of a committee which was raising funds for his favorite charity, the development of health care centers in Newark, and Ben had promised to sign a number of copies of a portrait of Dr. Martin Luther King, which were to be sold for the benefit of the charity. Now he could, from his hospital bed, keep that promise. These were the last prints he ever signed.

He had one further request. After receiving his doctor's permission to do so, he asked Larry Fleischman to rent a car so that they could go to Brooklyn the following day. The next morning, Bernarda and Jonathan, who were staying at Fleischman's apartment, joined Ben, Judy, and Fleischman for the visit. It was a marvelous outing for Ben. They visited the Botanic Garden and the museum, and ate lunch at Brooklyn's most famous restaurant, Gage and Tollner.

The following day, Ben was returned to surgery. The doctors had withheld from him the news that the previous operation had revealed a bladder tumor, which had to be removed. The operation went smoothly, but at eleven o'clock on the night of March 14, he suffered a fatal heart attack.

After his death, Bernarda was inundated with letters from all over the world, from friends and strangers who wanted to express their gratitude for Ben's great talent as an artist and his relentless battle against injustice. His achievements outbalanced by far his personal flaws. Of all the letters received, perhaps the most appropriate came from his old editor and friend, Russell Lynes, who compared his death to "the crash of a great town in the landscape, a part of our own world that we loved and took for granted as something to set our sights by, measure other things—people and ideas—against, a generous, affectionate, wise and humorous giant of a man."

Ben and Bernarda with their children Susanna, Jonathan, and Abigail.

Bernarda Bryson Shahn in Roosevelt.

SOURCE NOTES

These notes are meant to serve as an informal guide to the principal sources used in writing this book. Sources cited in the text are not repeated here, and complete citations can be found in the bibliography.

I have relied heavily on material found among the Ben Shahn papers, located at the Archives of American Art in Washington, and on the Shahn interviews that are part of the Columbia University Oral History Collection in New York, as well as on my own extensive interviews with Bernarda Bryson Shahn and Judith Shahn Dugan. I have also made abundant use of material found in Shahn's books *The Shape of Content* and *Love and Joy About Letters*. These sources have been utilized throughout the book to such an extent that I have chosen not to mention them in these notes to individual chapters.

CHAPTER ONE

For background material I have consulted Nancy and Stuart Schoenburg's *Lithuanian Jewish Communities* and Moses Rischin's *The Promised City*. Shahn recalled his own experiences in a seminar conducted at St. Olaf College, Northfield, Minnesota, in June 1960; there is also an unpublished manuscript titled "Autobiography." The author of this very useful document is unknown. It has sometimes been attributed to Edwin Rosskam (but never to Shahn).

CHAPTER TWO

Irving Howe's *World of Our Fathers* and Alfred Kazin's *A Walker in the City* are essential reading for a picture of Jewish life in New York at the turn of the century.

The most important source of information concerning Shahn's early years in Brooklyn are found in "Ben Shahn—His Background," an unpublished memoir by the artist's childhood friend William (Willy) Snow. Shahn himself spoke of those years in a series of interviews shown on CBS-TV in 1965.

His arrival in America is described in "An Interview with Ben Shahn" by Alfred Werner, *Congress Bi-Weekly*, March 7, 1966, and in the so-called "Autobiography." John Charles Carlisle's dissertation, James Thrall Soby's book on Shahn paintings, and Katherine Kuh's *The Artist's Voice* contain information about these early years. I have also relied on a letter to me from Gertrude Flax Gold and a telephone conversation with Sophie Rosenbaum.

CHAPTER THREE

John D. Morse's 1944 interview with Shahn, republished in Morse's 1972 anthology; Bernarda Bryson's "The Drawings of Ben Shahn" (*Image* no. 2, autumn 1949), the catalogue of the Philadelphia Museum of Art's Shahn exhibition (November 15–December 31, 1967), and Frank Getlein's "The Letter and the Spirit" (*New Republic,* January 25, 1964) all deal with this period of Shahn's life.

CHAPTER FOUR

Barbara Dunlap supplied information concerning Shahn's time at City College, and I found background material in S. Willis Rudy's history of the college. Patricia Dejohn supplied information from New York University, and Eulelie Drury uncovered material dealing with the artist's time at Woods Hole. Elliot Clark's history of the National Academy was useful, as were the archives of the Art Students League. Kuh's *The Artist's Voice* also contained valuable information.

CHAPTER FIVE

Morris Dorsky's excellent thesis was invaluable for this chapter, as was Snow's unpublished memoir. Other sources included Rodman's early biography of Shahn; Janet Flanner's *An American in Paris*; Dorothy C. Miller and Alfred H. Barr's 1943 MOMA catalogue; Morse's 1944 interview; Martin Bush's *Ben Shahn: The Passion of Sacco and Vanzetti*; and Shahn's afterword to his illustrated edition of Rilke's "For the Sake of a Single Verse."

CHAPTERS SIX–NINE

Dorsky's thesis, Carlisle's dissertation, and Rodman's biography were all useful, as was Shahn's essay "American Painting at Mid-century," from Bush's book on *The Passion of Sacco and Vanzetti*.

CHAPTER TEN

For information on Edith Halpert, I consulted Diane Tepfer's 1989 dissertation; "Edith Halpert," by Avis Berman, in *Museum News* (November–December 1975); the Edith Gregor Halpert papers in the Archives of American Art; and "Interview: Charles Alan Talks with Paul Cummings" in the *Archives of American Art Journal* XIII (1978).

Principal sources for Shahn and the Museum of Modern Art were Russell Lynes's *Good Old Modern*, Alfred H. Barr's introduction to the catalogue of the 1930 exhibition, and the CBS 1965 interviews.

I examined *Levana* at the Rare Book and Manuscript Department of the Firestone Library, Princeton University, and learned about Philip Van Doren Stern from Snow's memoir and from *Current Biography*, July 1955.

CHAPTER ELEVEN

The Trianon Press–Little, Brown edition contains essential material concerning the *Haggadah*, including Shahn's note, the preface by Stephen S. Kayser, and the introduction by Cecil Roth. Also useful were Dorsky's thesis, Rodman's biography, and the September 1963 issue of *Quest*.

Information concerning the Dreyfus series, the summer of 1931, and Walker Evans may be found in Rodman, Carlisle, Snow, and Dorsky as well as in *Artists in Their Own Words*, by Paul Cummings, and in Shahn's 1965 CBS interview. The excellent biography of Walker Evans by Belinda Rathbone has been the most reliable source of information concerning the photographer.

CHAPTER TWELVE

I consulted Dorsky, Carlisle, Rodman, and Morse's 1944 interview with Shahn, as well as Martin Bush's *Ben Shahn: The Passion of Sacco and Vanzetti*, Lincoln Kirstein's article in *Hound and Horn* (April–June 1932),

Edith Halpert's letter of July 10, 1959, to James Thrall Soby, and Brian O'Doherty's interview with Shahn on "Invitation to Art," WGBH-TV, Boston (n.d.). For background material I have used Paul Von Blum's *The Art of Social Conscience,* Page Smith's *Redeeming the Time,* and *Protest: Sacco-Vanzetti and the Intellectuals,* by David Felix.

CHAPTER THIRTEEN

The so-called "Autobiography," Russell Lynes's *Good Old Modern,* Alice Goldfarb Marquis's biography of Alfred H. Barr, and the anthology *By With To & From: A Lincoln Kirstein Reader,* edited by Nicholas Jenkins, as well as the exhibition catalogue, have all served as sources for this chapter.

CHAPTER FOURTEEN

Soby's 1947 *Ben Shahn,* Ann Abbinanti's "Shahn and Social Realism" from the March 1964 issue of the *Art Association of Indianapolis Bulletin,* and Shahn's letters to Soby of July 10, 1959, and April 29, 1957, were the principal sources for this chapter.

CHAPTER FIFTEEN

The story of Rivera's Rockefeller Center mural is best told by Irene Herner de Larrea. Bertram D. Wolfe's biography of Rivera and Hayden Herrara's biography of Frida Kahlo were also helpful. Other sources include Lucienne Bloch's "On Location with Diego Rivera" (*Art in America,* February 1986); Laurance Hurlburt's *The Mexican Muralists in the United States;* a January 17, 1965, interview with Shahn conducted by Eric F. Goldman for the TV program *The Open Mind,* a Lou Block interview of May 31, 1965, with Harlan Phillips; the Lou Block papers, in Louisville, Kentucky; and Shahn's letter to Soby of April 29, 1957.

CHAPTER SIXTEEN

Carlisle's dissertation; the "Autobiography"; the Lou Block papers in Louisville; Avis Berman's *Rebels on Eighth Street;* and Belisario Contreras's *Tradition and Innovation in New Deal Art* all give important information concerning the Prohibition mural.

In addition to the above, Greta Berman's two books and Diana Linden's dissertation have provided material for the Rikers Island section. I am most grateful to Ezra Shahn for showing me the Rikers Island sketchbook.

CHAPTER SEVENTEEN

In addition to my own interviews with Bernarda Shahn, sources for information concerning the artist's wife included an interview of April 29, 1983, which is at the Archives of American Art, Jake Wien's *The Vanishing American Frontier,* the June 17, 1979, edition of the *Trenton Sunday Times Advertiser,* and Francine Tyler's 1991 dissertation.

For background material I consulted Arthur A. Ekirch's *Ideologies and Utopias,* Contreras's *Tradition and Innovation in New Deal Art,* Charles C. Alexander's *Nationalism in American Thought,* and Tugwell's biography of Franklin D. Roosevelt.

The articles and books by Francis V. O'Connor are essential reading for those interested in federal art projects (above all, murals) during this period.

For information concerning Shahn's FSA trip through the South, I have depended on material found at the Library of Congress and the National Archives in Washington, D.C. For an understanding of Shahn's significance as a photographer, I am indebted to Susan H. Edwards.

The literature on the FSA photography project is vast. I have consulted the following books: R. J. Doherty's *Social-Documentary in the USA;* Fleischaven and Brannan's *Documenting America, 1935–1943;* James Guimond's *American Photography and the American Dream;* Milton Meltzer's life of Dorothea Lange; Belinda Rathbone's biography of Walker Evans; *The Black Image in the New Deal,* by Nicholas Natanson; *A Vision Shared,* by Hank O'Neal; *In This Proud Land,* by Stryker and Wood; *Symbols of an Ideal Life,* by Maren Stange; and studies of Shahn's photographs by Davis Pratt and Margaret R. Weiss.

CHAPTER EIGHTEEN

John Vachon's "Tribute to a Man, an Era, an Art" (*Harper's* magazine, September 1973), Roy Stryker's 1964 interview with Richard Doud, Walker Evans's 1971 interview with Paul Cummings, and Wien's catalogue essay on Bernarda Bryson Shahn all provided valuable information for this chapter. David Brinkley's *Washington Goes to War* is a lively chronicle of life in Washington during the Second World War.

CHAPTER NINETEEN

The most valuable history of Jersey Homesteads is Jason H. Cohen's 1994 Rutgers University B.A. thesis. Other sources concerning the town and Shahn's mural included Edwin Rosskam's *Roosevelt, New Jersey;*

Francis V. O'Connor's introduction to the catalogue of a Diego Rivera retrospective held in Detroit in February 1986; Carlisle's dissertation; "Four Million Dollar Village" (*Saturday Evening Post,* February 5, 1938); and "Stress on Home Values Urged by Ben Shahn," an article written by Gertrude Benson for the *Philadelphia Inquirer,* July 8, 1951.

CHAPTER TWENTY

For Shahn's trip through Ohio, I consulted *Ohio: A Photographic Portrait* by Carolyn Kinder Carr; *Ben Shahn in Ohio: The Summer of 1938,* edited by Robert W. Wagner; and Holly Fuhren's "Stranger in a Familiar Land: Ben Shahn in Ohio." Laura Katzman's excellent 1993 essay in *American Art* was helpful, as was material found in the National Archives and the Library of Congress.

CHAPTER TWENTY-ONE

Francis V. O'Connor is the acknowledged authority on Shahn's murals; I consulted his works whenever writing on the subject. Rodman's biography, Contreras's *Tradition and Innovation in New Deal Art,* Bernarda Bryson Shahn's 1972 book on Shahn, and "Shahn's Bronx Post Office Murals: The Perils of Public Art," by Carl Baldwin (*Art in America,* May–June 1967), provided valuable material, as did contemporary newspaper accounts. I also consulted the files of the National Archives.

CHAPTER TWENTY-TWO

Edwin Rosskam's interviews with Bernarda Shahn, Irving Plungian, Alfred Kastner, and others, used as the basis for *Roosevelt, New Jersey,* were an important source for this chapter, as were my interviews with his widow, Louise Rosskam. Pearl Seligman and Charlotte Safir also provided me with insights into the life of this unique town.

Soby's books and Carlisle's dissertation were helpful, as were Julien Levy's *Memoir of an Art Gallery* and Henry Brandon's *As We Are.*

CHAPTER TWENTY-THREE

Once again, Francis V. O'Connor's books and articles on Shahn's murals provided both information and insights, this time in my discussion of the artist's Social Security mural. "On the Walls" by Michele Vishnay (*Arts,* March 1987) and "The Benefits of Art" by Geoff Gehman (*The* [Allentown, Pennsylvania] *Morning Call,* December 15, 1991), were also consulted. I am especially grateful to Gehman for sending me a copy of a letter from John Ormai's widow (correcting Gehman's article) and for putting me in touch with Ormai's son, Ted.

CHAPTER TWENTY-FOUR

For material about the OWI, I made use of the production sheets at the National Archives in Washington. I also consulted the following books: *The Visual Craft of William Golden,* by Cipes Pineles; *V Was for Victory,* by John Morton Blum; *War and Society,* by Richard Polenberg; *Anti-Fascism in American Art,* by Cécile Whiting; *The Politics of Propaganda,* by Allan M. Winkler; and the following articles: an interview with David Stone Martin in *American Artist,* April 1950; "What to Tell America: The Writers' Quarrel in the Office of War Information," by Sidney Weinberg; *The Journal of American History,* June 1968; and "OWI on the Home Front," *Public Opinion Quarterly,* spring 1943.

I also conducted valuable interviews with Irving Geis, Bernard Perlin, and Raymond Gordon.

CHAPTER TWENTY-FIVE

An essential source for a study of the CIO-PAC is Joseph Gaer's *The First Round.* My own interviews with W. H. Ferry, Alan Reitman, Mildred Constantine, Gertrude Weber, and Estelle Thompson Margolis yielded much information, as did a letter from Hilda Robbins. Walter Abell's "Art and Labor" (*Magazine of Art,* October 1946), was especially helpful; Prescott's book on Shahn's graphic works, as well as the 1965 CBS interviews, contain information on Shahn's posters.

Frances K. Pohl's "Ben Shahn and *Fortune* Magazine" (*Labor's Heritage,* January 1989), and a March 24, 1969, letter from Dero A. Saunders to Bernarda Bryson Shahn contain material concerning Shahn's trip for *Fortune.*

CHAPTER TWENTY-SIX

The artist's own writings and already cited interviews as well as notices in the contemporary press were the sources for this chapter.

CHAPTER TWENTY-SEVEN

For information concerning the 1947 retrospective, I consulted Russell Lynes's *Good Old Modern,* the James Thrall Soby papers at MOMA, "Ben

Shahn" by Betty Chamberlain (*Art News,* October 1947), and reviews in the contemporary press.

CHAPTER TWENTY-EIGHT

John Bartlow Martin's *It Seems Like Only Yesterday* and Russell Lynes's *Confessions of a Dilettante* were important sources, as was Lynes's column "After Hours" in the December 19, 1957, issue of the *Saturday Review of Literature.* Shahn's correspondence with both Martin and Lynes, found in the Shahn papers at the Archives of American Art in Washington, was useful. Bernarda Bryson's "The Drawings of Ben Shahn" (*Image: A Quarterly of the Visual Arts,* autumn 1949) and "Ben Shahn's Mine Building: A Symbol of Disaster" by Carolyn Robbins (*Phoebus 5: A Journal of Art History,* 1988) were also consulted.

CHAPTER TWENTY-NINE

The Downtown Gallery and the Edith Gregor Halpert Papers in the Archives of American Art provided most of the material concerning Shahn's 1949 exhibition.

CHAPTER THIRTY

Frances K. Pohl's *Ben Shahn: New Deal Artist in a Cold War Climate, 1947–1954,* Serge Guilbaut's *How New York Stole the Idea of Modern Art,* and *The Flow of Art* (Henry McBride's essays) were valuable sources for this chapter. I also found material in the *Congressional Record* of March 11, March 25, May 17, and August 16, 1949.

For information about the State Department exhibition, I made use of material cited in Pohl's book, from *Advancing American Art: Politics and Aesthetics in the State Department Exhibition, 1946–48,* published by the Montgomery (Alabama) Museum of Fine Arts, January 10–March 4, 1984.

Shahn's relationship with the FBI and the U.S. Congress is chronicled in Herbert Mitgang's *Dangerous Dossiers.*

CHAPTER THIRTY-ONE

Shahn's correspondence with Selden Rodman and his comments on the manuscript of Rodman's biography are located in both the Shahn and Rodman papers in the Archives of American Art.

CHAPTER THIRTY-TWO

Examples of Shahn's advertising art can be found in *Great Ideas: Container Corporation of America,* edited by John Massey (Chicago: Container Corporation of America, 1976).

"Charles Coiner, Art Director" (*Portfolio* no. 2, summer 1950), and the anthology, *The Visual Craft of William Golden* were important sources.

I am grateful to Leo Lionni for sharing with me his memories of Shahn.

CHAPTER THIRTY-THREE

I consulted Shahn's own writings and lectures; material for this chapter was also furnished to me by Bud Stillman and Lorenzo Homar. Shahn's description of the students at the University of Colorado was part of a lecture given at the Franklin School in New York City in 1950.

CHAPTER THIRTY-FOUR

Martin Duberman's history of Black Mountain provided important background material, as did Mary Emma Harris's book. Tom Clark's excellent biography of Charles Olson and the published correspondence between Olson and Robert Creeley were most useful. I also consulted "What Moves You, Ben Shahn?" (*Responses,* vol. 8, no. 2, 1966) and "The 1951 Summer at Black Mountain College," by Betty Jennerjahn (*Dance Observer,* October 1951).

The quotation from Motherwell comes from Stefanie Terenzio's *The Collected Writings of Robert Motherwell.* The story of the encounter between Shahn and Rauschenberg at Black Mountain is found in *Rauschenberg: Art and Life* by Mary Lynn Kotz (New York: Abrams, 1990), and I interviewed Bernard Perlin about his relationship with Shahn.

CHAPTER THIRTY-FIVE

I consulted Haffenden's biography of Berryman and Charles DeFanti's biography of Dahlberg, as well as Reed Whittemore's books on William Carlos Williams. Williams's review of *The Sorrows of Priapus* was published in *Prairie Schooner,* fall 1958. Shahn's correspondence with Emilie McLeod of the Atlantic Monthly Press (publishers of *Ounce Dice Trice*), found in the Ben Shahn papers, and Leila Avrin's essay on *The*

Alphabet of Creation, published in *Hadassah Magazine* (August–September 1989), were also valuable.

CHAPTER THIRTY-SIX

Herbert Mitgang's *Dangerous Dossiers*, Fred Friendly's *Due to Circumstances Beyond Our Control*, and Frances K. Pohl's *Ben Shahn: New Deal Artist in a Cold War Climate* provided valuable material, as did my own interviews with Fred Friendly and Leo Lionni.

CHAPTER THIRTY-SEVEN

For information concerning Shahn's stay at Harvard, I consulted Scott Donaldson's biography of Archibald MacLeish as well as MacLeish's foreword to Davis Pratt's *The Photographic Eye of Ben Shahn*, Bernarda Bryson Shahn's book, and the Report of the Minutes of the Overseers' Visiting Committee Meeting at the Fogg Art Museum, December 3, 1956. Another source was Shahn's engagement book for 1956–57, which Mrs. Shahn allowed me to examine. Shahn's brilliant Harvard lectures, published by the Harvard University Press in 1957, are essential to an understanding of Shahn as a man and as an artist.

The best source for insights into Shahn's life in Roosevelt is Edwin Rosskam's perceptive study *Roosevelt, New Jersey*. Louise Rosskam kindly allowed me to examine her late husband's notes, used in writing his book, and she also furnished me with valuable information and insights of her own. I am also grateful to Pearl Seligman for helping me to understand the unique qualities of Roosevelt.

CHAPTER THIRTY-EIGHT

An important source for information about Shahn's Asia trip is found in the Edith Gregor Halpert Papers at the Archives of American Art, which contain letters from the artist to his dealer. Another source is "Ben Shahn in Japan," an article by Bernarda Shahn, published in *Global Courier* (Japan Air Lines), April 10, 1970.

I am indebted to Julie Fawcus for most of the information concerning Shahn's relationship with Arnold Fawcus and the Trianon Press. I would have been unable to write this chapter without her help. I am also grateful to Mary Laing, editor of the Trianon Press during this period, for her information and impressions.

CHAPTER THIRTY-NINE

Julie Fawcus was the source of most of the information contained in this chapter; I have also made use of my own memories. Arnold Fawcus generously allowed me to use a room in the Trianon office while I worked in Paris, and I was the "mediator" at many of the Shahn-Fawcus meetings in Paris as well as at the meeting at the Yale Club in New York.

CHAPTER FORTY

I spoke to Humphrey Burton about his visit to Roosevelt and his experiences there while preparing for the BBC television program, and I spoke to Richard Hudson about *Kuboyama*. I also consulted Bernarda Shahn's book, Katharine Kuh's *The Artist's Voice*, and Soby's book on Shahn's paintings.

CHAPTER FORTY-ONE

The main sources for this chapter were the Downtown Gallery Papers and the Edith Gregor Halpert Papers at the Archives of American Art, as well as an interview with Martin Bressler.

CHAPTER FORTY-TWO

Sources for this chapter included interviews with Shahn's sons and daughters, and with Martin Bressler, Pearl Seligman, and Louise Rosskam. Tapes of a long discussion between Shahn and Tony Schwartz, generously supplied to me by Schwartz, were most useful in this chapter and throughout many sections of this biography.

CHAPTER FORTY-THREE

Sources for this chapter included interviews with Martin Bressler and Lawrence Fleischman.

SELECTED BIBLIOGRAPHY

ARCHIVES

Brooklyn Museum, New York City. Ben Shahn file.

Columbia University, New York City. Oral History Collection. Interviews with Ben Shahn, by Dr. Paul Benison, October 29, 1956; January 5, 1957; February 9, 1957.

Museum of Modern Art, New York City. Ben Shahn file; James Thrall Soby papers.

Smithsonian Institution, Washington, D.C. Archives of American Art. Alfred H. Barr, Jr., papers; Black Mountain College papers; Downtown Gallery papers; Philip Evergood papers; Lawrence Fleischman papers; Clement Greenberg papers; Edith Gregor Halpert papers; Elizabeth McCausland papers; Ben Shahn papers; Bernarda Bryson Shahn papers; Raphael Soyer papers.

Whitney Museum of American Art, New York City. Ben Shahn file.

Stephen Lee Taller Ben Shahn Archive, Berkeley, California (to be transferred in 1999 to the Harvard University Fine Arts Library and the Fogg Art Museum, Cambridge, Massachusetts).

SECONDARY SOURCES

Alexander, Charles C. *Nationalism in American Thought: 1930–1945.* Chicago: Rand McNally, 1939.

Allen, Oliver E. *New York, New York.* New York: Atheneum, 1990.

Ashton, Dore. *The New York School: A Cultural Reckoning.* New York: Viking Press, 1973.

Baigell, Matthew. *The American Scene, American Painting of the 1930's.* New York: Praeger Publishers, 1974.

Baigell, Matthew, and Julia Williams. *Artists Against War and Fascism: Papers of the First American Artists' Congress.* New Brunswick, N.J.: Rutgers University Press, 1986.

Baldwin, Sidney. *Poverty and Politics: The Rise and Decline of the Farm Security Administration.* Chapel Hill: University of North Carolina Press, 1968.

Barr, Alfred H., Jr. *Masters of Modern Art.* New York: Museum of Modern Art, 1958.

Bayley, Edwin R. *Joseph McCarthy and the Press.* Madison: University of Wisconsin Press, 1981.

Berman, Avis. *Rebels on Eighth Street: Juliana Force and the Whitney Museum of American Art.* New York: Atheneum, 1990.

Berman, Greta. *The Lost Years: Mural Painting in New York City Under the WPA Federal Art Project, 1935–1943.* New York: Garland Publishing, 1978.

———, and Jeffrey Wechsler. *Realism and Realities: The Other Side of American Painting, 1940–1960.* New Brunswick, N.J.: Rutgers University Art Gallery, 1981.

Biddle, George. *The Yes and No of Contemporary Art.* Cambridge, Mass.: Harvard University Press, 1957.

Blum, John Morton. *V Was for Victory: Politics and American Culture During World War II.* New York: Harcourt Brace Jovanovich, 1976.

Bosworth, Patricia. *Diane Arbus.* New York: Alfred A. Knopf, 1984.

Brandon, Henry. *As We Are: 17 Conversations Between the Americans and the Man from the London Sunday Times.* New York: Doubleday & Company, 1961.

Brinkley, David. *Washington Goes to War.* New York: Alfred A. Knopf, 1988.

Brooks, Van Wyck. *John Sloan: A Painter's Life.* New York: E. P. Dutton, 1955.

Burnham, Sophy. *The Art Crowd.* New York: David McKay, 1973.

Bush, Martin H. *Ben Shahn: The Passion of Sacco and Vanzetti.* Syracuse, N.Y.: Syracuse University Press, 1968.

Canaday, John. *Mainstreams of Modern Art.* New York: Simon & Schuster, 1959.

Carlisle, John Charles. "A Biographical Study of How the Artist Became a Humanitarian Activist: Ben Shahn, 1938–1946." Ph.D. dissertation, University of Michigan, 1972.

Carr, Carolyn Kinder. *Ohio: A Photographic Portrait, 1935–1941. Farm Security Administration Photographs.* Akron, Ohio: Akron Art Institute, 1980.

Cassou, Jean. *Panorama des Arts Plastiques Contemporains.* Paris: Gallimard, 1960.

Castleman, Riva, ed. *Art of the Forties.* New York: Museum of Modern Art, 1991.

————. *Prints of the Twentieth Century.* New York: Museum of Modern Art, 1976.

Clark, Eliot. *History of the National Academy of Design.* New York: Columbia University Press, 1954.

Clark, Tom. *Charles Olson: The Allegory of a Poet's Life.* New York: W. W. Norton, 1991.

Cohen, Jason H. "From Utopia to Suburbia: The Architecture and Urban Planning of Roosevelt, New Jersey." B.A. thesis, Rutgers University, 1994.

Coke, Van Deren. *The Painter and the Photograph: From Delacroix to Warhol.* Albuquerque: University of New Mexico Press, 1972.

Conrad, Peter. *The Art of the City: Views and Versions of New York.* Oxford, England: Oxford University Press, 1984.

Constantine, Mildred, with Alan M. Ferm. *Word and Image: Posters from the Collection of the Museum of Modern Art.* New York: Museum of Modern Art, 1968.

Contreras, Belisario R. *Tradition and Innovation in New Deal Art.* Lewisburg, Pa.: Bucknell University Press/Associated University Presses, 1983.

Crowther, Prudence, ed. *Don't Tread on Me: The Selected Letters of S.J. Perelman.* New York: Viking Press, 1987.

Cummings, Paul. *Artists in Their Own Words.* New York: St. Martin's Press, 1979.

Davidson, Marshall B. *The American Heritage History of the Artist's America.* New York: American Heritage, 1973.

DeFanti, Charles. *The Wages of Expectation: A Biography of Edward Dahlberg.* New York: New York University Press, 1978.

Doherty, R. J. *Social-Documentary Photography in the USA.* Garden City, N.Y.: AMPhoto, 1976.

Donaldson, Scott, with R. H. Winnick. *Archibald MacLeish: An American Life.* Boston: Houghton Mifflin, 1992.

Dorsky, Morris. "The Formative Years of Ben Shahn: The Origin and Development of His Style." M.A. thesis, New York University, 1966.

Duberman, Martin. *Black Mountain: An Exploration in Community.* New York: E. P. Dutton, 1972.

Edwards, Susan H. "Ben Shahn: A New Deal Photographer in the Old South." Ph.D. dissertation, Graduate School and University Center, City University of New York, 1996.

————. "Ben Shahn: The Road South." *The History of Photography,* vol. 19, no. 1 (spring 1995), pp. 13–19.

————. *Ben Shahn and the Task of Photography in Thirties America.* New York: Hunter College of the City University of New York, 1995.

Ekirch, Arthur A., Jr. *Ideologies and Utopias: The Impact of the New Deal on American Thought.* Chicago: Quadrangle Books, 1969.

Encyclopedia Judaica, vol. 10. Jerusalem: Keter Publishing House, 1971.

Feldman, Edmund Burke. *Art as Image and Idea.* Englewood Cliffs, N.J.: Prentice Hall, 1967.

Felix, David. *Protest: Sacco-Vanzetti and the Intellectuals.* Bloomington: Indiana University Press, 1965.

Fleischhaven, Carl, and Beverly W. Brannan, eds. *Documenting America, 1935–1943.* Berkeley: University of California Press, 1988.

Franc, Helen. *An Invitation to See.* New York: Museum of Modern Art, 1973.

Fraser, Steven. *Labor Will Rule: Sidney Hillman and the Rise of American Labor.* New York: Free Press, 1991.

Friendly, Fred W. *Due to Circumstances Beyond Our Control.* New York: Vintage Books, 1968.

Fuhren, Holly. "Stranger in a Familiar Land: Ben Shahn in Ohio." Columbus: Columbus Art Museum, 1988.

Gaer, Joseph. *The First Round: The Story of the CIO Political Action Committee.* New York: Duell, Sloan and Pearce, 1944.

Galbraith, John Kenneth. *The Great Crash, 1929.* 3d ed. Boston: Houghton Mifflin, 1972.

Gambone, Robert L. *Art and Popular Religion in Evangelical America 1915–1940.* Knoxville: University of Tennessee Press, 1989.

Garraty, John A. *The Great Depression.* New York: Harcourt Brace Jovanovich, 1986.

Golden, Cipes Pineles, Kurt Weihs, and Robert Strunsky, eds. *The Visual Craft of William Golden.* New York: George Braziller, 1962.

Goodrich, Lloyd. *Three Centuries of American Art.* New York: Praeger Publishers, 1966.

Grosser, Maurice. *Critic's Eye.* Indianapolis: Bobbs-Merrill, 1962.

Gruen, John. *The Party's Over Now.* New York: Pushcart Press, 1989.

Guilbaut, Serge. *How New York Stole the Idea of Modern Art.* Chicago: The University of Chicago Press, 1983.

Guimond, James. *American Photography and the American Dream.* Chapel Hill: University of North Carolina Press, 1991.

Haffenden, John. *The Life of John Berryman.* Boston: Routledge and Kegan Paul, 1982.

Handlin, Oscar. *The Uprooted.* 2nd ed., enlarged. Boston: Little, Brown/Atlantic Monthly Press, 1973.

Harris, Mary Emma. *The Arts at Black Mountain College.* Cambridge, Mass.: MIT Press, 1987.

Hendrickson, Paul. *Looking for the Light: The Hidden Life and Art of Marion Post Wolcott.* New York: Alfred A. Knopf, 1992.

Hermann, Dorothy. *S. J. Perelman: A Life.* New York: Simon & Schuster, 1986.

Herner de Larrea, Irene. *Diego Rivera's Mural at the Rockefeller Center.* Mexico City: Edicupes, 1990.

Herrera, Hayden. *Frida: A Biography of Frida Kahlo.* New York: Harper & Row, 1983.

Hertzberg, Arthur. *The Jews in America, Four Centuries of an Uneasy Encounter: A History.* New York: Simon & Schuster, 1989.

Howe, Irving. *World of Our Fathers.* New York: Harcourt Brace Jovanovich, 1976.

⸻ and Kenneth Libo. *How We Lived.* New York: Richard Marek, 1979.

Hurlburt, Laurance. *The Mexican Muralists in the United States.* Albuquerque: University of New Mexico Press, 1989.

Hurley, F. Jack. *Portrait of a Decade: Roy Stryker and the Development of Documentary Photography in the Thirties.* Baton Rouge: Louisiana State University Press, 1972.

Josephson, Matthew. *Sidney Hillman: Statesman of American Labor.* Garden City, N.Y.: Doubleday & Company, 1952.

Kampf, Avram. *Jewish Experience in the Art of the 20th Century.* South Hadley, Mass.: Bergin and Garvey Publishers, 1984.

Katzman, Laura. "The Politics of Media: Painting and Photography in the Art of Ben Shahn." *American Art,* winter 1993.

Kazin, Alfred. *A Walker in the City.* New York: Harcourt, Brace & World, 1951.

Kingsley, April. *The Turning Point.* New York: Simon & Schuster, 1992.

Kirstein, Lincoln. *Mosaic: Memoirs.* New York: Farrar, Straus and Giroux, 1994.

Kisseloff, Jeff. *You Must Remember This: An Oral History of Manhattan from the 1890s to World War II.* New York: Harcourt Brace Jovanovich, 1989.

Kleeblatt, Norma L., and Susan Chevlowe. *Painting a Place in America: Jewish Artists in New York 1900–1945.* New York: Jewish Museum, 1991.

Klemin, Diana. *The Illustrated Book: Its Art and Craft.* New York: Clarkson N. Potter, 1970.

Klingaman, William K. *1929: The Year of the Great Crash.* New York: Harper & Row, 1989.

Kostelanetz, Richard. *On Innovative Art(ist)s: Recollections of an Expanding Field.* Jefferson, N.C.: McFarland & Company, 1992.

Kouwenhoven, John A. *The Columbia Historical Portrait of New York.* Garden City, N.Y.: Doubleday & Company, 1953.

Kuh, Katherine. *The Artist's Voice.* New York: Harper & Row, 1962.

————. *The Open Eye: In Pursuit of Art.* New York: Harper & Row, 1971.

Larkin, Oliver. *Art and Life in America.* New York: Rinehart, 1949.

Levy, Julien. *Memoir of an Art Gallery.* New York: G. P. Putnam's Sons, 1977.

Lewis, John. *The Twentieth Century Book.* New York: Reinhold Publishing Co., 1967.

Lichtenstein, Nelson. *Labor's War at Home: The CIO in World War II.* Cambridge, England: Cambridge University Press, 1982.

Linden, Diana Louise. "The New Deal Murals of Ben Shahn: The Intersection of Jewish Identity, Social Reform, and Government Patronage." Ph.D. dissertation, The City University of New York, 1997.

Lynes, Russell. *Good Old Modern: An Intimate Portrait of the Museum of Modern Art.* New York: Atheneum, 1973.

————. *Confessions of a Dilettante.* New York: Harper & Row, Publishers, 1966.

McBride, Henry. *The Flow of Art.* New York: Atheneum, 1975.

McCabe, Cynthia Jaffee. *The Golden Door: Artist-Immigrants of America, 1876–1976.* Washington, D.C.: Smithsonian Institution Press, 1976.

McElvaine, Robert S. *The Great Depression.* New York: Times Books, 1984.

McKinzie, Richard D. *The New Deal for Artists.* Princeton, N.J.: Princeton University Press, 1973.

MacLeish, Archibald. *Land of the Free.* New York: Harcourt Brace, 1938.

————. *Reflections.* Bernard A. Drabeck and Helen E. Ellis, eds. Amherst: University of Massachusetts, 1986.

McShine, Kynaston, ed. *Andy Warhol: A Retrospective.* New York: Museum of Modern Art, 1989.

Marquis, Alice Goldfarb. *Alfred H. Barr, Jr.: Missionary for the Modern.* Chicago: Contemporary Books, 1989.

Martin, John Bartlow. *It Seems Like Only Yesterday.* New York: William Morrow, 1986.

Meltzer, Milton. *Dorothea Lange: A Photographer's Life.* New York: Farrar, Straus and Giroux, 1978.

Miller, Dorothy C., and Alfred H. Barr, Jr., eds. *American Realists and Magic Realists*. New York: Museum of Modern Art, 1943.

Mitgang, Herbert. *Dangerous Dossiers: Exposing the Secret War Against America's Greatest Authors*. New York: Donald I. Fine, 1988.

Morse, John D., ed. *Ben Shahn*. New York: Praeger Publishers, 1972.

Naifeh, Steven, and Gregory White Smith. *Jackson Pollock*. New York: Clarkson N. Potter, 1989.

Natanson, Nicholas. *The Black Image in the New Deal: The Politics of FSA Photography*. Knoxville: University of Tennessee Press, 1992.

O'Connor, Francis V. *Federal Art Patronage: 1933 to 1943*. College Park: University of Maryland Art Gallery, 1966.

———. *Federal Support for the Visual Arts: The New Deal and Now*. Greenwich, Conn.: New York Graphic Society, 1969.

———, ed. *The New Deal Art Projects: An Anthology of Memoirs*. Washington, D.C.: Smithsonian Institution Press, 1972.

———. "The New Deal Art Projects in New York." *American Art Journal*, fall 1969, pp. 58–79.

———. "New Deal Murals in New York." *Artforum*, November 1968, pp. 41–49.

———. "WPA: Art for the Millions." *American Heritage*, October 1970.

The Ohio Guide. New York: Oxford University Press, 1940.

Olson, Charles, and Robert Creeley. *The Complete Correspondence*. 9 vols. Santa Barbara and Santa Rosa, Calif.: Black Sparrow Press, 1980–1989.

O'Neal, Hank. *A Vision Shared: A Classical Portrait of America and Its People, 1935–1943*. New York: St. Martin's Press, 1976.

Pohl, Frances K. *Ben Shahn: New Deal Artist in a Cold War Climate, 1947–1954*. Austin, University of Texas Press, 1989.

———. *Ben Shahn, with Ben Shahn's Writings*. San Francisco: Pomegranate Artbooks, 1993.

Polcari, Stephen. *Abstract Expressionism and the Modern Experience*. Cambridge, England: Cambridge University Press, 1991.

Polenberg, Richard. *War and Society: The United States 1941–1945*. Philadelphia: J. B. Lippincott, 1972.

Pratt, Davis, ed. *The Photographic Eye of Ben Shahn*. Cambridge, Mass.: Harvard University Press, 1975.

Prescott, Kenneth W. *The Complete Graphic Works of Ben Shahn*. New York: Quadrangle Press, 1973.

Rathbone, Belinda. *Walker Evans: A Biography*. Boston: Houghton Mifflin, 1995.

Rhodes, Anthony. *Propaganda: The Art of Persuasion: World War II*. New York: Chelsea House Publishers, 1976.

Rischin, Moses. *The Promised City: New York's Jews, 1870–1914.* New York: Corinth Books, 1964.

Rivera, Diego, with Gladys March. *My Art, My Life: An Autobiography.* New York: Citadel Press, 1960.

Rodman, Selden. *Conversations with Artists.* New York: Devin-Adair, 1957.

————. *Portrait of the Artist as an American: Ben Shahn, A Biography with Pictures.* New York: Harper & Brothers, 1951.

Rosskam, Edwin. *Roosevelt, New Jersey: Big Dreams in a Small Town and What Time Did to Them.* New York: Grossman Publishers, 1972.

Rudy, S. Willis. *The College of the City of New York: A History, 1847–1947.* New York: City College Press, 1949.

Russell, Francis. *Sacco and Vanzetti: The Case Resolved.* New York: Harper & Row, 1986.

Sanders, Ronald. *Shores of Refuge: A Hundred Years of Jewish Emigration.* New York: Schocken Books, 1988.

Schoenburg, Nancy, and Stuart Schoenburg. *Lithuanian Jewish Communities.* New York: Garland Publishing, 1991.

Shahn, Bernarda Bryson. *Ben Shahn.* New York: Harry N. Abrams, 1972.

Shapiro, David, ed. *Social Realism: Art as a Weapon.* New York: Frederick Ungar, 1973.

Smith, Page. *Redeeming the Time: A People's History of the 1920s and the New Deal.* New York: McGraw-Hill, 1987.

Soby, James Thrall. *Ben Shahn* (Penguin Modern Painters). Middlesex, England: Penguin, 1947.

————. *Ben Shahn, His Graphic Art.* New York: Braziller, 1957.

————. *Ben Shahn, Paintings.* New York: Braziller, 1963.

————. *Contemporary Painters.* New York: Museum of Modern Art, 1948.

Solomon, Deborah. *Jackson Pollock.* New York: Simon & Schuster, 1987.

Stange, Maren. *Symbols of Ideal Life: Social Documentary Photography in America 1890–1950.* Cambridge, England: Cambridge University Press, 1989.

Stebbins, Theodore J., Jr. *American Master Drawings and Watercolors.* New York: Harper & Row, 1976.

Still, Bayard. *Mirror for Gotham.* New York: New York University Press, 1956.

Stryker, Roy Emerson, and Nancy Wood. *In This Proud Land: America 1935–1943 As Seen in the FSA Photographs.* Boston: New York Graphic Society, 1973.

Tepfer, Diane. "Edith Gregor Halpert and the Downtown Gallery Downtown, 1926–1940: A Study in American Art Patronage." Ph.D. dissertation, University of Michigan, 1989.

Terenzio, Stefanie, ed. *The Collected Writings of Robert Motherwell*. New York: Oxford University Press, 1992.

Tomkins, Calvin. *Off the Wall: Robert Rauschenberg and the Art World of Our Time*. New York: Doubleday & Company, 1980.

Tugwell, Rexford G. *The Democratic Roosevelt*. Garden City, N.Y.: Doubleday & Company, 1957.

Tyler, Francine. "Artists Respond to the Great Depression and the Threat of Fascism: The New York Artists' Union and Its Magazine *Art Front* (1934–1937)." Ph.D. dissertation, New York University, 1991.

Von Blum, Paul. *The Art of Social Conscience*. New York: Universe Books, 1976.

Wagner, Robert W., ed. *Ben Shahn in Ohio: The Summer of 1938*. Upper Arlington, Ohio: Cultural Arts Commission, 1988.

Warburg, James P. *The Long Road Home: The Autobiography of a Maverick*. Garden City, N.Y.: Doubleday & Company, 1964.

Weiss, Margaret R., ed. *Ben Shahn Photographer, An Album from the Thirties*. New York: Da Capo Press, 1973.

Weller, Allen S. *The Joys and Sorrows of Recent American Art*. Urbana: University of Illinois Press, 1968.

Wheat, Ellen Harkins. *Jacob Lawrence: American Painter*. Seattle: University of Washington Press, 1986.

Whelan, Richard. *The Double Take: A Comparative Look at Photographs*. New York: Clarkson N. Potter, 1981.

Whiting, Cécile. *Anti-Fascism in American Art*. New Haven, Conn.: Yale University Press, 1989.

Whittemore, Reed, ed. *William Carlos Williams and James Laughlin: Selected Letters*. New York: W. W. Norton, 1989.

———. *William Carlos Williams: Poet from Jersey*. Boston: Houghton Mifflin, 1975.

Wien, Jake Milgram. *The Vanishing Frontier: Bernarda Bryson Shahn and Her Historical Lithographs Created for the Resettlement Administration of FDR*. New York: Wien American, 1995.

Winkler, Allan M. *The Politics of Propaganda: The Office of War Information, 1942–1945*. New Haven, Conn.: Yale University Press, 1978.

Wolfe, Bertram D. *Diego Rivera: His Life and Times*. New York: Alfred A. Knopf, 1939.

INDEX

Page numbers in italics refer to illustrations. Works of art are by Shahn unless otherwise noted.

ABOUT THE AUTHOR

HOWARD GREENFELD is the author of three acclaimed biographies, of Puccini, Caruso, and the art collector Albert C. Barnes. He was also the founder of Orion Press and lived in France and Italy for many years, where he published English-language translations of such writers as Italo Calvino, Primo Levi, Albert Memmi, and Jean Piaget. He became friendly with Ben Shahn in the last years of the artist's life and spent time with him in Paris, in New York, and in Roosevelt, New Jersey. Shahn's widow, Bernarda, herself an artist, agreed to allow Greenfeld full access to her memories and materials from Shahn, while placing no constraints on the book.

ABOUT THE TYPE

This book was set in Fairfield, the first typeface from the hand of the distinguished American artist and engraver Rudolph Ruzicka (1883–1978). Ruzicka was born in Bohemia and came to America in 1894. He set up his own shop, devoted to wood engraving and printing, in New York in 1913 after a varied career working as a wood engraver, in photoengraving and banknote printing plants, and as an art director and freelance artist. He designed and illustrated many books, and was the creator of a considerable list of individual prints—wood engravings, line engravings on copper, and aquatints.